D1738475

ENEMIES ON ALL Sides: The Fall of Yugoslavia

By Milija M. Lašić-Vasojević

Introduction by Dr. Milorad M. Drachkovitch

Illustrated By
Glenn L. Reitze

NORTH AMERICAN INTERNATIONAL

Publishers of Quality Books from Around the World
P.O. Box 28278, Central Station
Washington, D.C.

International Standard Book No. 0-88265-010-6

Library of Congress Card Catalog No. 76-41596

NOTE TO READERS: Additional copies of this book may be obtained, while the supply lasts, directly from the publisher for $10.00 postpaid.

North American International is a small firm with a name much too big for its present size. It was founded in 1971, and is dedicated to publishing quality books from around the world. If you would like information on other carefully designed, hand-crafted books as they are published, please drop us a letter or postcard. Have patience, however: we work quite slowly, doing all of the design work in our own shops, and publish only a very few books each year. Orders from dealers are welcome. Bulk discounts (available to anyone) begin at five copies of any one title.

THE SIGN OF THE SLEEPING MAN

NORTH AMERICAN INTERNATIONAL
Publishers of Quality Books from Around the World
P.O. Box 28278 Central Station
Washington, D.C. 20005 U.S.A.

ii

NOTE FROM THE EDITOR
OF THE ENGLISH-LANGUAGE EDITION

The manuscript presented here was written in the Serbo-Croatian language and translated by the author himself. Although the proposed book was greatly reduced in size and a considerable amount of editing was done, effort was made to leave as many of the author's linguistic peculiarities as was consistent with ease of reading and comprehensibility. Therefore the book preserves the flavor of the author's own speech patterns in English, and authenticity of language thus was preferred over a potentially standardized and homogenized prose.

I have added to this volume a series of maps, line drawings, and photographs, plus appendices on the historical and cultural background of Yugoslavia, with emphasis on the Montenegrin (Crna Gora) and Serbian sections. The reader who is unfamiliar with the history of this area of the world may find it helpful to read these appendices before beginning the book by Mr. Lasic-Vasojevic.

Glenn L. Reitze, NAI
Washington, D.C. 1976

TABLE OF CONTENTS

INTRODUCTION

By Dr. Milorad M. Drachkovitch
Director of Archives,
Hoover Institute on War, Peace and Revolution
Stanford, California

It has been said that history is written by the victors, and one may add that the dictum is even more applicable to victors in civil wars. But then, as Nietzsche observed, "victory is a liar," meaning that victors twist historical events, attributing to themselves purity of motives and behavior, and the opposite to their vanquished adversaries. Yugoslav communist historiography has faithfully followed that pattern, monopolizing for Tito's Partisans fighting patriotism, democratic aspirations, and popular allegiance, and vehemently denying all those qualities to their main enemies in the civil war under the occupation—the Chetniks of General Draza Mihailovic.

The present book—a much shortened English version of the unpublished original in the Serbian language—is an attempt to "tell it how it was" in Yugoslavia during the war. Perhaps the basic value of the book is that it is not written as a history by a person who interprets events molded by others; it is a personal narrative of what an individual citizen did and saw during some particularly bitter and complex phases of the war and civil war in Yugoslavia. The author of the book was well suited to write that kind of testimonial: as a seasoned high school teacher, and as a typical Serb very much interested in public affairs, he went into the war with the sharp eye of a keen observer. During the short engagement on the border of Albania, occupied by the Italians, and afterwards as a participant in the Chetnik-Partisan civil war in Montenegro, he was not in a position of higher authority where he would have been absorbed by everyday events and the responsibilities of leading men to action; he was, however, better suited to observe and remember being "in the middle"—between the professional officers in command of their troops (such as his own younger brother, Staff Army Major George Lasic, one of the most prominent of Mihailovic's commanders in the Montenegro [Crna Gora] section of Yugoslavia) and the simple fighting men. The military events were thus perceived by a participating civilian, who knew well and quickly understood the underlying political realities of implacable battles that raged in war-torn Montenegro.

There are essentially two interwoven themes in Mr. Lasic's book. One consists in vivid descriptions of his own war, civil war, and prisoner of war experiences. As the overwhelming majority of his Serbian compatriots, he rejoiced at the March 27, 1941 coup in Belgrade against the pro-Axis government, and joyfully demonstrated in the streets of Krusevac, a city in the heart of Serbia (also a part of Yugoslavia), where he taught. Mobilized soon afterwards, he went in high spirits to his native Montenegro, and anticipated with relish fighting the Italians on the Albanian border. Sudden retreat of his military unit from Albania (which he believes was caused by two treacherous Croatian communications officers) crushed his hopes, and he soon witnessed the collapse of the Yugoslav royal army and the dismemberment of his country.

Following the military dispersal, he briefly visited his native village, Kami, in the county of Lijeva Rijeka, a north-eastern region of Montenegro, inhabited by the proud Vasojevic tribe, whose virtues and customs he delights in describing in this book. From there he returned to Krusevac and therefore did not take part in the spontaneous popular uprising in Montenegro against the Italian occupiers in mid-July 1941, his brother George being one of its leaders. Early in August he was back in Lijeva Rijeka in Montenegro which he found devastated by the reinforced occupiers' punitive expeditions. The Italians had put down the uprising but had retreated to fortified towns leaving the countryside again relatively free. Then, in the fall and winter of 1941, Mr. Lasic was actively engaged in the organization of local self-defense units against the attempts by the disciplined members of the Communist Party of Yugoslavia to kill the most prominent nationalist leaders in order to assure their Party's domination in the resistance movement and the nation. When in June of 1942, after months of a cruel civil war, the bulk of the temporarily defeated Montenegrin Communist Partisans retreated to other parts of the country, the author returned once again to Krusevac in Serbia and briefly resumed his teaching duties. Suspected (rightly) by the German occupying authorities of being in touch with the underground organization of General Mihailovic, he was arrested, transferred to Gestapo headquarters in Belgrade and sent as a prisoner of war to various POW camps in Germany. He recounts his seemingly endless camp transferrals from one end of Germany to the other, and records his heartbreaking sorrow at the end of the war when he could not return to his by-then Communist-ruled native country. Arrested again, two months later, this time by the British as a potential "war criminal," he was released and in December of 1946 reached a big Chetnik camp in Eboli, South Italy, where he taught in an improvised high school. With the closing of the Eboli camp six months later, he was transported back to Germany, to the Munster camp in Eastern Westphalia, and was again interrogated by the British about his war experiences and political reliability. All these hurdles behind him, he stayed in Germany waiting for emigration to the United States. Finally, on October 10, 1951, he reached New Orleans, reemerging as a fully free man, with a terrible story of human sufferings to tell.

The second main theme of Mr. Lasic's writing concerns the collective side of that story, alluded to in the very title of the book. For indeed the enemies, foreign and domestic, were on all sides: the implacable and methodical Germans, shooting hundreds of Serbs for a single shot German soldier; the Italians, planning cunningly to subjugate Montenegro, and still being the softest, occasionally even humane occupiers; the Albanians, itching to settle old ethnic accounts with the Montenegrins; the Croatian Ustasi, who in their anti-Serbian genocidal fury had their criminal fingers around Montenegro, pitting the Yugoslav Moslems against their Orthodox Christian compatriots; finally, and particularly, the Communists, instigators of the supreme evil—the civil war. And still, castigating Serbian enemies in no uncertain terms, the author never indulges in chauvinistic recriminations. He does not identify the Croatian people with the Ustasi, and he mentions examples of Moslem kindness toward and solidarity with the persecuted Serbs. His rage against Communist terrorists, killing for the Party's sake, does not emcompass simple (Communist-led) Partisan fighters, many of whom he considers as being victims of Communist political manipulatons.

Nearly half of the book deals with the problem of Communism in the small area of Lijeva Rijeka, but this microscopic treatment has a much broader significance. Three elements emerge from the story, and if the author occasionally overwhelms the reader by citing numbers of personal names, as well as those of places, rivers, and mountains, their enumeration gives to the narrative the stamp of authenticity. The first element is the already mentioned incipient and functional Communist terror aiming both to liquidate local nationalist leaders and to frighten the population. (Tito himself, after the war, criticized these excesses of the Partisan behavior in

vii

Montenegro as politically harmful.) The anonymous terrorist actions, however, backfired and led to the creation, in the middle of December 1941, of the Battalion of Lijeva Rijeka with both military and political duties. The Communists were invited to join in the national effort against the occupiers, but were warned not to instigate internecine killings. The second element is a short-lived cooperation between the nationalists and the Communists, which the author illustrates with a series of vignettes about Montenegrin mentality and Communist duplicity which, according to him, made the cooperation impossible. It is significant for the Montenegrin concept of honor and the sanctity of the given word, that nationalist leaders refused to heed advice and liquidate Communist representatives when negotiations broke down and the latter were at the mercy of the former. The third element is the outbreak of full-fledged hostilities between the two camps, culminating with the Partisans' attack on St. John's day, January 20, 1942, when George Lasic, nationalist commandant, was greviously wounded (he was killed on May 5, 1944, during the bombardment of the town of Podgorica).

The author of the book was personally fortunate to leave Montenegro in the middle of 1942, at the time when Partisans' fortunes were at the lowest ebb. He therefore was not an eyewitness to the radical change of the situation which began with the capitulation of Italy in September of 1943 and escalated with the decision of the Western powers to give full support to the Partisans. However he includes in his book two detailed descriptions by survivors of the final debacle of the Montenegrin Chetniks, during their retreat northward within Yugoslavia in the direction of Bosnia. In the period between December 1944 and April-May 1945, thousands of fighters and their families were exterminated under the combined effects of separately attacking Partisans and Ustasi and the terrifying consequences of typhus, frost, hunger, and exhaustion. There was no pity and no relief for the Chetniks' youth regiment, which had been composed of 1,012 boys aged 15 to 17, or for about 100 girls who carried the wounded. And for a fitting description of how some of the Montenegrin freedom fighters perished the following words from one of the reports may serve: "We were in a triangle whose two sides were held by Ustasi, and the third by Partisans."

The reader of this book will realize that its author was not a morose and mysanthropic person, but on the contrary a gregarious fellow who enjoyed a good laugh and the warm company of other men. But they cannot miss a sentence, near the end of the book, when the author reflects on the outcome of the war: "Several months earlier all countries in Europe were enjoying the return of their sons from captivity, while we Serbians were not able to go anywhere: Fascism and Nazism had destroyed our country; the Allies had handed us over to Communists whose getting into power in Yugoslavia they had greatly helped from 1943 through 1945. This injustice was killing us." This is indeed the key sentence and the central message of this moving and important book.

Milorad M. Drachkovitch
Stanford, CA. 1976

SKETCH MAP OF THE BALKANS, 1941

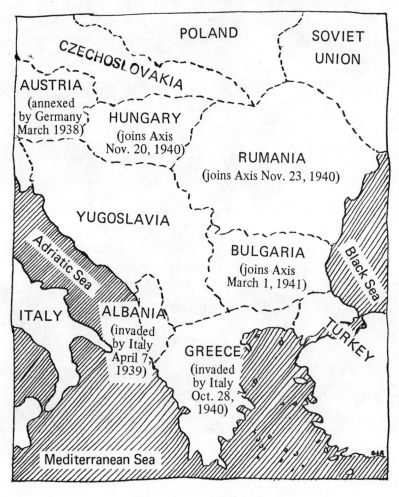

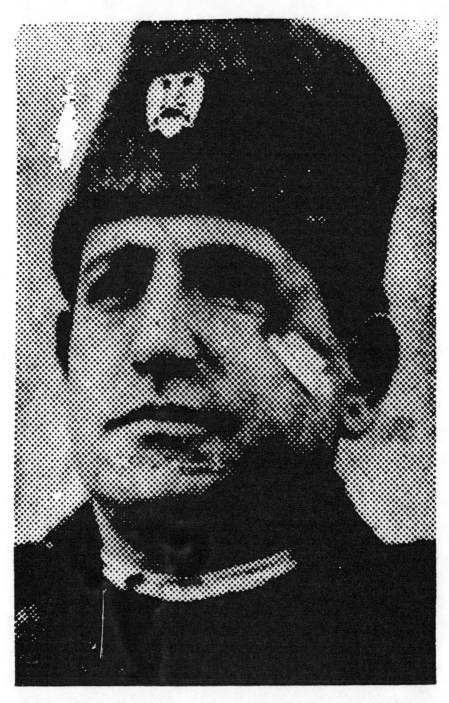

Major Djordje Lasic, showing bandaged wound near his eye.

PREFACE

The Serbians as a people survived many catastrophies during their tragic yet glorious history from the first days of their settlements on the Balkan Peninsula, some fourteen centuries ago. But the tragedy they experienced in World War II and immediately afterward and which has not yet ended, surpasses all of their earlier national tragedies; exceeding even the lost battles on the Marica River, 1371, and at Kosovo, 1389, during which the flower of Serbia's knighthood perished defending Christendom and the freedom of the Balkan Peninsula and Europe. This most recent martyrdom of the Serbian people may be better compared with the exterminations of peoples, for it included the annilhilation of small children, unprotected women, old men and other defenseless human beings by the Fascist-Nazi invaders of Yugoslavia and their satellites, as well as by others from within the borders of our country—the Ustasi (the Croatian fascists) and Communists.

The sufferings and the exploits of Serbs and Slovenes in the course of the last world war, unfortunately, are not yet known to the general public. They are not known even among well educated persons in the friendly nations of the West. Nor is it generally understood to what extent the actions of our old friends, particularly the English, contributed to the eventual tragedy, when Yugoslavia was turned over to the Communists.

This is the awful reality which we paid for by the sea of Serbian blood and 1,860,000 casualties. In addition, we—the Serbs, Croats and Slovenes of Yugoslavia—lost our civil rights and freedom.

History will show the responsibility of specific individuals for Yugoslavia's undeserved national catastrophy, but this will not correct what has been done. But our martyrdom should be a lesson to all.

To my personal misfortune and sadness, I was a witness of this greatest martyrdom of my people, as well as to trials of our people early in this century. Although I did not participate in the war of liberation from the Turks in 1912, nor in the defense against the Bulgars in 1913 (because I was not yet of age) I nevertheless was mature enough to comprehend and understand the enthusiasm and the strength of the Serbian people in those glorious days. But in the continuation of our struggle for freedom, during World War I, I was in the ranks of the army of Montenegro (later a part of Yugoslavia) from July 1914 to the end of 1915. I survived the horrors of the

2

retreat through Albania; I saw with my own eyes the tragedy of the generation, I saw the perishing of youths from Sumadija through famine and exhaustion in their vain efforts to escape the invading Austro-Hungarian armies.

The Second World War broke out when I was at an age of full mental and physical capacities, with enough experience and education to be able to understand the people and follow the development of events. Yet particularly because our country was so mercilessly broken by the armies of the Axis powers, it was not possible to see all. And even though I was often on the move in the central provinces of Serbia, I can not pretend to have been in position to have had a complete view of events happening in other parts of Yugoslavia at the same time. Thus in writing this book, a comprehensive view has not been my aim. Rather, my principal purpose is to give in this exposition what I personally saw and survived, and of the key events and happenings off of my path, to note the echoes of those events that were caused in the souls of the men with whom I was at the time.

My brethren from other Yugoslavian provinces should describe what they saw and survived, so that the new generations can have a complete view of all events that occurred in the nation during the last war, and have the opportunity to use it for their better understanding. This is my hope in having written this book.

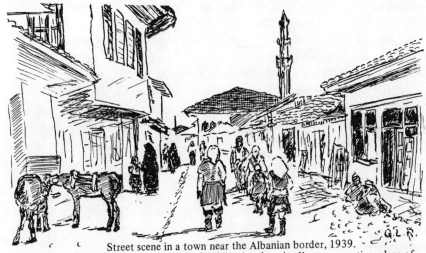

Street scene in a town near the Albanian border, 1939.
This small Montenegrin town near the Albanian frontier lies at a meeting place of cultures. Moslem women, clad in enveloping draperies, are seen side by side with Christian peasant women; the white skull cap worn by most of the men in the picture is said to denote Albanian origin. The flattish roofs and curved tiles of the buildings denote Mediterranean influence; the minaret speaks for itself.

CHAPTER ONE: YUGOSLAVIA ENTERS THE WAR

As soon as war broke out in Europe at the beginning of September, 1939 (when Germany invaded Poland) I was aware that Yugoslavia could not remain neutral. In this I shared the general feeling of most Serbians in the part of Yugoslavia where I was living. There was a popular story about a veteran of the First World War who was again on the Rhine River, and who asked a French companion: "Are there Serbian soldiers already at the front?" The Frenchman answered that there were not as yet. The veteran then told him: "Alors, pas de guerre!" (Then there is no war!) This story could well sum up the belief of large numbers of Serbians at that time. Simply put, our people were convinced that without us Serbs there could not be any war. Yet: "How can we remain neutral when our friends and allies of the First World War are falling like pears, shot down by the German tyrants?" was the question of the average Serbian man in those days. "It is better to die with one's friends than to live with one's enemies", was the conclusion.

The quick defeats of the French and Poles as well as the fall of Austria and Czechoslovakia did not destroy the spirit of the large masses of us Serbs. To me, those crushing defeats were merely evidence that the war would last longer. Knowledge of the First World War was the basis of this conclusion: the Axis powers could not win, even if Russia were neutral. Russia had shamefully left her (and our) allies in 1917, in the middle of the war, and yet the Allies won at the end. But the absence from the fighting of Russia at this time awoke the idea that the present war could be seriously prolonged, perhaps even for fifteen years!

The farce about our government's subscribing to the "pact" of the Axis powers was understood by the people as an attempt by our responsible statemen to avoid our getting into the war for as long as possible, until there would be some possibility of our getting help from our old allies. All of us were aware of this fact, and we were praying to God to remain out of the war for one or two years. In this context we understood the "salute" to Hitler after the fall of Austria in 1938, made by Dr. Stojadinovic, the Yugoslavian Prime Minister.

Although Yugoslavia was not actually to enter the war until 1941, it may be said that an isolated act of war had occurred much earlier. On October 9, 1934, Yugoslavia's King Alexander I, known as The Unifier for his work early in the century, was assassinated with the complicity of the Axis powers. In my opinion, this was the first major battle won by Fascism and Nazism in its impending conquest of Europe, and was a serious loss to the free men and nations striving to prevent war.

In Yugoslavia, the blow of King Alexander I's death was a severe one. The nation had from its inception after World War I been a constitutional monarchy, with the king merely a figure to "show the way" and ensure full and unbiased application of the laws throughout the land. At his death, Alexander was replaced by his 11-year-old son, Petar II, and (as temporary head of state during Petar's minority) by the assassinated king's second cousin, Prince Paul. Although these were both good men, they did not have the stature or military reputation of Alexander.

The coup d'etat on March 27, 1941, signified functionally our getting into the war. This was witnessed by the huge demonstrations and the enthusiasm of the people; there was a sense of relief, as though a stone had been taken off of our souls. On this day, as usual, at about 7:30 A.M. I was heading for the high school of Krusevac, where I taught. When I passed the Monument to the Heroes of Kosovo, I was joined by two younger colleagues, D. Vujsic and R. Medenica. After conventional greetings, they started to talk about what happened this morning to our Prime Minister, Dragisa Cvetkovic. Together we entered the nearby cafe restaurant; we heard King Petar's proclamation with great enthusiasm and relief, and then continued on our way towards the high school. From a distance we could hear a humming from inside the great four-story building, as though somebody had put inside numerous beehives.

In the large teachers' hall we met radiant faces on almost all of our colleagues. Any school work this day would be absurd. Instead, we left and joined the crowds streaming towards the Monument. All of these people, seemingly instinctively, then started to stream toward the nearby barracks of the 12th Regiment. The demonstrators asked for the appearance of the commandant Ilija Isailovic. Soon he was before us, standing on a wooden table. He was cautious in his words, but we heard him saying: "Our army had always been with the people, and this time they will also be with you. Long live King Petar II. Long live King Petar II. Long live Yugoslavia!" His words were repeated by the delirious crowd: "Long live King Petar II! Long live Yugoslavia!"

The crowd started out of the barracks toward the Monument to the Heroes of Kosovo. Some of us went to the headquarters of the Commandant to greet the army officers and thank Colonel Isailovic for his patriotic words. Then we rejoined the popular streams still moving on the streets. I spent all day in these celebrations through the streets of Krusevac, which lasted to the wee hours the next morning. In these streams of people, in front of you and in back, one heard mostly: "Better war than pact! Better war than pact!"

About midnight, there were some new ideas: "We want alliance with Russia!" I saw and felt deeply the joy and enthusiasm on all sides, beginning with veterans and spreading to the young men and children. "Pactasi" (advocates of the pact with the Axis) if there were any, disappeared suddenly, so that it was left to us to make jokes on their behalf. The rumor was passed that the druggist Krsta Novakovic managed his escape from Krusevac disguised in the clothes of a peasant (he was at that time a member of the House of Representatives). There was no known pro-"pact" man in Krusevac except Novakovic and his brother Nesa, a priest.

Watching what was happening in Krusevac, with the same sort of thing happening in other localities throughout Serbia, I was thinking of the moment when we would be attacked, or humiliated by some new ultimatum and compelled to enter the war. But a treacherous attack was not expected, for among us there was a belief in the chivalry of the German army, known from the Austro-Hungarian and German occupation of Serbia of 1916-1918.

Still tired from the demonstrations of the day before, I gave my lessons in the high school on March 28, then I came home to dinner and went to sleep. I slept only an hour or so when my wife Victoria started to pull my hair and my hands, and said: "Get up! Somebody is asking you to go to the City Hall; it's urgent! The army man is waiting outside." I got up quickly, put on my clothes, and met the military man, who handed me the order to present myself at once in the Military Department at City Hall. I was not surprised when I read in the telegram: "On April 1, 1941 at noon Podgorica-Mokra." That was the order of mobilization for my sharpshooters' company. Early tomorrow morning by the first train I would have to leave for the border of Albania, which had been subdued by Fascist Italy after its invasion of that country almost two years earlier, on April 7, 1939.

Except for the Adriatic Sea, Yugoslavia was now completely surrounded by hostile nations. To the northwest, it shared a border with Italy. To the west was the Adriatic, with Italy on the other side of the Sea. To the southwest lay conquered Albania. To the south Greece was largely in Axis hands, having been invaded by Italy on October 28, 1940. To the southeast, Bulgaria since March 1, 1941 was a member of the Axis pact nations, and seemed about to invade Yugoslavia. To the east was Rumania, which had been in the Axis group since November 23, 1940. To the northeast lay Hungary, which was pushed into the Axis pact on November 20, 1940. And to the north lay Austria, which had been annexed by Nazi Germany on March 11, 1938. Yugoslavia was surrounded, cut off almost entirely from the rest of the world, but we were preparing to fight.

Meanwhile, I did all I could to assist my family financially; then I got out my official documents and school and professional certificates, and put them into a cardboard box. I told my wife to keep it very carefully. She was astonished, and asked me why all this was necessary. I answered her: "You know, when one goes to war, very often one is supposed not to come back anymore. These documents will be of help to you and our children, if your Milija does not come back!" Her eyes filled with tears, but she understood my words and continued to prepare what was necessary for my journey.

On March 29, 1941, with my godbrother, Mr. Radivoje Jovanovic, a teacher in the elementary school of Krusevac, and my family and many friends and neighbors, we waited for our train. My godbrother and I took our leave and got into the train that had come from Stalac exactly on schedule, and we left for our destination. Later I learned that we two were the first from Krusevac to go to war.

On April 1, 1941, a little before noon, I arrived on the borders of my country against the upper northern point of Albania, on the border spot named Mokra, whose height from sea level is about 1,500 meters above sea level. At 1 p.m. I was in uniform, armed with a new rifle, supplied with 160 cartridges and two grenades or "kragujevke", which is what we used to call them after the place where they were made, Kragujevac, in the Sumadia province of central Serbia.

At the northern side of Mokra, near the wooded slope that decends to Verusa, was a small barracks for border guards that served as the center of mobilization for the 7th company of the 323rd regiment of our army. In this barracks there had been 15 frontier guards whose commander was Lieutenant Milicevic, born near Niksic. When Jovanovic and I arrived, only a few of our company were already there. The rest came in by groups for the next two days, mostly from Brskut, Stravce and Lijeva Rijeka. But by April 4, all of the company had arrived, except for our company commandant, First Class Captain Vido Lazarevic. Meanwhile our commander was Lieutenant Milicevic, who supervised the distribution of arms and other supplies. By April 4, the company was completely supplied and at full strength—about 260 soldiers, including the 15 frontier guards. On this day, near the barracks covered with deep snows, Lieutenant Milicevic, looking happy, mustered us and gave to us an enthusiastic speech. He said he was happy we were so quickly armed and ready to fight in the forthcoming battle. He stressed especially his happiness in having here veterans of previous wars, who know how to defend our country. From the successful attacks by Italy against Albania and Greece, as well as threatening events elsewhere around Yugoslavia, he was fearful that the arms at the barracks might have been taken virtually without our fighting, but that this danger had now been avoided.

Lieutenant Milicevic seemed a good and courageous young officer of about 25; all of his actions bespoke a man of firmness and resolve. In addition, he was very well acquainted with the border sector and the area of Albania on this part of the front. Unfortunately, he lacked the skill and knowledge to deal with the veterans, most of whom were over forty years of age—of my age, that is! This lack of knowledge of people showed itself one day when he came in conflict with some soldiers whom he found at some distance from our barracks on a road down the slope of woods near the few houses far below. Sharp words were exchanged, and discontent arose among the soldiers from Brskut. As soon as I learned of the incident, I went at night with Sergeant Aleksa Dujovic, my school mate from grade school, to see the men from Brskut, most of whom Dujovic knew by first name, whereas I knew only some of them by the names of their families. When we got among them, we started by talking of ordinary things, and making jokes. In this way, we approached the question of the "sharp words" of our Lieutenant Milicevic.

From our conversation I learned that a godbrother of mine named Jankovic was mostly responsible for the quarrel. This distant godbrother was from the village of Mrke in the lower part of Brskut. He knew that our godbrotherhood came from days of old, but he did not know how it began. Therefore, I told the whole story as it was kept as a tradition by us Lasic. These Jankovics are known among us under the family name of "Asanovic," a nickname of their ancestor Radoje, who was well known as a fighter against the Turks in the first decades of the 19th century. In those times "Asan" Jankov came to visit his friend Jovan Milojin, my great-great grandfather, to celebrate our patron saint, the Archangel Michael. When the guests were at the dinner table, a well-known foe of "Asan" crept secretly into the outer part of the house, and through an interior window shot our guest to death in our own home.

My great-great grandfather was extremely grieved by this tragic occurrence. He told his only son, Nikola, who was 19 years old, to mount his horse quickly and to go to the home of his dead guest to inform the family about the tragedy which took place in our home. He ordered this only son to ask the members of "Asan's" family to kill him in their home, for he could have no more honest outcome to pay for his humiliation not to have had protected and saved his friend and guest on his patron saint's day than to have his own son die in return.

The men listened attentively to my story and to many others of our native land. During these talks Dujovic and I thoroughly settled the "problem" of the quarrel with our Lieutenant Milicevic and Jankovic. My godbrother Jankovic told us jokingly that in his youth he was far more "troublesome" than our lieutenant. Lieutenant Milicevic, probably had been informed of our action; I noticed that he looked at Aleksa and me in a very friendly manner.

The company was divided into platoons. Every platoon had its own sheds that were used by shepherds in the summer time. The first platoon, including 15 border guards, was lodged in the small barracks. The mountain was still covered with deep snow, and often the new snow fell. Difficulties in obtaining food were eased by an abundance of potatoes kept by the frontier guard. I made arrangements with the guard to take my meals with them, paying according to the low price fixed by their authorities—one dinar per meal. In this way I was freed from preparing and cooking daily meals, and to have more opportunity to mingle with other soldiers. In addition there was the home of Punisa Marovic, a well-known hunter in Grla Veruska, as this area is called, down the slopes of the Verusa rivulet. At his home many of us were often invited to dinner and treated as if we were at home.

Many of us newcomers began to scout the frontier. Among us "old warriors" who went to patrol the frontier were Aleksa Dujovic, Punisa Marovic and myself; all three of us were once classmates in the elementary school at Lijeva Rijeka. We were joined by a second patrol of three frontier guards. The weather was very clear and the scenery marvelously beautiful, with the white snow glistening in the sun. The several peaks of the mountain Prokletije, on the other side of our frontier, looked as giants with snow between them. Some of us went to the Rikavac Lake south of Mokra; we even went to the border in a depression where the Vrmusa River turns and flows to the east toward the small Albanian town of the same name. During our scouting that first day we did not notice anything suspicious.

Although I was offered a job in the company headquartèrs, I preferred to be an ordinary soldier. But twice a day I used to listen to the radio in the lieutenant's office, and I related the news to the others with small comments. I used this opportunity to express my opinion on the dangers facing mankind from Fascism and Nazism, of the potential resources of our Allies in the West, and their certain victory against the Axis powers. The men liked it very much. My jokes and "complaints" against Sergeant Aleksa Dujovic, as well as his witty repartees, caused much joy among our fellows. As Aleksa used to sniff before speaking, it was easy for me to imitate him in that way, and to provoke my listeners to side-splitting laughter some-times without even my using any words. One of my imitations was of an incident that occurred in August of the year before, when I was with Aleksa on "trainings" in Podgorica. There he said: "Listen folks, I am a sergeant, and the professor is only a private. Thus I can use my military authority to tell him to take a single straw and to go down to the Moraca River and to throw it into the river so powerfully as to be heard by us in the army headquarters. Such is the 'authority' of a sergeant in the army."

The appointed commandant of the company, Captain Vido Lazarevic arrived on April 6, and immediately took command. The soldiers had already tried their rifles, almost all in their own way. I tried my own by "using" two cartridges to be sure that it worked all right. Each group of ten snipers got a machine gun and ammunition.

We were ordered to be ready to move early in the morning of April 8. I was assigned to the first platoon, headed by Lieutenant Milicevic. The commander of the second platoon was Reserve Lieu-tenant Garic. Reserve Lieutenant Markovic headed the third platoon, Sergeant Vidak Milacic headed the fourth. Two days' rations of dry food were given to all of us to take with us.

About 8 p.m. we started toward Albania. The fourth platoon was ordered to cross the Albanian line somewhat left of us in order to protect our main force. The remaining three platoons headed toward a plateau on the top of Mokra over a summertime horse path to Vrmusa. Having reached the small plateau, our first platoon left the other two platoons, and we headed down the long slopes toward Rikavac Lake. The remainder of the company with Captain Vido Lazarevic, continued in the direction of the Albanian border and Kunj-Vrmusa.

It was not easy to reach Rikavac Lake during the night because of the deep snow. The slope leading to the lake is very steep, so that it was dangerous to move straight down it. Especially on the lowest of the slopes, the snow had become soft, and our feet went deep into the snow. So I thought it was better to sit down on the snow and in this position to slide through the woods way down to the base of the slope. Most of my fellows did likewise. We were forbidden to talk loud, but there were many jokes on behalf of those fellows who asked for "help" to pull them out of the deep snow, or of those who supposedly lost boots.

When we reached the woods directly above the lake, moving forward became much easier; there was little or no snow. Exactly at 2 a.m., we regrouped on a small path above Rikavac Lake that leads toward the Vrmusa River. Then we entered the gorge along which the border was drawn. Instinctively, most of us took off our "sajkaca"—military caps—and made the sign of the cross on our chests and prayed, "God save us." I watched my fellows, and mused about the feelings that occur when men cross into foreign territory. Soon we reached the head of the Vrmusa River, along whose banks we continued for a long while, crossing it back and forth at fords. Our aim had been to support and protect the right wing of our company, and to reach and block the road—rather, a path—through the forest, heading from Vrmusa to Selca on the way to Skadar. We recrossed the meandering river by means of a large trunk over it, and continued to walk forward in complete silence. We moved up a long slope full of ravines on the right bank that was covered with a dense forest of birch and pine. We approached the road above us. Leading were Punisa Marovic, who supposedly knew the terrain best, and two of our frontier guards; we did not dare lose them from sight. At about 8 a.m., we heard two or three shots fired almost simultaneously—"Ta-tum, ta-tum." The shots were by our own men. Lieutenant Milicevic quickly gave orders to spread us into firing positions facing the road above, which we could barely see. Calmly I looked in the direction into which the shots were fired. The road by now was visible, but I did not see anybody. In any case, we took covering positions. In the younger soldiers one could notice emotion. The lieutenant loudly warned Corporal Militun Lasic, my cousin, who was standing against a pinetree trunk uncovered, trying to see somebody up there, to take cover. After a-while, we moved forward again. Smiling with a shade of doubt, I approached my fellow Punisa Marovic. He was eager to persuade me that they did not fire into "emptiness" or from being overcome by fear. He told me that they undoubtedly did see one Italian and two Albanians way up on the curve of the road. He was very happy when, a little later, we found numerous footprints in the snow on a ridge covered with short sparse bushes looking on our right toward Selca. It was clear that the three soldiers had been an Italian patrol, and as soon as they were fired upon, they came back to warn their main force, which fled over the ridge at our right.

We now approached the town of Vrmusa. From our position, we could see on the left, across the river, the bulk of our company coming to the first house. Far on the slope above Vrmusa, the fourth platoon was slowly descending toward the town. We too were moving to the left. There was no fighting We moved quickly and crossed the river to the left bank just below the town and soon entered Vrmusa. Before us appeared a large, three-story building of stone, property of the Albanian local chieften Prem Saljo, which was used now as a barracks for an Italian semi-military police force—"carabinieri." When our platoon arrived, at about 10 a.m. the bulk of our company was scattered around the "barracks." The officers and some soldiers were in the building, and the fourth platoon was approaching the town and soon joined our company.

I entered the "barracks." which was in great disorder. The Italians left this place quickly, leaving their trunks unlocked, open and disorderly, evidently grabbing out the things of greatest value. In their dining room were left unfinished cups of coffee and pieces of bread. The bakery was used by our soldiers as a welcomed supply of fresh bread. In the basement of the building there was a store of foods, including many large sacks filled with raw coffee, sugar and other supplies. Near the building there were left many unmilked cows.

Outside, our soldiers started traditional Serbian round dances, known as "kolos." I went into the building, into a room where our soldiers had made a fire in a fireplace, and I changed my sweaty underwear and socks. I spread my linen out on some empty chairs near the fireplace and let it dry. Leaving the underwear, I dressed and went out to mingle with my fellows. There, I saw four Albanians each carrying on their shoulders a ram. They wanted to give these rams as a gift to the captain and his company. They appeared sorry and hurt because our captain declined to receive their gifts but he told them kindly that we do not intend to cause any damage to the people or expose the peaceful Albanian people to expenses of any kind. "Our army has all it needs," he said.

We were at once aware that except for these four, the Albanians were nowhere to be seen. However, after a short while, they began to approach the town in small groups, and to continue their everyday work. We told them that we did not come to subjugate them, or to plunder their homes, but to expel the Italians, whose invasion of Albania meant slavery not only for them, but for all Balkan peoples. They trusted us wholeheartedly, and with radiant faces were listening to us and talking with us. To those who spoke our language fluently, we explained how the things stand now in the world and that our allies will again be victorious in this war. All of our soldiers were considerate of these peaceful and honest people.

At the invitation of Captain Lazarevic, we returned to the building, where we were distributing to all of our soldiers some cigarets found in the Italian magazine of supplies. While I was there, some soldiers from the upper story cried: "Fire! This building is on fire!" Captain Lazarevic gave orders to empty the building at once. Most soldiers had already got their portions of cigarets and were outside the building, warming themselves around the small fires in the large space around the building. A brief attempt was made to put the fire out, when it was beginning, but then nobody was willing to try to put it out. Instead, the soldiers still in there began to take out what they could find. Two or three of them were busily throwing through the windows some of the Italian wool-lined military overcoats. I hurriedly grabbed my rifle and haversack, and I left my underwear behind to burn.

The fire caught the roof of the building, and explosions of Italian ammunitions started. The explosions of the ammunition became louder and louder. Occasionally there were greater ones, apparently caused by grenades or by whole cases of cartridges exploding simultaneously. The explosions lasted a long while. Especially strong explosions were to be heard when the floor above the basement crumbled down. The fire later spread to some adjoining structures. As soon as these low structures caught fire, the greatest explosions were set off. There were countless cases of packed grenades in these small buildings.

These blasts did not cease as long as we remained in Vrmusa. As the building was crumbling and the explosions continued at varying intervals, our soldiers warmed themselves around fires far from the danger. Some of them went into houses which served as cafes. With two others I entered one of these. Here there was only an old woman and another in her forties. When we asked where were their men, the younger answered that they were somewhere nearby, doing some work. One of our frontier guards spoke Albanian fairly well, and he told them that there was no need for their men to fear anything. The women listened attentively, but their men did not show up as long as we remained.

After the fire, our company commander sought to find lodgings for our men to spend the night. There were four cafe-houses, in each one of which the soldiers were assigned by platoon.

The Albanian owner of the house had prepared a large kettle of boiled milk, and many of our men purchased cups of it. Some of us were warming our cans of foods to prepare our dinners. Our officers were seated at a table eating roast meat from the lamb that they bought about noon for 140 dinars. Aleksa Dujovic made jokes about this lamb. He was "astonished" why the officers did not get roasted lamb earlier by the huge fire in the building. Why do they torture the poor small animal turning it on the spike against the fire, and make trouble for the soldiers by preventing them from sleeping because of the scent of the roast lamb which was causing our mouths to water. Jokes and laughter are abundant so that even our Albanian friend enjoys side-splitting laughter. Our men joke with him, asking him, how in the devil did he dare to stay here alone with the men from the Black Mountains, or Karadak, as the Albanians call them, who

A tower-house or *kula*

Based on J. Cvijić, *The Peopling of the Serbian Lands*, Book 5, p. 14 (Belgrade, 1909). The *kule*, found principally near the Albanian border, were miniature fortresses.

can "cut off" his head as they did of old in similar situations. But the Albanian retorts wittingly: "Oh shut your mouth, you famous warriors were not able to cut off the heads of the rams we offered you in the morning as a gift; still less you would cut off the heads of us Albanians."

In the midst of these cheerful talks and laughter, an unknown soldier in a hurry came from outside and handed a small letter to the company's commander, Captian Lazarevic, who got up to read it close to the gas lamps. He read it many times and finally put it into the outer pocket of his uniform and sat on the chair. In his looks and gestures he was completely changed. To our jokes, which are still being told, he does not react. Already we have begun to make jokes about the "long" letter, about the impossibility to read such a "bull" so quickly. Some began among themselves to ask questions about our captain, as if he is illiterate. Where did he graduate from elementary school, and who was his teacher? All of this could not pull out our commander from his deep thoughts about the problem which, at the moment, oppressed only his mind. He got up again and reread the small letter, and again he sat down, putting his head between his hands, his face toward the floor. Many of us were conscious there was something very important in the letter that Captain Lazarevic had read so many times. We stopped our jokes and began to talk quietly about everyday matters.

Captain Lazarevic, after musing awhile, without changing his previous position, finally said as if in a delirium: "No, it is not possible, I will not. The men could not endure it." All of us who were still sitting by the fire, looked at one another. The captain continued to reflect; I got up and returned to my room to stretch myself a little on my "bed" which I had previously made. One of the soldiers who had been by the fire, or who was looking through the open door, said, "The captain is becoming insane! He is talking to himself."

In my room we started to guess where we would move. That we must soon move was clear. I began to express to them my strategic "knowledge". I was convinced that we were going toward Selca; this is the shortest way to Skadar. We knew already that our regiments had reached Skadar, encircling it from the west; the city was already in our hands. We were as happy and cheerful as little children. We foresaw in our discussions how many hundreds of thousands of Italians would be made war prisoners, because when our armies fall upon them they cannot escape, except to jump into the sea. However,

I was scared with a secret fear—this may be another retreat of our fighting forces through Albania. But I kept this to myself.

These guesses of ours were cut short by the company commander, who suddenly got up and loudly ordered us to be ready to move immediately. He sent some men to inform the other platoons. The company was ready to move within a few minutes. The third platoon was at a distance, but it was ordered to be the last out and to serve as the read-guard of the company. We started our movement, but—to our surprise and unhappiness—not toward Selca and Skadar, but back, up toward Kunj Mountain.

It was already dark at about 8 p.m. We forded a small stream and began up the base of the mountain before us. In the beginning our moving was easy, but the more we moved up, the harder was our advance, for we encountered deeper snow. The forest had always been difficult to get through at night. Some of us, looking for the right way, went astray, off the path, where the snow was softer and their feet penetrated deeper. It was especially dangerous if one stepped on a stump or fallen trunk, covered with snow; in that case some fell down deep to the middle of the body, and needed help to get out.

When we were somewhat midway on the mountain, a real January snowstorm set in. The men started to make caps out of their tent wings to protect themselves from getting wet, bacause the snow around the neck melted from the warmth of the body. The closer we got to the mountain top, the stronger the cold wind became, covering our faces with snow. The storm lasted until we came near the depression of the Mokra. Then the wind diminished a little bit, but the slope we had to climb was very steep. Very often we made a step or two forward, but then slid backwards the same distance. Our boots were frozen, so that you had the impression that you had on your feet small, very polished planks which were not flexible. In addition, the damned thirst and lack of sleep choked you! Most of us ate snow to kill the thirst. My knowledge and previous experience about the bad effects of eating snow were of no help to me—I ate it as if it were sugar.

About midnight, on April 9, our company was again on the plateau in the depression of Mokra, at the same place where we were the night before when we were headed for Albanian territory. Here came together the three mightiest foes of every soldier: exhaustion, thirst, and lack of sleep. I was hardly standing on my feet. Even now I do not know how I covered the distance from the plateau of Mokra to the barracks; in my ears I heard only the calling of those fellows who were more enduring: "Get up! We are going on!" I learned later, that it took us two full hours to cover the distance, which was covered with snow. It seems to me that I was striding on another's feet.

When we reached our barracks, I entered the large room, where there were some soldiers who were left at Kunj as rear-guard and did not go with us to Vrmusa. A fellow teacher, Milan Vesovic, offered me his place on the straw. I hardly had strength to take off my boots and put them behind my haversack that I used as a pillow. I was all wet from sweating, and the idea flashed through my mind that I ought to change my underwear because it was dangerous to lie down with them on; but sleep was stronger than the will to do so. I went to sleep as if I were dead.

I awoke about 10 a.m. When I opened my eyes, I saw many fellows lying on the straw around the room. Some of them were standing near the stove. In the room it was very warm. I felt well relieved —and thoroughly dry!

Many of our soldiers did not come back with us last night. The company's commander feared they might have been frozen, but fortunately, this morning the "laggards" have come. Feeling too tired, they entered the former Italo-Albanian barracks at Kunj and there they spent all night, and this morning they rejoined us completely relaxed and cheerful. Nobody reproached them for doing so. The other fellows, who covered so long a distance under most trying circumstances, were awfully exhausted. Strikingly they had lost their natural complexion because of the cold mountain air and wind which beat their faces. I did not see myself, but looking at them, I imagined how awful I must have looked.

After I washed my face, and took something for breakfast, my first thought was to learn about the cause of our sudden return from Albania. For this purpose I went to the headquarters of our company and entered the room of Lieutenant Milicevic. Captain Lazarevic and Lieutenant Garic were still lying on their beds, but Lieutenant Milicevic was already up and ready. The captain told me that our capital, Belgrade, was impossible to get on the radio; our transmission station was absolutely silent. He explained to me why we came back so suddenly from Albanian territory; the sub-commander of our police force in Brskut, a sergeant supposedly a Croat, had reported that Italian paratroopers had been parachuted on the soil of the Brskut community, to whose territory our company belonged, and therefore we were ordered to come back. The police force sergeant had got this order, supposedly from the commandant of the regiment—also a Croat! These things were at that time rather enigmatic to me; I felt that there was something deeper behind this "information" and military "orders".

The radio apparatus of Lieutenant Milicevic was on batteries which were already weakened, and their refilling was impossible. Therefore listening to the news was difficult; sometimes the first part was heard well, but later the voice became so inaudible that we could not hear the entire transmission. Since Belgrade was "silent", we tried to get London or Zagreb, far to the north. Out of some sentences from a Zagreb radio-station on April 10, 1941, it was clear to me: that Anton Pavelic's Ustasi Croats had shamefully betrayed their Croatian past.

However, we were unable to get a comprehensive view of our military situation. By telephone from Lijeva Rijeka, we were later informed by Bosko Orovic, keeper of the post office, that on April 12, our supreme military authorities had asked for an armistice. Even London was silent; nonetheless, as far as we could get some news from there, it was evident that our armies were in an awful situation. A suggestion from London that individual army commanders had received orders to resist separately wherever they found it possible to do so was another evidence of our defeat. Our only hope was that the main units of our armies would oppose the enemy somewhere deeper inland, where they would get a better strategic position. Privately I regretted not to be near the sea, to join those countrymen who would try to save some of our armed forces by escaping over water.

Our company remained in position; we continued to scout and to patrol the border of this section. At night a sentinel was put before the entrance of the barracks; during the day and night patrols were scouting the whole area. One day the afternoon patrol asked for reinforcements; they spotted seven armed men who were heading toward the Albanian border. The reinforcement consisted of soldiers dispatched in groups of three. The patrol, which was to prevent the deserters from slipping into Albania, encountered two Yugoslavs of Albanian descent; both were killed on the spot. Another patrol found three of our soldiers, also of Albanian descent; all three were killed on the spot.

The most interesting case happened to the third patrol, which cut off two men separated from previous groups of deserters. These two were heading back to their houses and were of our Serbian descent. One of them was a certain Kruscic from the village of Bjelo-jevici, community of Polja, district of Kolasin. The other was also from there, but his name was unknown. They declared they deserted from the front near Skadar as Communists. Both of them were killed on the spot.

When our patrols returned to the barracks, there was a discussion among our soldiers. They were unanimous that the patrols had done their duty. One of our soldiers asked: "Did Kruscic cry out: "Stop, folks, we will kill each other;" The men from Lijeva Rijeka explained that there is a branch of Kruscic whose custom was to cry so as soon as some other men were going to beat one of the Kruscics, in order to attract outsiders to come and protect him. To this Kruscic deserter such tactics would have been of no help. He paid for his having betrayed his fatherland and his people.

In such circumstances, beginning to lose every hope for a propitious turn on the battlefield for our armies, we remained on the borders of our country until April 19, 1941. At about 9 p.m., the officers had a conference. After their meeting, we were told that we had to leave our barracks and disperse. Captain Vido Lazarevic wanted to see us in the morning, and then to go with our fellows from Brskut toward Brskut-Kuci to Podgorica; Lieutenant Milicevic and Markovic decided to go through Moraca and Rovci to get to Niksic, where they had their houses, the frontier guards decided also not to be captured by our foes, but to disappear under arms; they had some friends or relatives, and made plans to go to them. For the Kuci from Stravce, fellows from Brskut and Bratonozici, who made the bulk of our company, it was very easy to scatter and go home. To us from Lijeva Rijeka, who were about 50 men, it was necessary to cross the highway leading from Podgorica to Kolasin-Andrijevica, if possible at night, to avoid being captured by German or Italian motorized columns and prevented from reaching our villages.

In the storeroom for military uniforms and boots there was disorder; Lieutenant Vidak Garic asked for some help. Somehow, order was restored and the soldiers took what they wanted or could grab. Grenades were also distributed very quickly.

During all of this tumult, I was calmly sitting with some frontier guards and other fellow soldiers in the small kitchen, all of us ready to go out. From nearby villages, especially Brskut, many people had come to take something from our barracks. The storeroom for foods was in front of the kitchen, on the other side of a small corridor with the kitchen door wide open. It was quite easy to see what was going on there. The "onslaught" began; they broke open our window and took out large cans of lard. With that, the barracks keeper opened even the door of the storeroom, and the people started freely to take supplies of food. A small fellow from Brskut grabbed so many strips of bacon that he could hardly move out. From the kitchen we cried in laughter, "Folks, help him: Do you not see that he will perish?" My Godbrother Radivoje Jovanovic, a teacher, just returned from outside, told us this: "Near the entrance was a human being with a big and heavy sack on his shoulders, and another at his feet. He asked me to help him put the sack on the ground over that which was already on his shoulders. I refused to do it, saying that I did not intend to load any jackass in this snow." All of this lasted until midnight.

The light in our kitchen went out; the lamp used up its supply of gas, and the other could not be found. We were sitting in half-darkness; only the open cover of the oven gave some light. A frontier guard complained in the darkness that his haversack was taken.

At about 1 a.m. on April 20, 1941, we set off down Grla Veruska. For a short while we were going on the left of a small stream, then crossing it on fords, we continued on the right side through the native village of my dear Godmother Zorka, who had so vividly told me about the suffering of the village during the First World War. The ground was not covered with snow. It was hard to go forward: the slopes were steep, and the upper soil had been defrosted whereas its lower layer was still frozen. We frequently fell.

Arriving at lower Verusa, it was daylight. We crossed the stream to the left bank. A little further, on Suvo Polje, we began to disperse—some went to the right toward Tara and Opasanica, and others on the left toward Lijeva Rijeka. There was no sign of any of the enemy's motorized columns, and we reached our villages under arms without any difficulty.

We arrived at Lijeva Rijeka at about 7 a.m., having walked six hours. There were already many of our soldiers here who were retreating from Podgorica, Kolasin and Andrijevica. Many of them were from Sumadija, central Serbia. Most of them were exhausted and unable to march because of calluses on their feet. Women from surrounding villages were bringing in small sacks of bread, cheese and other supplies to distribute to these soldiers; they quickly returned home to prepare new supplies for other groups who continued to come and go farther for many days.

After resting at Lijeva Rijeka, I went with two brothers, who had come to meet me, to our village to live with them for some days in the home of our parents. Almost all who were mobilized from our village, Kami, had returned. Veko Perkov Dadovic did not return; there were rumors that he was killed near Skadar. Later it was proved that he deserted his military unit with Communists, and with them was killed near Podgorica.

For regular army men and others who were born in our community, but who were scattered through the country, it was yet impossible to know about their fate.

In the house of my eldest brother Ilija, I found Vucic Dabetic, sergeant-pilot in our airforce. Vucic Dabetic was a good example of how we adapted to the new situation. First we ascertained that he could drive a motor vehicle, as his pilot's uniform, with some small alterations, could look like a civilian dress. We cut off the buttons of the uniform, and gave it to my niece to affix buttons used for civilian clothes. My eldest brother, who was a community official, obtained papers saying: "Vucic Dabetic, born at Lijeva Rijeka, where he is permanently living, chauffeur by profession." In this way his status as a military man was hidden.

From Vucic Dabetic I learned what all happened at the airfield at Niksic. There were many tragic occurrences, but King Petar II, head of the country and commander-in-chief of the armed forces, was successfully flown out of the country.

On Easter Day, I went into the house of my uncle Velimir. On a thick woolen mattress stretched on the floor near the stove, there was a young man deeply asleep. To my questions, they answered in whispers: "There have come to our village five Srbijanci from Leskovac; the young men are very, very tired. This one is somewhat sick; he could not even eat; we could barely get him to drink some warm milk. These soldiers had a horse, and they put on horseback the exhausted fellow, and the other four had to go on foot. All of them belonged to the battalion of the Royal Guard, which was in service for the protection of our King up to the moment of his getting to the airplane at the Niksic airfield. The villagers remembered these young men for a long time, always praying to God to protect them and help to reach their homes and to see again their parents. Old Milica Adzic would break into tears whenever, later, one mentioned her sick "Srbijanac"; her tears were a relief of her sorrows because of uncertainty of the fate of her only son, who did not return for a long time.

On the night of April 22, 1941, a great noise was heard coming from Raskovo Guvno. I was in my bed, absorbed in thought. I heard our people gathering in a hurry on the meadow behind our house; somebody said loudly: "Good Lord, what is it there? " They saw a German motorized column weaving from Verusa toward Lijeva Rijeka. From the window, I could see it, several kilometers in length, the beams of the motor vehicles projecting their lights, so that it seemed to form a long band of flame, which, threatening as a serpent, was coiling over the mountain and making a noise we could clearly hear. My niece Bosiljka, trembling and frightened, came in, saying "Get up, uncle, to see something never seen under Heaven! From the top of Viliste way down to the church there is a stream of fire. They are moving ceaselessly . . ." My niece again darted to the door repeating: "Almighty Lord, help us! Good Lord help us!" To the great surprise and bewilderment of my brothers, my sister-in-law and their children, I stayed on my bed, plunged into thoughts of our situation, and comparing it with the occupation of our country in 1916. The men, women, and children on the meadow behind our home were watching and talking among themselves for a long time. All were on their feet to see this "astonishment". I heard their excited breathing and repetition of prayer: "Good Lord, help us!"

This house in Crna Gora shows the flattish tiled roof which betrays Mediterranean influence. The lower walls are made of stone, the upper of adobe with a timber framework. The main living quarters are on the first floor, but not all the houses have balconies; stables, store-room and kitchen are on ground floor.

CHAPTER TWO: THE NAZI-FACIST OCCUPATION

The motorized German column that passed through Lijeva Rijeka on the night of April 22, 1941, left only a chilling memory and busted wall where a tank had slipped from the road. But on the following day, remnants of the column also passed through, but not so peacefully.

The first crime was the theft of a bale of hay from a farmer carrying it to his sheep. The second crime was the theft of a sheep. The third crime was the cold-blooded murder of a man—a Gypsy camped near the village of Lopate, who happened to have a rifle on his back. One of the Germans stopped his vehicle, took the rifle and broke it over a rock. Then he shot the man to death.

After the Germans had passed through, the Italians appeared. At first they were transporting our exhausted soldiers from Podgorica and possibly Niksic. They took them to Kolasin and Andrijevica, where the trucks were used to pick up Italian soldiers who had been captured early in the war by Yugoslavia's armed forces, but then left unguarded and without supplies after the defeat. This crisscross of war prisoners and former war prisoners lasted about a week.

I learned that my wife and children had gone finally to Bijelo Polje, where her mother lived. I decided to go there. Bus service was still available on the Podgorica to Berane line, and I stood in the crowded bus as far as Matesevo, where I got off to await the bus's return from its sidetrip to Kolasin. In Matesevo there was a sea of refugees, mainly farmers from the districts of Istok, Pec and Djakovica, who were fleeing bands of Moslem Albanians who had been armed by the Fascists. In Metohija, all of the homes of Serbians had been burned, and the food supplies and other possessions that were left behind were seized by the mobs. The story was virtually the same for numerous isolated farm houses and all of the villages in the border area except Vitomirica and Glavicica. These two had more numerous Serbian populations, were more compactly settled, and had organized armed resistance. However, the fate of these villages was still uncertain.

From the city of Pec the crowds of refugees, coming as a living human river, were walking over the road to Andrijevica. They brought only what they could take away in haste; some had saved a cow, some a sheep, pig or horse. There are more than 170 kilometers from Pec to Podgorica; the entire length of this way had been covered those days with these victims of war. Their rows thinned as far as they began to stride deeper on the territory that was Crna Gora before the Balkan wars, and where they gradually dispersed to seek shelter.

The hardships of these Serbian refugees were increased where they had to pass over two mountains, Cakor, with an altitude of over 2,000 meters, and Tresnjevik, about 1,800 meters above sea level. On April 27, 1941, when I passed, it was beautiful weather; but earlier and later it was raining or snowing on the mountains, so that the people, especially the children, suffered terribly. My godbrother, Radivoje Jovanovic, who covered the same way a few days behind me, told me that never in his life did he see anything more heart-breaking than the stream of refugees going up Tresnjevik. About half-way up the mountain, he encountered a group of refugees driving some cattle. He saw also a cow loaded with a blanket and some bed things. Some small children accompanied the cow. Each child carried something—one a small sack, the others some bundles. "I especially noticed," he said, "a small girl eight to ten years old. She was carry-ing in her left hand something wrapped in a white cloth. She had on a colored robe of a rather thin cloth. It was raining sleet very hard—rather, it was pouring, so that it looked as if her clothes were stuck to her very weak body, and the strong pouring of rain mixed with snow was dripping from her hair down her weak body." That was at the middle of Tresnjevik, but what would it be like on Cakor, on top of Tresnjevik this evening, when the night will surprise them soaked and exhausted on the road? About all this we could not talk any-more, but fell silent.

I arrived late in the evening in Berane and spent the night in the home of a relative, Vojko Vojnovic. The next morning I learned that the Albanians from Rozaje in great crowds were advancing toward Polica, a Serbian community about ten kilometers east of Berane. We feared that these Albanian mobs would kill all the non-Moslem, Ser-bian Orthodox population that they encountered. The Albanians from Rozaje, Pester and Sjenica were heading toward the Lim River under the leadership of a certain "captain" of theirs, who 20 days before was simply a gendarme in the ranks of our police force! It was known that the purpose of the Albanians was to fix old border lines between Crna Gora and Sultan Hamid's territory of old, or at least to "occupy all the territory up to the Lim River."

Italian occupying military forces were already stationed in

Berane at battalion strength. At the urging of local leaders, the Italians loaded some troups on their military trucks and sent them toward Polica to protect our peaceful population there from the Albanian armed mobs. The military trucks had machine guns in front ready for use. This action restored some order among the citizens; otherwise, if the Albanian mobs had advanced farther, it would have come to bloody fighting to repel them by our own means.

On April 28, 1941, late in the afternoon, I continued my journey to Bijelo Polje. There the situation was not noticeably bad. There were very few hot-headed Moslems hoping to get the opportunity to "sack" and "plunder" in this district, where the Orthodox population lived in a two-to-one majority. The bulk of the Serbian Moslem population, however, were willing to share with their Orthodox fellows our common fate. A platoon of Italian soldiers were brought here from Berane on demand of the citizens of Bijelo Polje to prevent the "Ustasi occupation" threatening from Prijepolje.

On May 2, 1941, I went back to Krusevac, which had been my home until one month before. At the Krusevac railroad station there were no Germans to be seen.

I went through almost deserted streets, even though it was only about 4 p.m. I saw that people were not completely downhearted, but they looked more restrained and silent.

Entering the courtyard around the house in which I lived with my family, I headed straight toward the entrance of my house. Upon opening the door, which was already a little ajar, my eyes encountered a German soldier sitting at a table in the living room. On the table there were two empty plates, a cover of a military cooking pot, a piece of bread and some other small things. I smiled bitterly, and in German told the soldier that this was my home, and that I had my wife and children whom I intended to bring back to our home. I asked him whether it was necessary for me to go to their command, or if he himself would ask that my house be freed. The soldier told me, as far as I could understand him, that I myself ought to go there to settle this question. Then I withdrew.

I went to our neighbor, the old lady Anka, who used to rent out a sleeping room. I agreed to rent this for 250 dinars per month. From the old lady Anka, her daughter, and grand-daughter, I learned what happened to my home after the leaving of my family for Bijelo Polje. The three German soldiers now occupying my home actually were the sixth party of them, who were lodged there successively.

Krusevac had been bombarded hard on April 6, 1941, early in the morning. At Obilic, near the city, and around Krusevac there were about 40 bombs of various sizes dropped, two of them on the city proper. Happily even these two did not explode, whereas on the military factories at Obilic they made an awful havoc, there having been many dead and wounded trapped in trenches or in shelters. Huge masses of citizens, including my family, had left their homes and fled out of Krusevac.

In the barracks of the 12th regiment, near the city, many of our army officers and soldiers had been made war-prisoners by the German military forces. Among them there was Army Major Gruja Bogdanovic, who had retired and had not reactivated for this war.

When the first German tank with some motorcyclists entered Krusevac as a vanguard, old Major Bogdanovic was among a group of on-lookers nearby. At the moment when the city's Mayor was to greet them and give them the keys of the city, Major Bogdanovic ordered the men around him: "Fall on the enemies, brave fellows!" At once a crowd of men barehandedly attacked the Germans, disarmed them, and took them as war prisoners. Two days later, stronger German military forces came to occupy the city, and to liberate their captured soldiers. When the German commander of this sector was told about this case, he ordered the white-haired Major Bagdanovic brought to him. The German commander looked at him sharply and asked how did he dare to do that. The old veteran answered: "I was ashamed that my city surrendered to so unimportant a military force of our enemies!" The German commander stretched his hand and congratulated him, saying, "Every good soldier would have done it!" The German commander gave him time enough to go to his home to put on his military uniform and to come back to join the other group of war-prisoner army officers. Old Gruja Bogdanovic went as a prisoner of war to Germany.

In our eighth-grade high school there were many changes. One was that on the big high school building a large Nazi German flag was fluttering, and there were many German soldiers inside. There were many new colleagues from all parts of Serbian territory: from South Serbia, Vojvodina, Bosna and Herzegovina. From conversations with them I learned more of our national tragedy. Those from South Serbia however, were comparably better off. They had been compelled to leave their homes and give up all they earned by hard work, but (at least at that time) there had not been killings by the invading Bulgars.

It had been different in "Independent Croatia" in the north of Yugoslavia, and in Vojvodina, occupied by Hungarians. In the school for girls' handy work there was employed a lady who escaped from the territory near Senta. Hungarian soldiers broke into her home after midnight; they took her and her husband (a teacher) with them, while the children were left weeping for their parents. On the place where the soldiers herded them she watched her husband shot to death with a revolver. Then she was allowed to return to her house and her children. Somehow, she managed to come with her children to Belgrade, and from there she was sent by the Commissar for public instruction to this school.

Petar Korac, a high school teacher in Subotica, was one among 18 Serbians whom Hungarian soldiers took to the Tisa River to kill them all. There they were called again by their names and ordered to get into the river. At that moment one of the Hungarian soldiers told Petar: "You are not a Serbian, you are a Croat; Koracs are Croats!" Maybe this Hungarian remembered the Croatian politician of that name and concluded that there was no such name among the Serbians. Only by this was he saved from certain death; all other 17 Serbians before his eyes colored the waves of the Tisa River. Such incidents were numerous in Vojvodina.

There was also ominous news of massacres in the territory under Ustasi rule: the Sava River bringing dead bodies of Serbians even to the city of Belgrade. Many of these dead bodies bore large inscriptions, painted on cloth: "Free ticket to Serbia!" The tidings also were coming to us of the massacres by Ustasi in Herzegovina, mainly about massacres near Mostar. We heard that Ustasi had put into chains 78 Serbians in one group and brought them to a precipice, where they killed them one by one, and pushed them into the abyss!

The stream of refugees toward Crna Gora, and especially toward Serbia, looked like a migration of nations. These people in flight from their homes were living witnesses of the beginning act of the tragedy of the Serbian people in this war.

All those who had been mobilized, or called to military "training," had to report to the mayor's military department by orders of the German authorities.Up to now we had been able to avoid getting directly into the hands of our foes, but now we were trapped. The opinion of many was not to report, but the majority thought it was dangerous not to report, as this could seem suspicious to the Germans, and provoke persecution of your family.

After the reporting the active army officers were taken to a separate room to get some special orders. Major Dragutin Keserovic told me that evening: that the "German did not take his eyes off me," and he told of his being informed that many Yugoslav army officers still would not admit that they were defeated in the war. Later, all of us who had reported were given a certificate that told us to behave as "war prisoners on leave".

Army Major Keserovic was living at that time in my immediate neighborhood, but we were never seen together on the streets. We met in the home of the 1st Class Army Captain Boza Bozovic, who lived in a very small house on Pec Street, near the cemetary. Before I returned to Krusevac, Bozovic somehow managed to be declared as being affected by tuberculosis. The sanitary commission to lodge German soldiers marked those homes not fit for their purpose with a yellow circle, signifying dangerous to live in. At the entrance of this lane lived Steva Vlahovic, sanitary II class captain, and a little farther, Milovan Ivanovic, head of the circuit court, and Radomir Saicic, state's attorney. All of us every day about 6 p.m., before the BBC news from London, used to go there to visit our sick friend Bozovic.

In this way for almost three months we followed the BBC transmissions from London. Bozovic had a radio of medium size, but very good. One minute or two before the start of the transmission, we quickly pulled out the radio from under the bed: "This is London . . . We give you our first evening transmission in the Serbo-Croatian language . . . ."

On May 8, 1941, we learned that Colonel Draza Mihailovic had not been captured and that the flag of his regiment continued to flutter in freedom somewhere in the western part of pre-Kumanovo Serbia. The people believed he was either on Rudnik Mountain, or Ravna Gora or even on the Kopaonik Mountain even closer to us. We were aware that under today's circumstances it was impossible to keep together in any place such military forces, because of the impossibility of supplying them. However, the number of armed forces under his command was growing from day to day. Colonel Mihailovic thus even at that time had many hundreds of thousands of willing soldiers in our country, but it was necessary to get them together and organize them to be ready for military action.

On the subject of organization we often talked with Major Keserovic. On May 12, 1941, he told me: "Do not worry! We are getting orders and instructions from above; plans are already made to organize and link together our military forces within the country."

There had not been open flight into the mountains as yet. Under the circumstances, it would have been harmful, as our forces could be discovered and exposed to the danger of being annihilated by the occupiers. At the most propitious moment, we would get instructions of what to do. We were very cautious. One could talk only with his most trusted friends.

Our sorrows grew intensely from the awful explosion which occured on June 3, 1941, at Smederevo. The freight cars loaded with ammunition at the Smederevo railroad station exploded that day, killing about 5,000 Serbians and 950 German military men, and destroying the old fortress of Djuradj Brankovic on the Danube River. The train was ready to leave for Belgrade, and the Smederevo railroad station was crowded with men, women and children who came to accompany the members of their families and bid them good luck. The blast lifted the whole train into the air. The bodies were flying and falling on the ground all around.

In the city of Krusevac, there was almost no open activity at all. On the streets one could see men in a hurry who were going somewhere. Cafes and restaurants were almost empty. In the hotel-restaurant "Paris", where there usually had been many people before the war broke, one could see few guests in the cafe; they had drunk a cup of coffee, put 2 dinars aside and were talking in a low voice. In the main hall they were setting tables, with much care, for the German under-officers, who took their meals there regularly. They were sitting calmly and without any talk among themselves; as if they were conjuring to do some new evil to us. Before them on the tables one could see in abundance cookies, wine glasses and big cups for coffee. The owner was complaining, in whispers, that they paid for all this in occupation marks, or in many colored papers as he called them.

In the beginning there had been some "promenading" about, as was the custom everywhere in our cities before the war. Local police authorities stopped such walking completely.

By the end of June, 1941, we learned that a great number of Slovenes were compelled to leave their homes and their fatherland where their ancestors had lived for many centuries. The German occupiers had annexed a great part of their native homeland, Maribor and other surrounding lands, and asked them to make their choice:

to become the citizens of the "great German Reich" or to leave their homes. We learned that about 60,000 of these honorable people had arrived in Belgrade and that they would be immediately resettled within the borders of pre-Komanovo Serbia; in Krusevac and the surrounding area about 3,000 of them were to be resettled. When this number of Slovenes were due to arrive at the Krusevac railroad station, a modest greeting was set, but their greeting was most solemn. In conversations with them we became aware of the awful ransackings in Slovenia and plundering of their homeland by Germans. Being now in Serbian environments, these brothers of ours felt the warmth of soul, and from the very start of their living here there was no difference among us.

In the first days of the occupation the farmers used to come to the market places in great numbers and bring their products to sell, but Germans came and bought what they wanted at a price fixed by them and payed in the occupation marks. In the following days there were fewer and fewer farmers, and finally they disappeared from the market. The city dwellers began to buy "underhand," or they themselves used to go to the villages to buy. The prices for goods were rising.

My family was still in Bijelo Polje. About the end of June I went to the special department in the City Hall, which had charge of the required papers to bring them back. As my family was living in a "foreign country" (because of the Italian occupation) and I would have to get through "Independent Croatia," through Sandzak, my petition had to be sent to Belgrade. Finally the papers were issued.

I set off by passenger train from Krusevac on August 1, 1941. Between Pozega and Uzice I started a conversation with a postman. He, whispering, told me that recently two Germans were wounded near Kosjeric. The morning after their being wounded, there had come to Kosjeric a detachment of German military, who gathered 100 men from this small town. The postman vividly described how they blockaded the town, went into a cafe-house and private dwellings and into the offices of civil authorities, and counted out 100 men, all peaceful persons who did not even know what had happened yesterday on the highway. Then they shot them all on the spot in retaliation for the wounding of the two German army officers!

The commissar of the border police unit of "Independent Croatia" was Mr. Ilic, a rather young man, very considerate and thoroughly informed about the suffering of our people on the other

30

side of the "border-line"; he was absolutely against my continuing farther. He affirmed that even yesterday in the Croatian police prison at Visegrad three Serbians from Crna Gora were simply choked. This information he got from our railroad personnel who were running the trains going to Sarajevo as far as Visegrad, where Croatian personnel took it over. When we took leave for this time with the commissar of the border police station, Mr. Ilic, he told me, with his eyes filled with tears: "Mr. Lasic, please go back. Do not let them take you life in vain!"

Nevertheless, I continued the next day, and my German-approved papers proved sufficient to get me through on the train.

In the late evening, on August 2, 1941, Vukosav Radovic, a policeman from Krusevac with whom I had travelled, and I arrived in Bijelo Polje, which some 20 days before had broken off the Italian military hold. We were met on the road by three of the "insurgents," who recognized us and greeted us warmly. We were in territory that at least temporarily was "free".

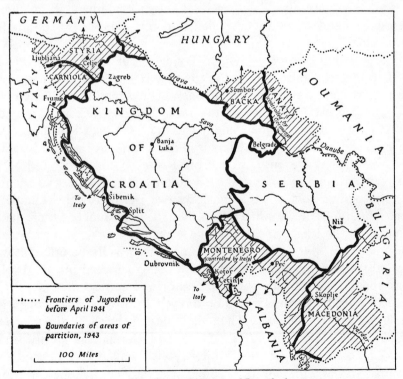

The dismemberment of Jugoslavia, 1941
Based on official sources.

CHAPTER THREE: REBELLION AND REPRISALS

Hatred of the invaders mounted, with the discontent growing rapidly ever since the annexation of Boka Kotorska and parts of Dalmatia, as well as the changing of Serbian names throughout the annexed zone. But the Fascist attempt in June and July of 1941 to establish an "independent" Crna Gora had brought large numbers of persons to outright desperation. The people of the Serbian Crna Gora and (Brda) Mountains simply could not allow such an act because they were aware that by so doing the enemy was separating them from their brothers.

The first flame of the general uprising could be considered the attack on a small Italian garrison at Vir Pazar during the night of July 12/13. The garrison was a small one, probably of company strength, and its soldiers were annihilated. The insurgents first killed the sentinels at the bridges, and quickly penetrated to the military barracks there, and put them on fire. The Italian soldiers within were burned alive. The leader of the insurgents was Rasko Vukasevic, a Yugoslavian Army Reserve Officer.

The second attack against the Italians occurred on the highway at the eighth kilometer from Cetinje to Rijeka Crnojevica, at the turn below Mekovac Hill. The insurgents of the upper Ceklin, Dobarsko Selo, and the upper Dobarsko Selo had been ready since July 11, and had given orders that none of the villagers could go to Cetinje. The attack occurred on July 13, 1941. The leader of this group of insurgents had been Andrija S. Pejovic, army officer in the reserve of our army. Pejovic spread his forces on the line Dobarska Ploca-Debeljak-Mekovac-Prijevor, and on the line Dobarska Ploca-Han Masanovica. The Italian column consisted of ten trucks, which had left Cetinje at 2:00 p.m., and came to the place of attack at 2:20. The attack started first from Debeljak, and then from all sides. The fighting lasted until 6:00.

The Italians had been taken by surprise, but defended themselves courageously. They had about 70 soldiers; all but 15 fell in battle. The 15 prisoners were taken to the village of Donje Ulice. An attempt by the Italians to come from Cetinje to the rescue of this detachment was unsuccessful, because the insurgents had forseen such a possibility.

Among the Yugoslavians to die in this fighting at Dobarska Ploca was our finance comptroller Matovic, who had written much about our "twenty years of slavery" (while Croatia was a part of Yugoslavia), and who was thought to have been the writer of the first article published in the insurgent newspaper of the time *The Voice of Crna Gora*.

The uprising broke out through the entire territory of Crna Gora and Mountains. The garrisons at Savnik (300 men), at Zabljak (30), and at Goransko (25) had been quickly taken. In all this district of Savnik, national unity had been established under leaderships of army officers. At a meeting at Bukovica, Major Jakov Ostojic was selected as commander of all these forces, with Captain Mitar Pejovic, the battalion commander at Piva, Captain Ivan Ruzic in Drobnjak, Captain Zeko Trebjesanin in Uskoci, and Captain Nahod Djakovic in Saranici. These forces moved in two directions: those of Saranci, under the leadership of Captain Nahod Djakovic and Bosko Bojovic toward Lever-Tara to protect our forces from Pljevlja; and the others toward Niksic.

Fierce fighting started around Danilovgrad in Bjelopavlici, where there had been an Italian garrison of about 1,200 men who had artillery. Bajo Stanisic, an army colonel, was the insurgent leader, with Captain Milos Pavicevic and Lieutenant Dusan Bozovic as his aides. The commander of the Kosovaluka battalion was Major Nesko Jovovic, and for the Martinicki battalion, Captain Todor Ivanovic. On the left bank of the Zeta River was a smaller group of insurgents led by Lieutenant Risto Perovic, with Arso Jovanovic as his chief of staff; both had been opposed to Colonel Stanisic being the commander-in-chief of our armed forces around Danilovgrad, but they had not been able to impose themselves on a majority of the insurgents. Their "youth" battalion had grouped predominantly the Communists from this area.

After the fall of Spuz, the belt was tightened around the Italian garrison at Danilovgrad, and the general onslaught occurred on July 17, in the morning. The garrison was taken with great losses on both sides.

In this respect, the attack at Danilovgrad differed greatly from that of Bijelo Polje. The main forces of insurgents for the attack on the Italian force at Bijelo Polje on July 16, 1941, came from Ravna Rijeka. A few days before the uprising there had been some stirrings which showed up openly at meetings in various communities. At Zaton, the only community of the district on the right bank of the Lim, some hundreds of men, who gathered under the leadership of Major Milan Bandovic, an army officer who lived in Zaton, marched to Ravna Rijeka, where they joined the insurgent groups coming from Mojkovac. The insurgents from Sahovici and Pavino Polje crossed the mountains and came down to Ljesnica. The insurgents from Nedakusi and Sutivan advanced up the Lim River to Pruska, a suburb of Bijelo Polje.

The farmers had been organized into companies and battalions under the direct command of active or reserve army officers in the area. More than 2000 men were organized in this manner. The others with the insurgents were very young men and old ones, all of whom had a rifle or some other weapon.

At night the insurgents blocked the city from all sides. The Italians had about 400 well-armed men in Bijelo Polje, who were well intrenched and fortified in the center of the city, at the high school, on a hilltop. They occupied and blocked main entrances to the city, and on the marketplace in front of the Hotel Radovic they had installed many machine guns and mortars. The insurgents were armed mostly with rifles, with little ammunition, a few machine guns, some hand grenades, and only a few were without firearms. The fighting began at dawn, with attacks from all sides. The first breakthrough occurred in the lower section of the town, so that the insurgents' main forces quickly stormed the city from that side. The Italians' machine guns and mortors had not time enough to show their full effectiveness; the main entrances to the city were also overcome, and the belt tightened around the main Italian force. They defended themselves with firing in all directions from their trenches around the high school. The insurgents issued a call for surrender to the Italian commander which read: "Surrender to us; do not lose your lives! Our forces are very great—8,000 well-armed men!" After a while the garrison surrendered.

After the surrender, all Italian soldiers and army officers had been disarmed and were strictly treated as prisoners of war. Enlisted men were lodged at the elementary school; the officers at the hotel Radovic. The supplies of foods as well as the sanitary facilities and other necessities were organized. The insurgents formed a guard which was regularly relieved. The Italian losses were one dead and six wounded; the dead soldier did not fall at that battle, but he was killed by a farmer later to revenge his brother killed by the Germans somewhere near Berane in April. All of our men deplored this killing, and the murderer barely escaped being punished for his act. The insurgents suffered only some slightly wounded. The Italian and insurgent wounded were treated by doctors in the local hospital.

Having captured and freed Bijelo Polje, all insurgent military forces moved toward Serbian villages on the right bank of the Lim River, organized previously into military units, and set the front against the Albanians in Sjenica district and further right on the bank of the Lim River as well as against the Ustasi who had occupied the whole district of Mileševo. The Moslems on our side were peaceful and loyal, except a few individuals who had earlier ran to the Ustasi occupied territory; our Moslems were treated as the other citizens among us. There was hard fighting to save Serbian villages in the Low Kolasin (the upper valley of the Tara River), especially the three communities there inhabited by a purely Serbian population, which had preserved their Serbian name and customs for centuries even during the darkest Turkish rule. The insurgents front against Albania and Croatian fascist Ustasi was a deep-rooted expression of self-defense and protection of the Serbian population.

Thus Italian garrisons in Kolasin, with about 600 soldiers, in Andrijevica, with about 500 soldiers, in Berane, with 1,500 men; and in Bijelo Polje, with about 400, had been taken in the uprising. Although common farmers did most of the fighting, they were led by both active and reserve army officers. Among these, as well as those already mentioned, were Captain Pavle Djurisic, and my brother, Staff Army Major George Lasic.

The uprising against the occupiers had been realized under most trying circumstances. It was a great moral victory of Crna Gora and (Brda) Mountains, which were now in freedom, and those of the occupiers who had not been killed, we now guarded as our prisoners of war.

They were not guarded for long, however. The Italians still held Bar on the Adriatic sea, as well as Cetinje, Podgorica, Niksic, and Pljevlja. And strong military motorized units were concentrating to rush on this small area of Serbian land to extinguish the spark of liberty. Some parts of these troops had been on the eastern coast of the Adriatic, ready to take a rest in their native Italy, after long efforts made to conquer parts of the Balkans. These military units had been embarked on ships. Informed there was an uprising behind them, their troops returned in fury to pacify Crna Gora and Mountains in fear Il Duce would die from hurt pride, due to his not being able to impose his Fascist creed on the "develish Montenegro."

The forces of the punishing expedition were concentrated in Podgorica, coming from Skadar, and in Pec, coming from Prizren, and in Djakovica, coming from the south of Albania. It was believed at this time that in Podgorica alone there had been, or passed through the city, about 120,000 soldiers. The first troops, belonging mostly to the "Pusteria" Division, were forcing their way toward Cetinje by July 20. The vanguard, about 1000 strong, reached Koscele four kilometers from Rijeka on the route to Cetinje at 1 a.m. on July 21, 1941. Here insurgents led by the First Class Army Captain Jakov Kusovac attacked from all sides, beginning a battle which lasted more than eight hours. About 120 of the Italians were killed, and a great number wounded: the rest were made prisoners of war. Later, the main bulk of the Italian division succeeded in forcing its way forward to reach Cetinje, strengthening their earlier force in that city. Along its advance, these troops made an awful ransack of inhabited places near the highway, starting from Kokote some 16 kilometers from Podgorica all the way to Cetinje: killing men, women, and children on the spot, burning homes, and mercilessly destroying the harvest in the fields all around.

The second troops of the punishing expedition set off from Podgorica toward Niksic, through the valley of the Zeta River in the direction to Danilovgrad. The new forces of re-occupation were very strong, and the insurgents were not strong enough to resist them any longer. The population fled as far as possible from the main highway linking Podgorica, Danilovgrad and Niksic, taking with them what they could as their homes were burned by the invaders. Other Italian armed forces moved on the route Dubrovnik—Trebinje—Bilece—Niksic.

The third group of the Italian punishing expedition set off from Podgorica at the end of July to force its way toward Kolasin into the direction line Podgorica—Bioce—Vjeternik—Lijeva Rijeka, then through the valley of the Tara River—Han Garandzica—Matesevo—Kolasin, and farther on. These forces also made a terrible ransacking of the countryside; dense smoke and flames engulfing homes on this sector indicated to the frightened inhabitants how far the invaders had come. Many of our people were killed during this advance.

With the news of the approach of the Italian motorized units in the fourth branch of soldiers of the punishing expeditioin, our military forces started back from the front lines and began to cross the Lim River to disband into the villages, each man to his home. Fear reigned in the city proper. Late at night, Andro Stanic, one of the delegates from this district, had returned from the general meeting that was being held in Kolasin. I went to see him. His opinion, he said, had been "to give a resistance somewhere between Podgorica and Vjeternik, but the majority did not consent." It was not difficult to conclude that the Italians had already broken the uprising.

Italian forces from Podgorica and Pec broke the Serbian defense lines, and the insurgent forces were compelled to retreat and disband. The motorized Italian forces appeared at Cakor on August 6, 1941, and began shelling our forces. Meanwhile, Albanian incendiaries, numbering more than 3,000 men armed by the occupiers, went forward and began putting fire to village houses. All 350 homes in the county of Velika were destroyed. From Cakor the Italian forces with Albanian mobs continued putting fire to other villages as far as the county of Ulotina in Polimlje. The inhabitants fled into the mountains to save their lives, and if possible, some of their sheep and cattle.

The main insurgent forces retreated under fire until it became evident that any further resistance was in vain; from Murino they began to break their lines, scattering through villages to save their families.

A delegation of distinguished men in Vasojevici was organized to ask the Italian commander to stop further putting fire to homes. In this delegation were the Archpriest Bojovic, Milan Popovic, a teacher, Milutin Jelic, high school principal and former member of the house of representatives, and Dr. Kaberice, from Andrijevica. They took with them an Italian ex-police chief who had been captured by the insurgents and kept as a prisoner. The headquarters of the punishing expedition were still at Cakor.

The delegation set off on August 7, early in the morning and barely got through the Albanian and Italian lines. They were received immediately by the commander, but a cease-fire could not be achieved quickly. They were compelled to stay on the mountain, standing during the night. About 3 a.m. they were called again to the headquarters and to receive the conditions imposed by the Italians. The principal purpose of the delegation had been to stop the firing of homes and to get the Albanian incendiaries to leave the territory. In this they were successful, thanks to the Italian ex-police chief taken with them; he certified that the insurgents had humanely treated about 500 Italian war prisoners at Andrijevica, and that none of the captured soldiers were killed. On orders of the Italian commander, the putting of fire to homes was stopped, and the Albanians were forbidden to go further as vanguard of the punishing expedition. About 1,800 homes had been burned already, mostly in the area of the Upper Vasojevici, district of Andrijevica.

The Italian punishing expedition, without the Albanians, continued advancing down the Lim River valley. There had been little resistance on our part. But far from Andrijevica, in the mountains in Sekular county, an Italian detachment surprised a group of men in a shepherd's hut. Among these was Army Major Milicko Jankovic, who was a very courageous army officer. At the uprising he had been the commander of the Velika battalion. He was brought to Andrijevica to be shot. At the shooting field, he showed a manly attitude; he did not allow himself to be shot in the neck, from the rear, as the Italians (and later the Communists) generally used to do, but was shot in the chest. He fell with these last words: "Long live King Petar II! Long live Yugoslavia!"

The advance of the punishing expedition was awaited with great apprehension at Berane. Here the Italians had at the time of the uprising a garrison with about 1,500 men. In attacking this, the insurgents had killed some 90 men. Some 42 of these had burned alive in the barracks. Though they were allowed to surrender, they did not (as other groups of the garrison did), but, kissing the photographs of their children and wives and giving the Fascist salute, they were consumed by the flames. The new occupying forces immediately put on fire all the empty houses in Berane whose owners had fled. The house of Dusan Popovic, a judge, was also put on fire, although his family lived within, because the freed Italians saw that an insurgents' machine gun had fired from its balcony at the Italian garrison barracks.

Six citizens were taken immediately to the shooting grounds. Among these were the only daughter of Army Major Milovic. Milovic came forward and was allowed to replace his child and be killed in her stead.

From the military standpoint, this uprising gave our Allies, the English, French and Americans, about 200,000 fewer soldiers to fight against, since these were engaged in "pacifying" Yugoslavia!

The occupation was not easy for Yugoslavians.

A sorrowful case occurred on September 20, 1941. A certain Moslem highwayman from Korita or Ivanje shot one of our gendarmes, wounding him in the arm, at Rasovo on the Lim River, downstream from Bijelo Polje. The wounded man had enough strength to get to the nearest Serbian home, and then all the village of Njegnjevo went and encircled the killer in the bush below the village school.

The villagers could not approach him bare-handed, but they set up a watch all night, patiently waiting to kill him with stones or by other means. The next day, early in the morning they came to ask the Italians for help. A company was sent. When they came on the spot, the Italian Army officer ordered a gendarme of ours to go ahead of him and to throw a grenade at the place where the highwayman was hiding. The gendarme went forward to throw the grenade, but at that moment he was wounded by the killer.

The Italian Army officer then went on alone, and threw a grenade, but the criminal fired again and killed the officer. After that, the company left, carrying the dead body of their captain. Not knowing this region, they picked seven villagers from those remaining on guard and took them along to Bijelo Polje. The next morning at Nikoljac near the church, they shot one of them, a young man named Furundzic, known to be feeble-minded. For many days afterward there was a simple chair at the spot on which the young man was sitting when the soldiers shot him in the neck. Later, people used to come to this place, and pray to God to grant his innocent soul ever-lasting life. The other six were taken to Berane, where two more were shot to death, and two others each in Andrijevica and Kolasin. The Italians were convinced Serbians had killed their captain.

Yet back where the criminal was surrounded, the next morning Radojica Orovic came to the spot from the village of Ostrelj. He was well-known as a sharpshooter. He remained through the next night on watch with other villagers, but before dawn the next morning he loudly told all present to go to their homes and not to waste their time. He himself skillfully hid near the criminal. As soon as the villagers were some distance away, Orovic fired his rifle, killing the criminal.

CHAPTER FOUR: COMMUNIST TERROR

In addition to our troubles from the Italians, the Germans, the Ustasi Croatians, and the Albanians, Yugoslavian-born Communists began assassinating men of importance. First killed was Tomica Cukic, mayor at Haremi in Budimlje County, near Berane.

Soon after, on October 17, 1941, Milovan Andjelic, mayor of the county of Polja Kolasinska, in the district of Kolasin, was assassinated by his fellow Communists on the bridge over the Tara River. Some 600 Communists had been celebrating the Bolshevik revolution in a cafe-house at Mojkovac, district Bijelo Polje. They invited their "comrade", Andjelic, a long-time Communist *of old* and ex-member of the House of Commons in Belgrade, and one of 54 Communist representatives before the suppression of the Communist Party in Yugoslavia in 1922. "Comrade" Milovan Andjelic made a short speech: "Comrades, you are involving the people in blood and suffering before the right time. Your action is but a foolish game, which will incur a disgrace to our communist idea. I remain a Communist, but I will not go with you; I will not take any part in a round dance of criminals. Long live Comrade Stalin! Long live the Red Army! Long live the Communist Party!" Then he calmly stepped off the rostrum, took his rifle, and left the meeting without saying goodbye to anyone. With his brother, he headed to the bridge over Tara. Some of the younger comrades had been quicker, and by short cut, came to the bridge, crossed, and waited hidden. When "Comrade" Milovan was crossing, he was shot dead.

The third victim was the mayor of the county of Sekular Bozovic, Andrijevica District, who was from a very distinguished family. By the assassination of Mayor Bozovic our resistance against the Albanian mobs was weakened. The Sekular men were famous for their centuries-long struggle against oppressors, even under Turkish rule, and had lived in freedom since 1854, when Upper Vasojevici succeeded in liberating itself and joined Crna Gora. Living in freedom, they had been sharp borderline fighters, living continously under arms and ceaselessly fighting against the Turkish power. Vaso Laban, army first class captain in retirement, had come to the burial of Bozovic with a group of men from Polimlje. In his speech at the grave of Bozovic, Laban had warned the people and urged them to defend themselves against the new foes who had begun to appear. In returning home, he was mysteriously shot to death.

Laban's assassination had terrible consequences for the organization of the resistance against the foes of our people in this area. The Albanians in Plav rejoiced as did the Communists.

In spite of these first assassinations of our leaders in this region, the people remained inactive. In the district of Kolasin, Nikola Jovanovic, representative in Parliament, was killed. The people remained with their hands crossed.

The Communist terror reigned in full force during the fall of 1941, but from December, 1941 to February, 1942, it was at its most bloody peak.

In districts of Niksic and Savnik the Communists had surpassed all one knew about atrocities, even the beheading of our leaders in Sumadija in the beginning of the 19th century by the Turkish *Dahija*. The "red-dahijas" of our time massacred numerous prominent men. One of the first was Ceda Milic, a well-known patriot from Herzegovina, who escaped from the Croatian Fascist terror there. The Communists took hold of him in the Piva Monastery, and brought him to Gornje Polje near Niksic, and slaughtered him there. Then followed a long string of murders: Blazo Visnjic, sous-prefect, with his 19-year-old son; Army Captain Tadic, killed at Laticko between Piva and Golija; Army Captain Stanko Radulovic with his daughter, killed at Zavrb, near Niksic; retired Army Captain Joko Jovovic, killed midway between Glibovac and Gornje Polje; Army Captain Damjanovic, with many other men, killed in Brocenca Village; the brothers Novica and Blazo Kovacevic, at Grabovo, along with Army Captain Markovic and many others.

In the districts of Pljevlja, Cajnice and in the counties of Sahovici and Pavino Polje, the Serbian Orthodox people were continuously fighting the Ustasi, who had been strengthened by the arming of the Moslems. The position of Orthodox populations in this area was almost unbearable.

At the end of November and during the month of December, 1941, several thousand Communists from the pre-Kumanovo area of Serbia, were driven out when the people destroyed their infamous "Republic of Uzice". They fled en masse toward the territory of Crna Gora and Mountains.

The arrival of several thousand Communists in this area spread the communist terror. With these Communists from all other parts of Yugoslavia, and the local Communists under Arso Jovanovic, the slaughtering of the prominent men increased greatly in the districts of Savnik Niksic, Danilovgrad, Kolasin and a part of Podgorica district. This is the time of killing over 40 Karadzics in Drobnjak, 82 men, including many Dzakovics, in Boan, as well as men in Moraca. A massacre took place in Kolasin, where 264 men were killed.

In the districts of Berane and Andrijevica, of the Vasojevici, there had not been until this time any mass killing. In Kuce, there were only 22 locally born Communists, and these had been ordered to live in peace, else they incur on themselves any evil. In our neighboring county of Bratonozici, there were about 120 Communists properly organized under the leadership of two of our former gendarmes, Dragisa and Ljubisa Milacic. The districts of Bar and Cetinje, in part, were under the would-be leadership of Krsto Popovic, known as a separatist. But we knew that the death orders were falling as rain for men throughout this part of our country. Our great hope had been the prominent men in the district of Kolasin: Batric Rakocevic, circuit court judge; Army Captain Leka Vujsic; Mileta Pekic, judge in Gornja Moraca; Army Colonel Radovan Radovic, in Kolasin; Sava Dzajov Lazarevic in Gornje Lipovo; Army Colonel Veko Bulatovic in Rovca, and others in this neighboring area.

On November 30, 1941, I ate my supper, and went to bed. About midnight the loud voice of my sister-in-law Jelena awoke me: "Brother, get up; there is a noise up there near Uncle Jovan's home!" I started getting ready to go there, when I heard some men hurrying by our house already going that way; these were our neighbors Radevics from the lower part of our village, who were going armed toward the home of Uncle Jovan, at the extreme west end of the village. With my eldest brother Ilija, I went by short cuts through fields in the same direction. We both went armed.

When the two of us arrived, our neighbors were already gathered on a small meadow by Uncle Jovan's house. Among them there was our Godbrother Miras K. Radevic, a refugee from Metohija with his eight family members, living now with his parents and his brother. He had been to visit his in-laws in the village of Duske today, and at night was coming back home. When he was near our village, he heard some noises and undistinguishable talking up above him on the other path. From this he concluded that there was a rather large group of people. He told us he hurried on and by-passed the house of Uncle Jovan. However, when he had covered a small distance, he changed his mind to come back to tell the sons of the late Savo Radovanov Zecevic, whose home is close to the house of Uncle Jovan, of the matter. They talked it over, and decided to alarm all of the neighbors. The villagers feared it might be a patrol of the Italian armed forces, which should be watched during the night.

We patrolled, heard men in the darkness, but they eluded us.

In the morning, on December 1, 1941, I was still asleep in my bed when my sister-in-law frantically ran in and told me: *"Brother, get up! Milic Orovic has been killed at Bucin Potok tonight! Our villagers are getting ready to go to express their condolences; we ought to go with them."* I quickly got up, and we joined a large group to go to Bucin Potok, which is near Lijeva Rijeka. On the way we speculated about the cause of the killing, but nobody was able to give a reasonable explanation, because nobody could imagine a motive to kill this man, who as a settler in Metohija escaped the fury of the Albanian mobs and had come with his wife and two small children to live with his brother on the farm of their mother; their father had been killed in the cause of freedom in January, 1913, in the battle of Skadar.

Coming in sight of the rather large, well-built house of stone, some of our group began the customary lamentation; one by one expressing loudly the virtues of the dead, as well as the merits of his close kin in the past during our struggle for freedom. It was easy for the mourners to speak well of Milic Orovic. The Orovics had been known of old as good men among our tribe of Vasojevici; they had been courageous fighters and wise men. Milic's grandfather on his mother's side had been one of the greatest heroes of the battle of Vucin Do, and had received on the spot the Medal of Obilic from the prince of Crna Gora and Mountains. After these solitary lamentations, the lamentating of women at the house entrance began in chorus.

In the house, in a spacious room on the right, on a long table, the body of Milic Orovic was lying with his arms crossed on his breast. Seen by the morning light, penetrating the room through a large window at the left, he looked as if he were asleep. To the left in front of his coffin, his mother Milja was standing like a stone statue; his wife was in a mourning dress, the tears running profusely down her face. The men began to express their condolences in sorrow. I approached to do as was customary, first to Aunt Milja. Even before I stretched my hand, Aunt Milja looked at me and said: "Son, they killed my Milic!" My voice choked, and I was barely able to reply: "May God save your other family, two sons, daughters-in-law,

and grandchildren." Milja Orovic looked as a wounded tigress awaiting a moment to rush with all her remaining strength against the
attacker.

Other groups of villagers arrived all morning. Their lamentations
were heard approaching the house. We got up to make room for
others, and went out. All around the house in the upper courtyard
men were sitting in groups, talking about this first killing in our
county.

In the company of some friends, I went to see the place where
Milic had been killed and to get more information about the circumstances under which he was killed.

Yesterday, on Sunday, after supper, Milic Orovic with his wife
and two small children went to spend some hours in conversation
with his aunt and her two daughters, because her son was not here
these days, but had gone to Andrijevica to buy some food for their
family. The aunt with her daughters had been very pleased by this
visit, and they were sitting around the room, while Milic, with his
clothes on, was lying on the bed. The womenfolk were talking among
themselves. So they spent a pleasant evening, and the baby went to
sleep.

At about 10 p.m., the womenfolk heard some loud noise as if
breaking the door of the house, and believing that the head of the
household had come back, the elder daughter quickly left the room
to open the entrance door. As soon as she had opened the inner
door, she saw a group of men on the fireplace in half-darkness. Frightened, she recoiled, having no time to shut the door of the room
behind her. The four men were already in, immediately approaching
the bed where Milic was sleeping profoundly. The men quickly fired
some revolver shots at him. With the first shots, the lamp went out.
In complete darkness, the killers left the room, and, together with
those who had been in the fireplace room waiting for them, left in
an unknown direction. The women lit the lamp, and quickly approached Milic, who already was dead. They noticed an inexplicable
stain of blood on the floor spreading through the kitchen and even
over the threshold of the entrance door. The women immediately
informed the neighbors. During the night the news spread very
quickly through the villages nearby and even through the neighboring
counties.

Many questions were discussed repeatedly, and the opinion
became conclusive: The Communists killed him. Mirko Vesovic and

Scepan Djukic had shed the blood of our brother."

Returning to our village with my close kin, I was in a group of villagers from Ptic, Stup, and Krkor-Dujovici, Radevici, Mujovici, and Milikici. Among us was Aleksa Dujovic, a former secretary of the county, and Miro Dujovic, a First Class Army Captain. We decided that it was urgent to organize immediately to prevent the sort of catastrophe which had engulfed the greater part of Crna Gora and Mountains—we must defend ourselves by the force of arms against the communist criminals. Special couriers had been already dispatched to find Army Major George Lasic in Vasojevici over the mountains Komovi. Aleksa Dujovic was thundering: "We will not let them slaughter us as one kills oxen!"

We learned on December 3, 1941, that one of the four killers had been the son of Ananije Milosevic, a medical student, from Tara, near Matesevo. He had been shot in his thigh in the darkness, and his blood left the stains on the floor. When the others were carrying him toward the hamlet of Radunovici, down Rijeka, he cried out because of the pain. They had been compelled to leave him in a house in Radunovic. From a 13-year-old shepherd boy named Radunovic, we learned the name of the wounded, as well as that there had been 18 in the group of Communists who took part in the crime. Eight of the men had entered the house, four into the room to perpetrate the murder, the other four as guards within. The other ten were standing guard around the house. The scout-guide of these criminals had been the step-son of Bosko Orovic, whom Bosko's wife brought with her when he was one year old, after she remarried after the death of her previous husband, Sekulovic from Brskut. This young man grew up in the home of his step-father who was caring for him as if he had been his own son, and these last years Bosko trusted him so the youth became the manager of his possessions. Nevertheless, on November 30 in the afternoon, Bosko's step-son spyed on the movements of Milic. Through the uncurtained windows on the room, he had recognized the brother of his step-father lying on the bed, and he himself told to the murderers the "most propitious moment" to kill the brother of him who included him among his sons and had trusted him wholeheartedly. This was the "new ethics".

CHAPTER FIVE: THE TERRORISTS RESISTED

On December 3, 1941, several of us got together and discussed the problem. At the meeting were George Lasic, staff army major; Aleksa Dujovic, former secretary of the county; Miro Dujovic, army captain, first class with the Upper Military School; Krsto Radevic, a farmer and distinguished veteran; Nikola Lasic, sous-prefect (constable) from Bitolj; Branko Radevic, army captain, second class; Milisav Radevic, army captain, first class in reserve, and myself. Aleksa Dujovic told us that 198 men were already committed to take arms if another murder occurred in any village in the area. We decided the men of each village should be organized in a military manner.

The traditional military organization would be utilized. For example, it was accepted that Boricici, Dujovici, and Mujovici belonged to the third company; Milosevici, Vesovici and Djudici to the first company; Dabetic-Lasics, Kojici, Radevici, Adzici and Milikici belonged to the second company, and so forth. This organization corresponded to the territorial disposition of villages: in Ptic and Duske, neighboring villages, inhabitants were almost exclusively Dujovici and Boricici, and similarly with other villages. The soldiers in any company would alone choose their company captain. Then the program of this military organization was drawn up as follows:

"The battalion of Lijeva Rijeka is formed for these purposes:

1. To protect against all the *honor, life and property* of any inhabitant of Lijeva Rijeka;
2. If there is any evidence that anyone does anything contrary to the *honor, dignity*, and the *traditions of the people* of Lijeva Rijeka and our tribe, Vasojevici, *he will be tried exclusively by an appointed popular court but not by any irresponsible group of men;*
3. In this organization are included all capable able-bodied men of Lijeva Rijeka from 18-70 years old;
4. This organization has no party designation, but only a common national aim;
5. In this organization are to be included all brotherly popular forces to prevent their use in vain and any weakening, as well as to protect themselves against any evil which might come from without;
6. This organization *forbids any internecinal killing of men and any activity which could endanger the existence of our nation;*

7. Each member of this battalion has to be sworn to the people that *he should sacrifice his life for their honor* and their good, *and that he should tenfold avenge any fallen inhabitant of Lijeva Rijeka* [the words . . . "and that I will tenfold avenge any fallen inhabitant of Lijeva Rijeka" were added on January 5, 1942, when we had been sworn in complete formation before the church at Lijeva Rijeka] and,

8. At the head of the battalion is the headquarters of the battalion, that is, the commander and his adjutant; the appointed popular court, and the committees for supplies and help for refugees.

Made in the village Kami, county of Lijeva Rijeka, on December 3, 1941."

As soon as we finished drafting this document, messengers were sent to call meetings. On the appointed hour, there had been 31 men under arms: 11 Dabetics (2 Kojics and 9 Lasics); 9 Radevici; 2 Zecevici; 7 Gogici; and 2 Milikics from Krkor. The proclamation was read, and everyone was asked if he agreed to it. Anybody who would not consent was free to say it. None left. That same night we began to patrol and protect our village.

Then George Lasic, Branko Radevic, and Nikola Lasic, with some villagers as their guards, went to the village of Duske, where messengers had already been sent. They found there 72 Boricici and Lakusici already under arms. Similar to the procedure in our village some hours earlier, the proclamation was read and explained. When they were asked who agreed, 71 Boricici and Lakusici wholeheartedly joined our ranks.

Thursday, on December 4, 1941, we went, as it was previously agreed, to the village of Ptic. When we arrived at Ptic, we found there a great number of Boricici too. Aleksa and Miro had already settled that we all had to go to Stup. There we met all Dujovics, Radevics, and Mujovics—all under arms. By 3 p.m. on December 4, 1941, we had 177 armed fighters ready to oppose the killing of men by Communist terrorists, or for any other eventuality.

Now, it was necessary to go to organize Malo Slacko, the neighboring village northeast of Ptic. There Adzics from Siralija, all Milikics and Dabetics, from Velje Slacko, headed by army captain Novak Milikic, joined us cheerfully and wholeheartedly. Now we were an armed force with over 200 men. The meeting broke quickly, and we headed to our homes.

On December 5, 1941, early in the morning George Lasic, Aleksa Dujovic, Nikola Lasic, Miro Dujovic, Branko Radevic, and five witnesses from previous meetings, went to Kolevice. In Kolevice, and on down to Rijeka, lived Zecevics, Orovics, Tomovics, and Mitrovics in greatly scattered homes. There were 25 men, and Vidak had already visited and enlisted them. Therefore, it had been unnecessary to stay here any longer.

On December 5, 1941, in Lopate village, some 36 Milosevics, Djukics and Vesovics-Popovics, joined us.

The next day, on December 6, we went to Verusa through Grbi-Do and Planinica to organize some 15 Zecevics and Vesovics living in Verusa. Then we went through the mountains to Tusi, where we met in the elementary school building. Milosevics and Djukics lived in this village. We saw Army Lieutenant Colonel Radivoje Milosevic, who looked like a lost man, and learned that Mirko Vesovic's Communists last night, in this very room, had held a meeting and that "death sentences" poured like drops of rain! There had been about 40 men from our batallion "sentenced to death"! Our men laughed until their sides were aching with laughter. From Vukadin Djukic we learned that all Djukics in Tuzi were against the Communists, and that they did not care a bit about Communist "sentences" or "trials".

So we continued to Uac and Vucetin Kami in the valley of the Upper Tara River. At Uac, late in the evening, we came to the home of Radisav Milosevic, district sous-prefect, who had already been informed about the organization, and had organized all Milosevics in Tara as well as some living in Tusi who could not expose themselves there bacause of the frquent meetings of Communists there. He gave to George a list of 25 men. It was necessary to leave Uac quickly, because we were near the highway, and feared that some Italian military force might surprise us. Toward Opasanica we set off very cautiously, using special patrols to protect us from any surprise from Communists or Italians.

In Opasanica lived Radunovics, Dabetics, Gogics, Kruscics and Lasics, and we knew that there were 52 able-bodied men here ready for military service. The villagers awaiting us had foreseen that we might have supper and spend the night with them. In the house of Labud Kruscic, all 52 village men attended the meeting, in addition to us 20 or so visitors. Aleksa Dujovic, Nikola Lasic, and Milovan Radunovic took part in the discussion of the Communist terror which raged throughout this part of our country. Afterward, George

Lasic read the resolution for the organization of the battalion, and explained it point by point. Finally, as at the previous meetings, he asked: "Who is willing, of his own free will, to join us to defend any brother against the violent and criminal actions of these irresponsible men?" Immediately 27 villagers wholeheartedly consented, while 25 others went into a caucus. Left alone, their final decision was unanimous to join our organization immediately. The villagers of Opasanica elected Vojin Gogic, our Army Lieutenant, as their company commander, acting on the recommendation of Radisav Kruscic, First Class Army Captain, both of who lived there on their own homesteads.

Delighted in having accomplished the task so quickly, we began to talk of the troubles of our country. We were then surprised by the arrival of Milos Dujovic, Aleksa's brother, with some 14 other Dujovics and Mujovics. They had been informed that the Communists were ready to kill us all when we separated and went to sleep in the various homes of our hosts. This changed our plans. Milos Dujovic argued that if we started to fight the Communists in Opasanica, it would take long to arouse our men, but that our leaving would disrupt their plans. After a short deliberation, we, about 35 men, left in fighting formation. Milos Dujovic with two others was at the head; about 30 villagers from Opasanica accompanied us to Han-Garandzica in Tara, and their patrols followed even up Verusa until we went through two most dangerous gorges on our way.

When we were nearing Suvo Polje in Verusa, a storm with strong winds began beating us on the face. There were no houses nearby, because they had been burned last August when the Italian punishing expedition had passed through. We got some shelter around the walls of the late Janjo Dabetic's home; Dabetic had been captured by the Italians last summer while his house had been in flames and taken to Podgorica, where he had been shot to death. After the storm slowed down, we continued to Velje Slacko . Here we from Kami–Radevics and Lasics–parted from Dujovics and Mujovics, and came to our village somewhere about 4 a.m.

While we had still been at Uac, George Lasic had sent instruction to Majo Milosevic, Otas Zecevic, First Class Army Captain in reserve, and Jevto Djurovic, an industrialist, to organize our men in that part of the county of Lijeva Rijeka. This company enlisted 20 workers in the Djurovic Sawmill near Matesevo.

Now, on December 6, 1941, the complete organization of the

battalion of Lijeva Rijeka had been achieved, the first military organization on the territory of Crna Gora and Mountains, ready to oppose the criminal Communist terrorism in this area. The fighting strength of this battalion, based on the information given by each individual company, was 469 soldiers. According to Radivoje Milosevic, an Army Lieutenant Colonel, this was the same number as the battalion of Lijeva Rijeka was in 1912, when they went to fight for liberation from Turkish rule.

The organization having been achieved, we began living as armed camps. In my village, 31 men of us under arms used to gather either in the house of Krsto Radevic in the lower village, or in Kojic's and Zecevic's at the upper village; other nights we camped in the house of Velimir Lasic, or Kosto Radevic's. The choice was among the houses with a big room, in which 25 to 30 men could gather. Two patrols of three men each continously crossed the village and were relieved according to the weather: if the weather had been mild, they were on duty for two hours; if it was cold, for one hour. At these camps the soldiers elected their company captains. For the First Company, the captain elected was Petar Milosevic; for the Second, Novak Milikic; for the Third, Miro Dujovic (until the middle of January, 1942, and since that time, Marko Boricic); for the Fourth, Vidak Zecevic (until the middle of January, 1942, and since, Zarija Zecevic); for the Fifth, Vojin Gogic; and for the company at Matesevo, Otas Zecevic. Although it was felt generally that George Lasic should be elected as the battalion's commander, he chose to let that be decided at a general meeting later.

Throughout all of our villages security had been restored. The company captains forbade any crossing of suspicious persons through our villages. During the day, the men were doing their usual work without any fear that somebody would enter his house and kill somebody. The Communists retreated to other counties, or secretly met in Tuzi.

But they were never left in peace even there, not because we had been after them to persecute them, but it was enough for them to fear Bosko Orovic alone, the brother of Milic Orovic, with his fourteen-year-old son. One day, at about 7 p.m., Bosko Orovic entered our house and started to shout: "Shame on you, stupid ones! Why didn't you shutter the windows? The Communists could have thrown a bomb through the window and killed your children; I do not care for you grown-ups, but I do care for the little ones." He quickly slammed the door, and went on. I was told by my folks that he had gone toward the home of my uncle Velimir. I went to find him there, but I was told that he came in to bid them goodnight and went out.

The next morning, I met him in a house of Radevic in the lower village, and I asked him: "How quickly you left, and did not stay with us for even a few minutes?" He looked at me calmly, and started to list the names of villages and places where he had been last night. First he went to Malo Slacko, where the Communists met sometimes in Adzic's; then with his boy, he had gone over the hills to Tusi, some five to six hours of walking, and he did not find them there either. I understood what was the matter and gently asked what he could have done with his boy, if he had found "them"? "You know", said he, "what I could have done: I would be able to sneak to their meeting, and start to throw unscrewed bombs among them, this I could have done." "In this case," I continued, "you and your boy would have been killed together with them." "Eh, this is not your business," answered he. "I want to revenge my Milic, whom they killed against God's justice, even if I must together with my son be turned into pieces." It was hard for me to look at a man whom sorrow and injustice had broken and put out of bounds of any normal thoughts and feelings; I knew him from his earliest childhood, and I never noticed in him any bad inclinations. This change in him had not come up from any fault in his character, nor from any inclination to do evil; on the contrary, in him awoke the deep-rooted human willingness to fight against the criminals, who could be named as murderers, gangsters, or Communists, it did not matter. In the days of lawlessness, these avengers had taken the place of law; they make order and peace among men.

The partisans in our county had been aware of the sense of revolt which spread through our villages. I believe there had been some men in their ranks who did not approve the killing of Milic Orovic, and maybe tried to soften our wrath through the men in their ranks who were not Communists before. In this way we construed the letter of Lieutenant Radivoje Milosevic, who invited me to come to see him in Malo Slacko on December 8, 1941, in the afternoon. We decided that some villagers ought to go with me, even George himself. When we arrived at the house of Milos Pavicev Adzic about 1 p.m. we found Mirko Vesovic, Radivoje Milosevic, and an unknown man, sitting at the dinner table. In front was Mirko, on his left Milosevic, and on the right the stranger. As customary, we greeted them in the name of God, and they asked us to sit at the table with them to eat. "We had already eaten, thank you." I said. On the left of us there were sitting or standing around these at the table about 15 men, and in the courtyard before the entrance maybe again as many of them. We took some seats on the right. I noticed among them Otas Lakusic, and began to joke with him.

After they finished eating, and the table was cleaned, Radivoje Milosevic got up and turned to us, looking more at me than at the others, saying: "I invited you, Milija, to talk with you a little about our present problems. I have read many books, and some of them about Communism, and I do not know what Communism is." I ran out of patience, I could not let him further talk nonsense, and interrupted him with these words: "Listen, uncle, you never knew anything good, and the least you know is what is Communism; your knowledge consists of turn to the left—turn to the right— attention, and that is all. But this lawyer here, pointing my finger at Mirko sitting head down, what kind is he to kill our brothers in our villages?" Looking at Mirko, still with my finger pointing at him I continued: "You have to tell, before all of us, and give any reason for the killing of Milic Orovic." On my right I felt a stirring, and George, holding a paper, told me: "Look at the reason", and he began to read out loud: "On November 30, this year, we killed the 77th traitor of our struggle, Milic Orovic from Lijeva Rijeka, a well known fifth columnist man, spying for former Yugoslav regimes, and a man who made ambushes to our men." He stopped reading and continued talking with extreme wrath: "It is shameful that someone dared to slander a plowman, a Serbian, to be a 'fifth columnist' and spy against Yugoslavia. And as to the ambushes of your men, or of you, this was not necessary for Milic Orovic; at any moment he could openly approach you, and twist your neck as a chicken." Among all present, there was a breathless silence. Radivoje looked at me astonished, but George continued to read from the Communist "Bulletin of Radovce" of December 3: "sentenced to death are well-known fifth columnists and traitors in Vasojevici: Milutin Jelic, Filip Cemovic, and George Lasic."

I disdained to talk any more, and I got out to the courtyard. I shook hands with all of them there, maybe mostly partisans. Soon out came Otas Lakusic, whom I took by the hand and we separated from the others in the courtyard. Immediately I told him: "Listen,

Otas, and this you should say to your older brother Mijat: because of your lawlessness in the last war you were in jail 16-18 years. Don't do some foolishness again and earn some ten years in jail after this war. Put in your mind that this war too will not last forever, this will also be called yesteryear, and I would like both of you to meet later as men with shining faces, and not be sentenced to jail." Otas was listening to me very excitedly, and answered: "I beg you as my brother to be assured that neither my brother nor I will ever be the killers of our brothers! Be assured that none of us had been involved in the killing of our brother Milic Orovic. We two knew about this killing only as any of you Lasics or other men of Lijeva Rijeka. I repeat to you that Otas Lakusic will never be the killer of our brothers!" After this conversation "in seclusion" we mingled with the others.

Before long our villagers emerged from the house of Milos Adzic, and we headed in the direction of Velicin Do, and continued toward our village Kami (the Rock), talking about the men we left. George Lasic told us that the local Communists had been ordered to conduct terrorist actions or be striken from the Party. This had been the direct motive of the killing of Milic Orovic. And Mirko Vesovic was not a Vesovic to oppose "the order" from Radovce; rather he had been a "Petrovic" and began to spread the Communist terror in Vasojevici. We returned to our village late in the evening, and went to our homes to eat supper and to reinforce the ranks to protect our village.

The partisan headquarters these days roamed around Lijeva Rijeka constantly. In the middle of December 1941, an official letter from the staff of the Battalion of Lijeva Rijeka was sent to the partisan headquarters with the following content:

1. That on the whole territory of Crna Gora out of reach of the occupiers (should) be formed a National Committee, whose members the people would elect by a general secret ballot in the counties (and this committee) would immediately exclusively take over government in Crna Gora and exercise it during the occupation of Yugoslavia by our enemies;

2. In this committee would be organized a military department with only expert (military) men at its head, to which could be admitted representatives of partisans, if they want to be inculded. The expert military men would form the general popular military organization in the whole territory, so as to be ready for any military action at the most propitious time and hour for it;

3. The internecine killing of men by the irresponsible elements must be stopped. Investigation of present crimes as well as the punishing of the accused men should be postponed to a later time, when the legal public order is restored in our country after the war. Until that time the accused person could peacefully remain in their homes, under condition that we could not free them from their responsibilities before the regular courts in freedom;

4. That in all counties, out of the reach of the occupiers, should be formed the popular courts with the task to discuss the responsibilities of those persons suspected of collaborating with the occupiers, and to undertake necessary steps to prevent such ignoble dealings;

5. To form a special committee to help the refugees, and the support of poor people in general, and,

6. To give the Communists the unbound freedom to peacefully express their ideas, either in written way or by brochures and books or in speeches at meetings and in their conferences.

In the name of the battalion of
Lijeva Rijeka,

George M. Lasic,
Staff Army Major

Aleksa Dujovic,
former County Secretary

On the basis of this proposition as well as the invitation of George Lasic and Aleksksa Dujovic, a common meeting was held in the village of Ptic on December 16, 1941, in which about 400 men from Lijeva Rijeka took part under arms, and about 150 partisans from Lijeva Rijeka and other nearby localities. The meeting was held at 2 p.m. At the appointed hour there were about 350 of our men and about 120 partisans. We arrived by groups somewhat before the appointed time, and filled up the hall of the building of the elementary school at Ptic, where we took our seats in the classroom benches. Soon some partisans, one by one, began to enter with the red star on their cap. I was sitting in the first row with "the Uncle" (Milisav Radevic) on the right. The first partisans greeted us with: "Death to Fascism!", and the Uncle touched me with his forearm saying: "This one is from Brskut, or Bratonozici." Then another entered and greeted us: "Death to Fascism!", and the Uncle explained to me: "This one is from Moraca, or Rovca!" He sorted them by their accents, and never was mistaken. Our men from Lijeva Rijeka objected: "Eh, you men, greet us in the name of God, as it is fit to a man; we know that Roosevelt, Churchill, and Stalin have already sentenced your Fascism or Naziism to death!"

Outside the rain was pouring. They told us a large group of partisans had arrived. A stranger got in among us on the benches. He had on his head a fur cap, probably rabbit. Milisav Radevic told me: "This is Blazo Jovanovic in person, a lawyer, the brother of Arso Jovanovic. Immediately we began our task. Our men by acclamation elected me as the chairman of our meeting. I thanked them and greeted the "guests". In a few words, I expressed my wishes that God would give us all enough moral strength and wisdom at the meeting that day so that we would pass a resolution to restore unity of purpose and to prevent any bloodshed of innocent people. Then, by common consent of all present, I called upon Mr. Blazo Jovanovic, the lawyer from Belgrade, as to our common guest. Blazo Jovanovic really made a patriotic speech: "Brothers of Lijeva Rijeka, I am happy to be here among you to have an opportunity to tell you the views of our partisan forces on the territory of Crna Gora. Our forces are not in any way contrary to the interests of people and their wishes. We are, as all of you, for our King Petar II and for our Government in exile." Then he continued in a highly laudatory tone to speak about the Vasojevici clan. He cited many famous battles in the past wars, recent and old ones, in which Vasojevici had given full measures of their heroism: Vucji Do, Novicic, Bukova Poljana, Kolasin, Bardanjolt and Glacinac, all from Kosovo to our times! Finally, he said that he was a Communist by his political conviction, but he was not opposed to any social political system of the contrary according to the wishes of the majority of the people. He finished his speech that he had come with the hope that our forces unite in the struggle for freedom. His words: "Long live King Petar II! Long live Yugoslavia! Long live the people!" were greeted with an enthusiasm by all of us at the meeting.

Because the rain had stopped outside, and the sunshine returned again, we decided to go out. The mass of people made a semi-circle on the meadow before the entrance of the building. Other speakers spoke from the small steps before the entrance. I called upon Aleksa Dujovic, a former county secretary, my classmate in the elementary school, and co-fighter in this war.

Aleksa Dujovic began first to tell us what Vasojevici had done in the uprising against the occupiers on July 13 of this year:

"Within twenty-four hours, without any help of the others, we took over all garrisons of the occupiers on our territory. The garrison in Berane was the strongest in all of Crna Gora, but it was subdued with great casualities on both sides. After that we were compelled to turn our front against the Albanians from Plav, all the way to Bojana and Bihor. We had to do this, because these occupiers' slaves tryed to profit from our fighting against the foreign invaders and to drive us even across the Lim River, being surely incited by their fascist masters.

"When the Italian punishing expedition assailed us from Cakor and Podgorica, we were exposed to an awful destruction. Entire counties and villages went up in smoke; about 1,800 homes were burned, and the sacrifices in blood cannot yet be evaluated, because the ruthless occupiers are still killing and inflicting tortures, and the Albanian mobs with still more ferocity assail us from the east all along our borders. I ask you now, you other fellows of Crna Gora, what do you ask more of us Vasojevici? While we Vasojevici did our duty in the uprising, you other fellows of Crna Gora surrounded Niksic, Podgorica, Bar, and Cetinje and began to slumber around the Italian garrisons—you managed to disarm none of them, except that Bjelopavlici subdued a greater occupiers' garrison at Danilovgrad. You should know that we are even today in great danger, not only from the occupiers, but from their Albanian incendiaries. Therefore I warn you this day, you other fellows of Crna Gora, to let us be in peace!"

The timbre of Aleksa Dujovic's voice was strong and vigorous. He was not "setting" or sorting his ideas as do the men without conviction: his words came from his heart and his thoughts went in their logical order from his experience and convictions. With the same strength of conviction, he spoke about the killing of Milic Orovic on November 30. This time he turned more to the fellows of Lijeva Rijeka and let them remember that the killers of our brother had been Communists from our area, and the order of execution was given in person by Mirko Vesovic, lawyer from Podgorica. By instinct of self-defense, the people rose in arms to protect themselves against the killers. With this Aleksa Dujovic finished his speech, greeted by loud applause from our men. What the partisans felt I do not know!

After the audience calmed a little, I called upon Mirko Vesovic, lawyer from Podgorica. He was shaken, and did not look straight at the mass of people before him, but his gaze was directed at the group of his men. Our men were swallowing him with their eyes, but they were warned in advance not to disturb the speakers, and they were calm, except that one felt the breath of the listeners. The speaker talked about the merits of Communists in the July uprising, but he did not mention the fighting against the Albanians nor the flight of Communists before the appearance of the punishing expedition at Cakor. Then he told us about the "success" of the partisan organization in Crna Gora. Although he told us at the meeting in Stup two weeks ago that their forces had 10,000 men, and I answered him we would organize the remaining 30,000 men, he now affirmed that their forces had 30,000 men, though these last days all their headquarters were roaming around Lijeva Rijeka, or were in the villages nearby in Bratonozici and Lutovo. His thoughts were evasive, and his voice was colorless and unconvincing. He withdrew almost unnoticed, and did not mingle with the people but remained in the corridor.

The next speaker called on was George Lasic, staff army major, assistant of the chief of staff of the Drava Division in this war and chief of staff of the upper Vasojevici forces in the July 13 uprising. I went to mingle with the audience before the building to better look and listen. First he gave an expert critique of the organization of the first July uprising, as well as the attitude of individuals and groups during the uprising: "The organization of the uprising had many flaws from the military point of view. The main fault had been in not having a general plan to attack the occupiers, so that there had been no timely onslaught on them, nor were the uprising forces arranged according to the strength in some places of the enemies; in addition, our military forces had not been regrouped but remained aside, which in the future must not happen."

Then he explained many mistakes made on the front against the Albanians. "Communists in our ranks were concerned with their propaganda among the fighting forces," he said, and continued: "In the rear, they had been more concerned with coming to power and in giving our uprising their Communist color. But the fight against the occupiers and the Albanian mobs to them had been of little importance. We have to know that even the few of them in the ranks of our fighters scattered and left our forces in the days before the appearance of the vanguard punishing expedition at Cakor." He gave as an example Mirko Vesovic, who left Andrijevica in a hurry on

August 3, while the punishing expedition appeared at Cakor on August 6.

"As to the punishing expedition forcing its penetration inland from Podgorica toward Kolasin and Vasojevici," continued George, "the best positions to resist their advance—gorges and narrow abrupt slopes from the bridge at Smokovac at the end of Dobjane, some 20 kilometers long—had not been used profitably." Making no reference to the murder in Bucin Potok on November 30, he continued: "The organization of the battalion of Lijeva Rijeka has been accomplished with the purpose of preventing the killing of innocent men by the irresponsible elements and to prepare our military forces for the fight against the occupiers at the most propitious moment to annihilate their military forces. To all of you who are opposed to the internecine killings and are willing to fight *only* against the occupiers, the door is wide open to freely join us. The partisans could be included with their separate companies, or they could individually join our companies to be together with their kinsmen. Their representatives may be in our headquarters under condition that no action could be undertaken without his consent. For the purpose that all of our military forces on the territory of Crna Gora may be organized and ready to fight as a whole against the invaders of our country, a proposition had been sent to the headquarters of the partisan forces, which I here, before you and their delegates, publicly repeat. Our proposition reads as follows" (he then reads in full the text of the proposition printed above).

Aleksa Dujovic asked to add something to the previous proposition. Immediately he emphasized that the Communists were deceiving our people by claiming that we were against the Russian people, and that it was their intention to make trouble among us. He moved that a seventh point be added to that resolution, as follows: "If, after the liberation of our country from Fascism and Nazism, there would be any question of uniting our country and our people with Russia, this committee, elected by the free will of our people, be authorized to unify our country with Russia—without the consent of our people! But not with Bolshevik Russia." The men at once understood that the speaker was clubbing with a heavy hammer those who were pretending to be "better Catholics than the Pope", and broke into laughter.

After this "completion" of the previous proposition, Novak Djukic, first class captian in reserve, from the village of Tusi, was called. He expressed his happiness that the staff of the battalion of Lijeva Rijeka had undertaken the necessary steps to unite forces from the whole area in the struggle against the occupiers, and he warned those who strove to prevent us from achieving this goal. "I am living in the immediate neighborhood where some 'death sentences' have been executed those days, but I am not intimidated at all, and I join the ranks of my brothers who are making peace among us," he concluded, with the general approbation.

Then, Vuko Pavicev Adzic was called upon—a well-known gusle player in this area, who also asked for peace and unity. He talked loudly, ceaselessly, gesturing a great deal, which later served to inspire jokes on his account, especially because it was known that all Adzics had joined the partisans.

Finally Nikola Lasic, a sous-prefect, was called upon. In his speech Nikola made a comparison of declarations of different speakers at this meeting from both sides, and stressed the proposition to unite all our fighting forces in this part of the country under the leadership of the national committee. He found that the substance of all this was: the stopping of killing by irresponsible elements, or simply said, by the criminals; and the preparation of military fighting forces for any action at opportune moments against the invaders of our country. He moved that the men from both sides be appointed to sum up our wishes expressed at this meeting and write them down in the form of a common resolution.

His proposition was unanimously adopted, and the election of the delegates was immediately undertaken. The partisans elected Blazo Jovanovic and Mirko Vesovic, and our men, George Lasic and Aleksa Dujovic. It was cold and almost dark, and we had to break up to leave. The men from the nearby homes and nearby villages took with them those whom they liked. The men from outside talked with the Dojovics and went home with them. Blazo Jovanovic went to Vule Dujovic's home, where that night the delegates' conference would take place.

To spend the night, according to the plan of our Dujovic hosts, I went with my brother George to the home of Milos Dujovic, my younger classmate in the elementary school long ago, brother of Aleksa. I asked him at what time to come to eat, and he answered me: "The table plate will be turned over, if you do not come at 8 p.m.; he went home, and I went to mingle with small groups settled in the nearby houses. The men were together everywhere; there had been no division among them. They made jokes, and the friendly conversation went on. Among the partisans one could notice their red stars on their caps with the initials above the Yugoslav tri-color, and our men had on local caps with the initials P. II. Special care had been taken that the intials of "Petar II" be strikingly visible, so that the caps almost reached the eyebrows. Djoko Lasic, otherwise army officer in reserve, long ago had bought a special local cap, on which was embroidered a large Yugoslav crown with "Petar II" on it. He wore it aslant on the right side of his forehead. By the light on the fireplace in the house of Vule Dujovic, his cap with crown on was glowing with many changes of color. In addition, he had put on an army officer emblem of an extraordinary size. All this had been done to suppress the red star, which had been made of some red rags.

Here by the fireplace were sitting the group of partisans, and "men of Lijeva Rijeka", who were peacefully sitting together and talking in witty jokes. The conversation went on, and there had been some discussion about how could be taken most easily the Italian "fortress" in Lijeva Rijeka. Some gave plans according to their best knowledge, and Djoko Lasic developed his plan, which in his opinion would completely be successful with fewer casualities on our part. He said that for this purpose 60 men would be needed—30 of them partisans. He positively claimed to be able to introduce all 60 men with him at their head into the "fortress", knowing in detail the disposition inside: where and when the Italian army officers are together, where their trenches were very weak, and where were to be found the "dead fields" for the fire of arms. His group would attack from inside and deprive the Italian battalion of their commanding staff; meanwhile our forces from outside would have the opportunity to penetrate in without losses: "Now, if these 'headquarters' give us an order to go, I am ready to sacrifice me and my men—if you are ready to go with us. However, we must die there," stuttering as usual, he concluded.

The partisans were speechless and thoughtful. "It is impossible to make war by casual shootings from the top of Djurilovac (some two kilometers away from the "fortress"), and then scatter back and flee, allowing the enemy to put fire to the poor mens' homes and to kill women and children," he went on.

I made a tour of the other houses, and everywhere the conversation and jokes were going on. All Dujovics, who are otherwise known as courageous and intelligent men, were striving to treat our men kindly, especially the "foreigners".

In the morning, at about 9 o'clock, Aleksa came to us. All of us had been ready, and were talking after breakfast. Aleksa and I left the Milos' home, and headed toward the house of Vule Dujovic. On the way, we were joking as usual, and judging from his looks, there would be something good to come out; surely, they had come to the understanding according to the proposition made on our part. When we got to Vule Dujovic's home, cheerful and smiling, I entered frist. In the fireplace room, I greeted the owner and his son captain Miro, and entered the big room. Near the stove, on the left, Blazo Jovanovic was sitting on a chair looking down and thoughtful. We greeted very cordially, and I went to greet Miro's mother who had been sick these last days and was still lying in her bed on the right in the room. As accustomed, I came in cheerful and started to joke with the "lawyer". Blazo Jovanovic did not react in the same way. Soon Aleksa Dujovic entered; Mirko Vesovic was still late.

Sitting at the table, I asked Miro Dujovic to bring me some paper and an inkstand to have ready when all of us four would be at the same table, and Miro brought all that was necessary. In the best mood, turning to Blazo Jovanovic, I said: "Let us see what you delegates have decided last night, and we will write it all nicely on paper and get your signatures." Blazo murmured: "When Mirko comes." Not waiting for his arrival, I set off to write:

> " The delegates appointed at the popular meeting, held in the elementary school building in the village Ptic, county Lijeva Rijeka, district of Andrijevica, on November 16, 1941, in the afternoon, to wit: In the name of the battalion of Lijeva Rijeka, George Lasic, staff army major, and Aleksa Dujovic, a former county secretary; and in the name of the partisan forces for Crna Gora, Mr. Blazo Jovanovic, lawyer, and Mirko Vesovic, lawyer, met this same day in the house of Vule Dujovic, at 10 p.m., and had come to these conclusions:
>
> 1. . . . ."

Now I was expecting Blazo Jovanovic to tell me what they had decided last night, but he was waiting for Mirko Vesovic. Finally, Mirko came in. He immediately told me that "they" also accepted all conclusions they came to last night, except that the battalion of Lijeva Rijeka should be called the partisan batallion. The men there began to protest. I turned to Mirko with these words, among others: "Listen, Mirko, be sensible. You ought not to lie even to these men around us. The men of Lijeva Rijeka will not be called partisans as long as the majority of Vasojevics will not agree. You know as well as I that we are hardly the twelfth part of our tribe, and if Vasojevici as a whole decide by their majority their armed forces are to be called partisans, or Communists, or anything else, the men of Lijeva Rijeka will submit to the decision of the majority." George Lasic and Aleksa Dujovic had left last night this question to be decided later by the majority of Vasojevics. In this discussion with Mirko Vesovic we spent a few minutes, but he was stubborn. I took the sheet of paper with the head note already written on it, crushed it and threw it in his face, saying: "Shame on you!" Blazo Jovanovic did not utter a single word. Very probably both of them had decided to make this alteration in the final text, that our battalion should be called a partisan battalion, and it was unnecessary for him to interfere.

Outside, there was a loud noise. The owner of the house whispered something in Aleksa's ear, and Aleksa darted to the door and left in a hurry. Mirko left after him. I stayed for a little while to think, but soon I went to see what was going on, leaving Blazo Jovanovic alone. I saw Aleksa Dujovic way down by the stream behind the house of Djoko Dujovic, on my left. I heard him crying in the full volume of his voice: "This should not be done! Oh you men, we could not allow the shame to incur on us!"

On the other bank of the stream I saw a large group of men under arms; these were mostly the soldiers of the Third Company of our battalion—Boricici, Lakusici and Dujovici. Captain Miro Dujovic was before them, facing them, explaining something to them as though to prevent them from going farther. I went down to see Aleksa. He was already in front of the group and was explaining to them: "We will not plunge into the blood as the Communists have already done! We will defend ourselves, but will not strike first. Especially we will not allow you to kill any men who are guests in our homes."

Mirko Vesovic had immediately disappeared somewhere with his men, but Dujovici accompanied and protected Blazo Jovanovic until he was out of danger somewhere in nearby territory. All of us on this side of the stream crossed to the other bank, and mingled with them. There were about 100 men under arms. We began to convince them that we were trying to come to the understanding by peaceful means, because in this way we would gain more. Under these circumstances, we should not put a blemish on our honor by killing men from outside, but Mirko should have atoned with his head for the crime which had been done by his orders some weeks ago. So the opportunity was missed on the part of men who looked farther into the future; the opportunity to prevent further murders by Communists in Crna Gora.

At the village of Ptic we dispersed to go to our villages. Our villagers from Kami, Radevics, Lasics, and others returned late in the afternoon, and went to our homes. This same evening, on December 17, 1941, after supper we gathered together in the house of Branko Radevic and his uncle Krsto Radevic. As we were still in the course of grouping, two militia men came from the Italian "fortress" at Lijeva Rijeka, and told us that Nikola Lasic, George Lasic, and Milija Lasic, ought to present themselves to the commander of the Italian forces there! A little confusion set off among us, but we quickly found a solution: the militia men would report that they did not find George in the village, but Nikola and I were following them and pretty soon would come to Lijeva Rijeka. We two immediately set off with much foreboding, because we feared that the Italian authorities knew something about the activity through our villages.

Fortunately, just as we were going in the dark down the slope of Lijeska, toward Lijeva Rijeka, two other young men from the militiamen met us and told all three of us that we should come tomorrow at 9 a.m. So we came back. In the course of our conversation that night at Radovic's we concluded that the Italian commander did not ask us because of some information about our actions in the village, for it was positively known that all the time of their being in Lijeva Rijeka, the Italian military authorities could not find a single informer among the population in this area. In the beginning they looked for nine Communists, whose names they got from a list gotten from confidential archives at Cetinje or elsewhere, but the local civil authorities refused to comply, insisting that these nine persons had been either some young boys, or one or two old men, and the occupiers dropped their demands. Among our men in the civil service, who by their functions were compelled to come in contact with the Italian authorities, the rule had been as a law: *never denounce anybody*. Nikola and I were calm. That night we thought that we had been summoned because we came from Serbia, although we did report regularly on our arrival. Nevertheless, Nikola and I decided to comply with the summons; if they asked for George, we should say he was not in the village and we were unable to inform him about the summons.

The next morning, on December 18, 1941, we two went earlier to arrive exactly at 9 o'clock to see the commander of the Italian military forces at Lijeva Rijeka. Going down the abrupt slope, called Lijeska, toward the "fortress", we were rather thoughtful and silent. But Nikola, who was going before me, all of a sudden turned to me and said: "What do you think, should we take with us one small trunk and put in the most necessary things for both of us, or take each one his own?" I did not understand him immediately, and answered him laughingly: "What is the matter with you, may God help you! About what trunks are you talking?" He continued: "Listen, all this looks like when I was taken a war-prisoner when I was a Serbian army sergeant in the last war. Just when I recovered a little from wounds, the Austro-Hungarian military authorities ordered all of us who had been in the Serbian army to be picked up and sent to Cetinje, then to Hungary. That time I took a small trunk, maybe less than ten pounds, but I had great troubles. My hand pained me, and the baggage became heavier and heavier where we were marching under the guards. We will be deported, and it would be better to profit from my previous experiences and get one small trunk for both of us. When one of us gets tired, the other would carry it, and so forth." I answered him: "Let us see, Niko, and we will solve this problem to your satisfaction, if they, in such a case, would allow us to inform our relatives where they sent us."

So, in such conversation we arrived at the "block" in Lijeva Rijeka. The sentinels moved aside the block, opening the gate, and we got in. Last night we had been told that the commander would receive us in the cafe-house of Radule Popovic, in which he lived. At exactly 5 minutes to 9 a.m. we entered. The owner told us that the commander would show up soon, because he used to leave his private apartment exactly at 9 o'clock. Just at the appointed time Giovanni Ferro, the Italian army major, entered the cafe-hall and greeted us very politely. He asked us if we spoke Italian, I explained to him that I would understand it in a broken way, but that I spoke French rather well. He started in French almost fluently. His first question was: "Why did the Major not come? Though I lied a "little", I told him that George had gone a few days ago to visit our sister married to a man living in another district, and we could not let him know about the summons. The Italian army major bit his lower lip, then continued: "Gentlemen, I have summoned you only to fulfill a formality—to answer my superiors that I have seen you in person and had talked to you. Many a time the headquarters of our division in Berane had warned me that somewhere around Lijeva Rijeka had come from Serbia for some political reasons a "professor" and a "sous-perfect". Through the local civil authoirities we have information that you have been home to live with your families and your close relatives." To prove that his private information had been right, I pointed at Nikola, and told him: "My cousin has his parents still living, and his family had come before the war here, so his children are living now with their grandfather and grandmother; my situation is similar to his. I am living with my brothers in our common house, and on our common farm." Somehow at Lijeva Rijeka the news had spread that Giovanni Ferro was an anti-Fascist, and feeling that he well understood our hardships, I ventured to remind him that Italy had been our ally in the last war. Major Ferro told us that he had been a cadet or lieutenant in Albania in that war on the left wing of the Serbian armed forces. I became more sincere and openminded, and I told him in the most friendly tone that Italy was on the wrong side in this war, but I pray to God that we will be even for two days on the same line in this war. The Germans are dangerous for Italy and for Yugoslavia, if they come to the Mediterranean Sea permanently. As a good army officer, he did not make any comment, but only slightly shook his shoulders. Finally, I thanked him because his battalion, though being a detachment of the punishing expedition, up to now did not make any retaliation against the people in this and surrounding counties. And this was true: this battalion had not shot any man at Lijeva Rijeka. Before my arrival, the villagers managed to save the life of a young man from Lopate on whom the Italian soldiers had found a bomb. All had been prepared to execution, but the commander intervened in the last minute and prevented the execution, and the young man returned home that same evening! One must tell the truth even for a devil.

Major Ferro took leave with us very politely and friendly and went to his headquarters, and we two remained in the cafe-house for a short while. From the owner of the house, Sveta Popovic, we learned much interesting "local news": by barter many individuals could get tobacco, and many kinds of liquor, coffee and other things. The most successful in this sense had been Milos Lalovic, from Jablan, a neighboring county, who by the intervention of an Italian driver had bartered 600 kilograms of potatoes for 600 kilograms of Italian corn. He wondered how he was successful. She told us that among us here it was customary to get one kilogram of corn for two kilograms of potatoes. Both of us did not go further into explanations of the owner of the cafe-house, but immediately went out and headed to the barbed-wire block in order to quickly get out of the "fortress."

As soon as we were enough away, we started to talk freely. I made some jokes about "one or two trunks", about which he had talked to me sometime earlier, and then we discussed the cause of our being summoned this morning. As an experienced policeman for so long a time before the war, and well acquainted with the events happening now in this part of our country, Nikola came to this conclusion: that the communist agents, well masked, are able to break us down by the occupiers; they are frightened by the revolt of large masses of our people, and may try to drive out from this area all men whom they cannot attract to them or did not kill openly, and do this aided by the occupiers; they succeeded in infiltrating their agents even into the headquarters of the Italian division in Berane. After that, we began to discuss the "barters" which the cafe-house owner mentioned a few minutes earlier. Both of us knew that out of ten Lalovic from Jablan, in the neighboring county, two of them—Veselin and Milos—long ago joined the partisan company in Brskut under the leadership of Ljubisa Milacic, and it was clear to both of us that they make their supplies in foods and other necessities through the occupiers. Milos Lalovic had a contract to supply meat, potatoes and wood for the Italian garrison at Lijeva Rijeka; all this business was done at Jablan, county of Brskut, out of our reach.

However, we returned to our village joyful and satisfied, and all were extremely delighted. The "uncle", Milisav Radevic and his brother Krsto Radevic were especially delighted because their advice, that Nikola and I should report, turned out satisfactorily.

The rumors spread that soon the Italian garrison at Lijeva Rijeka, Matesevo, and from all areas of Lijeva Rijeka and Kolasin, would leave. We hoped that the situation would improve when the occupiers' armed force were far away.

On our terrain, there had been no new terrorist crimes perpetrated, but we learned that Communist "sentences to death" had been falling as rain drops. Our men had brought complete security to our area. The popular court in the battalion's headquarters was effective. Two of its members were two experienced jurists—Nikola Lasic, and Radisav Milosevic, and 19 other members were representatives of their close relatives. This court, by a majority of votes, took a decision to leave aside the killing of Milic Orovic to wait for the regular proceedure of our courts after the liberation of our country at the end of this war, because it was done after the organization of our battalion.

For this time the occupier was our greatest concern. We did not know what would be the attitude of their military forces during their forthcoming retreat. For any emergency, we called on "partisans" to be ready, if the occupying military forces started to "put fire and destruction" on our villages in their retreat. In the very beginning of January, 1942, we learned that the Italian troops from Matesevo were maneuvering in the upper Tara River, and this meant that they would come to help their forces at Lijeva Rijeka. Our battalion was ready. In the case of close fighting, our situation became worse. On January 3, 1942, about 100 partisans from Brskut, coming over Planinica and down Verusa, attacked the almost unarmed Italian soldiers, and killed 13 of them. It seemed clear to us that the intention of partisans: they wanted to incite the occupiers to start to put on fire the homes in our villages tomorrow while retreating. The staff of the battalion concentrated our main forces on the left around the village Lopate, and on the right along the retreat of the Italian battalion. In advance the company captains were orderd: as soon as the first house in lower Lopate was put on fire (even though the first house in line happened to belong to Scepan Djukic and Mileta Djukic, both partisans, and the first of whom was known as a killer) we would attack from all our positions to discourage further burning of our homes.

On January 4, 1942, it was a beautiful, cloudless day: the sun was reflected off the light snow on the hills surrounding Lijeva Rijeka, and the Italian battalion left their barbed-wire "fortress" in the town. The vanguard passed the first house without harming it, and then the builk of the Italian troops also passed. Just at that moment the Italian soldiers set off a mortar barrage toward the mound known as Ikovik above Lopate. We thought at first that they had panicked out of fear. Later we learned that a small group of armed partisans had let themselves become visible to the Italians, and that the Italians had therefore fired at them. The seven partisans there were unharmed, but the mortar fire slightly wounded six men nearby in First Company, including Captain Petar Milosevic, who was wounded in the buttocks, and the priest Nikola Milosevic. (We were also told that "casual shooting" at the Italians by partisans had occurred elsewhere.)

But the Italians left Lijeva Rijeka without setting fire to a single house, and disappeared from sight toward Raskovo Guvno and Verusa to join other Italian forces in the upper Tara region.

That afternoon, people from all over the region came to dismantle the Italian barracks and carry away the planks for their own use. When our armed men returned to the town, we could see the barracks disappearing, several of them at the same time. About 6 p.m. I went to the school courtyard where the twenty barracks had been and chatted with the villagers. One of them told me: "Listen, it is better to destroy the barracks as soon as possible; the Italians could change their minds and come back."

To celebrate Christmas (January 7th on the new calendar) the villagers made preparations in their homes as usual. My sons went very early with their uncles and their cousin to bring home oak Christmas trees. I got up also early to greet them on their return according to the custom. I could read happiness on the faces of all our family. Especially my neice Bosiljka was in a holiday mood, because the women had made everything inside clean and shining, so that it looked as before the war. The "big room" looked as a room in the city: the floor was covered with a thick carpet; the cupboard was shining; King Petar's II portrait was turned out as before (up to now it was turned backward and looked as a carton neatly stuck in the upper left wing of the cupboard), and now Bosiljka had put it right like it had been before. On the caps of my sons and my nephew, when they came back with the Christmas tree, I noticed the Yugoslav colors embroidered above "Petar II". All of this had been done yesterday on their own initiative.

After the customary leaning of the oak Christmas tree against the house near the entrance, the eldest brother brought in a big loaf, out of which he cut off a small piece and put it on the large oak Christmas tree that he himself had brought this morning, as our eldest in the home, and all of us sat around the round table to breakfast. Today on the Eve of Christmas we were fasting all of us, except Milica who some days ago was one year old. My sister-in-law Jelena found for this occasion enough walnut and dried plums. I wondered where she hid the walnuts out of reach of her "soldiers". All day had been spent in happiness. The Christmas tree brought by Ilija, by his right of being the eldest brother, and the male-folks cut wood, sorting it by the entrance to be ready tomorrow to take two small pieces to stir the fire in the fire-place and greet the Christ's Birthday and wish happiness to all in the home and those related by kinship.

At supper, as usual, Jelena sat at the round low table with all the children, and the other grown-ups at the table. The whole-wheat loaf, beans, and plum marmelade were the main and only dishes at the supper, but had an extraordinarily sweet taste, and all the family was delighted and in a shining mood. After supper we grown-ups at the table got into a conversation, while the children sat on the straw spread on the floor, or went to the fire-place to see if the "beard" on the Christmas tree had been separated. This event ought to be announced by firing rifle shots—in the name of the Father, Son, and the Holy Ghost, and the eldest brother would take it to the cornfield, throw it into the air, and ascertain if the "Christmas tree beard" fell on the flat part or on the opposite side, accordingly he will know if the next harvest will be abundent or poor. Then he will make a large circle around it with straw; in the middle, again with straw, he will make a cross, on whose center the "Christmas tree beard" will remain to the next spring. At about 11 p.m., this customary act was done, and in our home there started a general rejoicing among our family. This act was announced by rifle firing in the other homes all around.

On the Orthodox Christmas Day (January 7, 1942), all of us males were on our feet very early and ready to bring in the ceremonial Christmas firewood logs. First Ilija, the eldest son, brought in his log, stirred up the fire, which was already quite large, and greeted all of us with "Christ is born. Merry Christmas to all of you! May every one of you have as much happiness as there are sparks." Then others brought their logs, and we soon had a huge fire. Some said: "As many as there are sparks, so many may there be sheep, or cattle", and so on. After this ceremony, all of us embraced each other separately and thanked the holy day, wishing good health and happiness to each other, and sat at the table to breakfast. My sister-in-law, Jelena, had prepared for the children first a cup of milk for each one, then ham, cream, cheese, and whole-wheat bread. We had the same on the table for the grown-ups, in abundance.

We took our breakfast in joy, knowing that in all the homes of our village there was the same happiness as in ours, except in the house of the late Veko Dabetic, but that had been the judgment of God to whose will we are all submitted. We were awaiting the "polasajnik", the first person outside from our home, who would come to felicitate the Christmas Day. Soon we heard some talking outside, and got up to greet our brother with his small son. They were about to come in to congratulate us on the holy day. Milicko instructed his boy how to stir the fire and what to say. The little boy did it very deftly, and came to us, while his father did it alone; "To all of you I wish Merry Christ's Birth; how many there are sparks, so much happiness I wish to all of you. Christ is born!" Almost simultaneously we answered him: "Indeed He is born!" And all of us in turn embraced him, while my little nephew was warmly kissed by his aunts, and his uncles, and cousins. In the most holy day mood, we continued our conversation at the dinner table covered with various foods; meanwhile my sons and eldest nephew had gone to visit their Aunt Divna nearby. There also was rejoicing and happiness. After dinner we would visit only our close relatives; it is customary on the first Christmas Day. However, these days could be some exceptions; we are more closely knit than by the bare kinships in the past.

While still at the table, we were told that Ljubisa Milacic, the leader of the partisans group in Brskut, was in our village and wanted to visit us. Our patrolmen at Lijeva Rijeka had caught him at night in the house of Nikola Orovic, and held him under watch all night with an order to leave in the morning from the terrain of our county. Without being asked by the company captain at Lijeva Rijeka, he offered the information that he had not come to kill George Lasic; he never had a thought in his mind to kill anyone in Lijeva Rijeka, and least of all to kill any Lasics, and asked to be allowed to visit us.

When he arrived at the lower village, Radevics did not let him go there without our consent. George, undisturbed, told: "Let the men in peace, and allow Milacic to visit anyone he wants to". Among us there was laughter and joking. From sheer curiosity, I went out behind our house to see that "mountain wolf" Milacic who had been terrorizing Brskut for a few months. From afar I saw two men approaching our home. On the fence before the house I had put my rifle, and when they were closer, I started to aim at a small flat stone, emerging from the snow in front of the house, at a distance of some 600 to 900 feet. As soon as the unknown got into the courtyard, I liesurely left my rifle against the fence, approached them and politely greeted them with: "Christ is born!" They both answered: "Indeed He is born!" We shook hands, and they introduced themselves: "I am Ljubisa Milacic"; "I am Novelja Musikic" (or Musikin, I did not hear exactly). I let them before me to enter the house, and showed them into the big room, where we offered them seats at the table, on which there was much food and drink. They greeted all members of our family by shaking hands and giving Christmas greetings, and took their offered seats. George was smiling and scrutinizing them. Ilija and Milicko began to joke even when they were offering them food and drinks, but I noticed the the ugly Novelja "attracted" our looks more. Milacic was of middle stature, stocky in build, of a rather square face, more fair, with small eyes, and abstruse look. Novelja was an extraordinary creature: small in stature, skinny, bent, with a small round head, a furtive look, rarely looking at you squarely—a real monster; if you found him in your cabbage field, you would not tell him go out.

Ljubisa was the speaker, drinking to our health, praising to extreme our family. He was hurt that anybody could think he was plotting to kill George Lasic, or any one of the Lasics. They abode by us longer, and my two brothers, Ilija and Milicko, choking with laughter, were offering them food and drinks all the time, they themselves were drinking to their health, saying: "To your health, Ljubisa Milacic, to you who are the 'ruler' of Brskut these days; not even Sekulovics there are heard to be alive!" He was somewhat pleased with such words of praise, but cooled down when Ilija added: "Go slow, this is not yet the end. Sekulovics, Dedics, Cadjenovics, as well as the majority of Milacics, have something to say!" I asked Ljubisa: "Why did you not come with us to attack the occupiers when they were retreating from Lijeva Rijeka two days ago?" "We would not have done it because we buried my close relative, who was badly wounded in Verusa and died that same night". Already they expressed their wish to visit others of our relatives. Especially they wished to pay visit to my Uncle Jovan and my Aunt Miruna, born Sekulovic in Brskut. They got up, greeting all the members of our family, took their arms, and went out to the courtyard, and I jokingly said to the "powerful" leader of partisans in Brskut: "You know, we also have here our arms; let us see who is better sharpshooter. I had previously set up that flat stone emerging from the snow." Ljubisa and Novelja consented; both used Novelja's rifle, because Ljubisa was armed with his machine gun. First Ljubisa aimed and fired without any evidence that the shot came near the stone; then Novelja got his turn and aimed for a long while, and again nothing! I told them: "Now, look how we here are shooting!" I aimed about a foot below the target, telling to myself I could over-shoot. I fired on my turn, and immediately was looking if the shot had left some mark, at least to be sure that it did not go "way up the hill". Luckily, the shot hit at the base of the stone and shattered some snow, so that they knew that "we were able to shoot!" Ljubisa, quickly, recognized it saying: "My goodness you hit it."

I took my rifle with me, and went with them, telling the family not to wait for me for dinner. We went first to Milicko's house, who was certain they would visit him, and was waiting before the house. Here too they were treated well. Then we visited some other farmers abiding for some minutes, and soon came to the house of my Uncle Jovan. Even from the other end of the courtyard, I called: "Aunt, here are coming two 'well-known' gentlemen from Brskut!" I let them before me, and we entered. We greeted all with "Christ is born— Indeed He is born!", but my aunt looked at me aslant, and we sat at the table richly garnished with foods and drinks. Here we found Djoko, the youngest son of my uncle Jovan. He immediately offered food and drink. He drank to the health of the guests and made longer speeches. "To your health and welcome, you 'Uncle Ljubisa', and to you, Novelja Musikic; you know, I . . . I . . . I . . . a . . . am shuure that taken together twooo by twooo, there aaare not twooo bettter meen than youuu I . . . I . . . I . . . haad ever met in all this area!" Uncle Jovan sternly looked at Djoko, took his glass and seriously told: "To your health, both of you and welcome!" We remained here much longer. My aunt asked the guests about many of her kinfolk in Brskut, about her close relatives Sekulovici, and others living there, and Ljubisa answered her. In a good mood the time was spent quick-ly, it was about 4 p.m. The guests told us that they wished to leave, so as not to be late. They got up, gave parting greetings to all mem-bers of the family, and Djoko and I accompanied them a little while. All of us took our arms. Uncle Jovan and Aunt Miruna accompanied us to the courtyard, again wishing them good speed, and we contin-ued with them. When we were above the house, from where they could go back down to the village, or on the right by shortcuts toward Nozica, Ljubisa said that it was better to go by shortcuts. But Djoko, in the most friendly terms, told him, "You know, uncle, our men are scattered in all thiis aarea tooo Noozica, aand I wouuld noot like if they meeet you; there aare oover fourty meen, aand you know aamong them there aare of men of different moods. However, how you want . . .", Ljubisa and Novelja were somewhat confused, mused for a while, and Ljubisa said: "All right, it is better to take the same way, but we will not go to Lijeva Rijeka to encounter again the watchmen, we will go to the right!" We accompanied them to the middle of our village, greeted them, wishing them good speed. On our return to our homes, I asked Djoko: "About what men did you talk about a few minutes ago scattered in the area down to Nozica?" Djoko answered me: "For goodness' sake, there is not a living soul there, but I wanted to know what kind of courageous men are these 'tailwaggers' ", said Djoko, choking with laughter. When we got to our house, Djoko told them the tale about "40 men who were criss-crossing", and they laughed till their sides were splitting.

The second and third day of the Christmas holidays we spent in peace and joy. All of us wished to visit and greet our kinfolk with: "Chirst is born—Indeed He is born!" Early in the evening on January 9, 1942, George Lasic recieved a letter of the leading men in the district of Andrijevica. They asked him to come to a meeting which was called for January 14 (our New Year's Day) in the elementary school building at the village of Kralje. At the same time he got a letter from Artillery First Class Captain Djeranic, by which he let him know that he had to transmit something very important, and would wait for him in the village of Kralje. The preparation for the trip had been made. On January 12, 1942, with George Lasic, some 150 men left, among whom were Aleksa and Miro Dujovic, Nikola Lasic, Vidak Zecevic, as well as all army officers. The weather was very bad: a strong western wind was blowing and it was snowing with large flakes throughout the day.

The men living at Matesevo, and all over in this area of the Lijeva Rijeka county, as well as Jevto Djurovic, industrialist, originally from Boka Kotorska (Bocca di Cattaro) with his 20 factory workers in the sawmill near Matesevo, had gathered together to spend the night with them in conversation about the present day situation in this part of our country. The next day, early in the morning, they headed forward to Kralje, increased in number by our men in Bare Kraljske with Dmitar Vukicevic, a teacher, in the lead.

On the Yugoslavian New Year's Day (January 14), 1942, a conference was held in the old ammunition barracks in Kralje, attended by 162 military men. In the course of the deliberations and discussions, First Class Captain Tomica Jojic stood up and declared: "We have no need of the King!" He was joined immediately by First Class Captain Batric Zecevic. This resulted in tumult. To prevent further undesirable consequences, George Lasic, staff army major and chairman at this meeting, left the rostrum, took both by their hands and brought them to the door, saying: "Out, before we tear you to pieces!" The remaining army men continued their work in complete understanding. The conclusion of this conference was the unanimous election of George Lasic as commander and organizer for the resistance against the Communist terror.

Meanwhile, great masses of people gathered in the courtyard of the school building, while outside were 135 armed Communists with Mirko Vesovic and certain Keljanovic at their head—their entire forces in the Upper Vasojevici at that time. The villagers already had been arguing with them, and some proposed that the Communist rabble be beaten with wooden sticks.

After the army officers came out of the ammunition barracks and mingled with the people, George Lasic came closer to the Communist partisans and told them: "You must immediately break up and return to your homes, where you may abide in peace. But if you want to fight, we will fight!" Then the people gathered in the village hall, or at least so many as would fit. Many were in the corridors, or outside by the wide-open windows to listen to the speakers. The meeting unanimously endorsed George Lasic as commander-in-chief of the military organization. He then appointed brigade and battalion commanders, and company captains by the traditional territorial military system. These appointees had, each in his area, to muster all men fit for military service on the next Sunday to take the oath.

Having spent the night again in Kralje, on January 15, 1942, George Lasic returned to Lijeva Rijeka with his followers, who now numbered more than 1,000 armed men. They accompaned him to Matesevo, where another meeting had been held, with the speeches ending with: "Long live King Petar II! Long live Yugoslavia!" These speeches were accompanied by enthusiastic approval of the masses of the population, giving a volcanic strength to the movement. The Communists were nearby, and surely understood the revolt of the people against them.

On the return of Pavle Djurisic, First Class Army Captain, from the national headquarters of our military forces, where he had met General Draza Mihailovic, the organizing was furthered. On January 17, 1942, the hall of the elementary school at Zaostro was filled with the elite of the population from this area—Dobrasinovics, Joksimovics, Bozovics, Cemovics, Miladinovics, Micovics, Obradovics, Bojovics, Popovics, Dabetics, Pesics, Zecevics, Bukumiras, plus representatives of numerous other families. They confirmed Pavle Djurisic as their leader in this area. From Lijeva Rijeka on the extreme west to Sekular and Velika on the southeast, and from Zaostro to Plav, the people almost unanimously resolved "not to let the Communists kill us as oxen."

The situation at this time within Crna Gora and Mountains as well as in Sandzak had been this: The Italians still kept the cities and towns—Podgorica, Bar, Cetinje, Niksic, Pljevlja, Bijelo Polje, Berane and Andrijevica. We were far from the Italian garrisons—42 kilometers from Podgorica, more than 100 kilometers from Andrijevica, and still farther from Niksic. All territory between Podgorica-Cetinje-Niksic on the west, and Pljevlja-Bijelo Polje-Berane-Andrijevica on the northeast and east, was completely free of the occupying Italians, since the withdrawal on January 4, 1942.

The districts of Bar and Cetinje, as far as the inner situation was concerned, up to now they were under Krsto Popovic, an army officer serving as an Italian puppet who was a well-known separatist (or federalist). But he was of little concern to us; we were more interested in Vukotics, Petrovics-Njegos, Martinovics in Bajice, Plamenacs Djurovics, Ozrinics and other large family tribes living in these two districts, who constitute the main national strength in the ancient Crna Gora; they, for sure, were not pro-Krsto Popovic nor pro-Communist.

The valley of the Zeta River from below Podgorica, Kuci from Tuzi, or better from Doljani to Brskut, were the most resistant to Communist-partisans; there had been no killing by Communists. Even Bratonozici and Brskut, bordering us on the west, were more than 80 percent against the Communists' acitivity; the communist partisan group under Ljubisa Milacic would be scattered in the least general uprising of the people there.

Those most oppressed by Communist terror were in the districts of Pljevlja, Cajnice and Bijelo Polje and the people were doubly oppressed, from Communists and from Moslems under the Ustasi from the north and the east. The suffering of people there was greatly increased by the flight of about 8,000 Communists from Nova Varos, where they had been penned after being driven from pre-Kumanovo Serbia. The Communists' terror especially broke down the district of Kolasin, neighboring Vasojevici from the north all along the borders, and one simply could feel that the people living there were sinking under the Communist terror. We learned that

Gornja Moraca had been broken completely, as well as Rovca and Donja Moraca, though our neighboring counties Prekobrdje and Recine were still, led by Sava Dzajov Lazarevic and the men of Gornje Lipovo, courageously fending off Communist terrorists.

The hardships of people under the terror could be felt when talking with men who escaped from those areas most affected. These men at first looked as if they were chased by wild beasts and overcome by fright, fleeing their persecutors. They used to live for months in some hideouts, or they fled from one village to another, where they thought the terrorists could not find and kill them. One night Batric Rakocevic, circuit court judge, came to our village with seven of his followers. Our villagers took them two by two to spend the night in their homes. Rakocevic told us about the partisans: "In their speeches and leaflets they deceive the people, telling them they are fighting against the occupiers. But we saw with our own eyes that they turned their back to the occupiers and attacked our villages which are on the average more than 100 kilometers away from the Italian garrisons."

In Bjelopavlici, we learned, Colonel Bajo Stanisic was still resisting. His tribe was exposed to the wild onslaught of the Communist rabble, who had killed some 800 men in the villages. Mijuskovics in Strasevina near Niksic also were resisting. At this time, Colonel Stanisic had about 200 fighters around him, and those of Mijuskovics were about the same. Returning to Lijeva Rijeka, George Lasic immediately set to work in his capacity as commander-in-chief for Grna Gora to organize for defense and liberation of this part of the country from the communist terror. After his return from the meeting at Kralje, the fighters were singing:

From Kom Mountain the nymph called,
O Lasic, young army major,
You are the hope of Crna Gora!
Rouse all your armies against the Communists,
And their tail-waggers, the partisans,
Who are plundering all around,
And killing all living things!

The Communists on January 15 and 16, 1942 had formed four special "trojka" to assassinate George Lasic. The "trojka" that succeeded in killing him, would get a reward of 250,000 Italian lires, or that value in dinars. In addition, the Communists concentrated their best fighting forces in Kolasin to overcome the Vasojevici that he led. Their plans were disclosed in a confidential document that Army Colonel Relja Piletic managed to get and later give to George Lasic himself. The document told of the formation of their battalion in the county of Vrazegrmci below Ostrog on January 13, 1942. After the writer had related who was the battalion commander and political chief, he added a postscript under his signature, to wit:

"P.S. The Italians have evacuated Grahovo, Lijeva Rijeka and Kolasin. In Grahovo and Kolasin we installed our authority, but to Lijeva Rijeka we dispatched our best fighting forces to capture and kill the Lasic brothers."

Pro-Government resistance leaders gathered in the Herce-govina region early in the war. At center with cane is General Blazo Djukanovic; to his right is Major Djordje ("George") Lasic, and in front of Lasic, reclining, Colonel Bajo Stanisic. To Gen. Djukanovic's left, on a level with him, is Captain Pavle Djurisic, and between these two immediately in back of them is the priest-army officer Perisic. Reclining in front is Major Petar Bacevic.

CHAPTER SIX: BATTLING THE COMMUNISTS

The Communist forces to the west and northwest or us, along the borders of the Kolasin District with Andrijevica and Berane consisted of 5,000 to 7,000 men. But we were aware that this included some who they had deceived or put by force into their units, and we did not especially fear these units. We knew that the neighboring county, Prekobrdje, was resisting, and that Rakocevics and Vujsics, under the leadership of Batric Rakocevic and Leka Vujsic, had decided to defend themselves by all means.

We also obtained information that we were to be attacked from Podgorica through Brskut and Pelev Brijeg, where 1,200 men had gathered, and from Rovca, where 400 to 600 more were grouped. But in checking out this information with Pero Cadjenovic Military Court Army Major, and Vlado Djukic, Staff Army Captain, as well as through our scouts near Rovca and Moraca, we learned that where the partisans claimed to have 1,200 men, there were more like 120; and when they said they had 400 men, there were less than 40.

At night on January 17, 1942, Army Captain Veljko Tomovic, coming directly from Matesevo, arrived at our headquarters to see George Lasic. He informed us that partisan forces, coming from Kolasin, earlier that same day had crossed the bridge over Drcka, and simply stormed some 70 men of ours in Matesevo. They took them to Kolasin Majo Milosevic, or killed them on the way; Jevto Djurovic and Company Captain Otas Zecevic were seen surrounded by partisans.

Tomovic told how he saved himself. "Jevto Djurovic and I heard their yelling after us as though we were strayed dogs. Djurovic was already very exhausted, and when we were past the tunnel under the highway in the vicinity of Jasen, he slipped off the road, and did not appear up anymore. I told myself he was overcome by exhaustion, because he was rather fat. I supposed he was already dead, and I told myself it was better if he died here than to be tortured by these wild beasts. When I reached Jasen, and got out of sight of my pursuers, I turned in a hurry to my left to the snow-beaten path along a long, high stack of dry wood. At the end of this, on the other side I simply fell buried into the snow.

"I heard this mob asking where is Djurovic and the unknown man with him. They did not mention me by name; so, they did not know who I was. For a long while they searched the few houses there, around the houses outside, even along the long stack of wood

I passed a few minutes earlier. I had been lucky, because nobody had seen me. It was easy for inhabitants to say truthfully that no living soul had been seen on the highway, and to prove that they weren't hiding anyone in their houses. When the noise diminished a little, I heard their steps turning and disappearing toward Matesevo. Then I got up to shake the snow off my clothes. It was dark.

"To warm myself a little, I entered a house on the upper side of the highway, wherein I got some warm milk, and then I hurried upstream to Tara, not entering any house along the entire route until here. I am very sorry that these criminals may torture Jevto Djurovic, but I pray to God that he dropped dead before he got into their hands."

Fortunately, as we learned sometime later, Jevto Djurovic had crept into the tunnel under the bridge, where it was a little warmer, and he lay in the water on his belly. At that time he was unaware of what was going on in the houses of Jasen and did not know if his companion Veljko had been able to escape the Communists. He had heard the noise of their feet on the highway above him, but their voices diminished quickly and they were lost in the darkness of the night. When he was reasonably sure they were far away, he got out of the tunnel and went toward the left bank of the Tara River, which he forded to the right bank near Milosevic's house. He knew the head of the house and his household were friends. They immediately got him out of his wet clothes, which the womenfolk in the house set to wash and dry near a good stove. After supper, at about 10 p.m., a partisan patrol came unexpectedly from Matesevo. They were coming along the right bank of Tara in this direction. Partisans with red stars on their caps entered Milosevic's home, searching, and for a long while talked with the members of the family. All this time Jevto Djurovic was lying on the floor under a large bed, under which there were some sacks filled with raw wool, and in front of which sacks with potatoes and corn had been set. His clothes and underwear had been left drying above and around the well-heated stove, without causing any trouble.

After the departure of the patrol, Jevto Djurovic tumbled from underneath the bed and sat among the family members. The womenfolk ironed his clothes and underwear, and he soon got into them. The eldest son of the family head then accompanied him through the woods to Bare Kraljske, out of reach of the Communist patrols. The men there were glad he had been saved, and they cheered him greatly.

In the villages of Lijeva Rijeka reigned a perfect peace and security. On January 19, 1942, the majority of our villagers had been to the church, and all of us remained there under arms. We learned that about 200 partisans were coming from Tuzi and would get through Lijeva Rijeka on the highway. About 6 p.m. in the evening many of them went home. With George Lasic, a large group of us headed to the bridge near Popovic's cafe-house. We heard behind us the hurried steps of a large partisan force headed by Lieutenant Colonel Radisav Radevic. Soon we almost mingled with them. George suddenly entered the cafe-house, and the partisan column got through and continued on down river, toward Nozice Leaving their ranks as if in a hurry, Otas Lakusic told those who continued forward: "I must get some water; I am thirsty." Then he quickly entered the cafe-house, and I followed him, because George was still there. George was standing alone, and Otas Lakusic asked for a glass of water and immediately bent slightly toward George and told him something in a whisper. As soon as the cafe-house owner handed him the glass of water, he quickly drank it and darted out of the cafe-house. My brother and I slowly went out. Then, with our men who were waiting outside for us we went by groups into our village.

On the way back I asked George what Otas told him, and he smilingly said: "You know Otas and his jokes! He told me that tonight we will be surrounded on all sides; partisan forces in greater numbers are coming against us through Bratonozici Their general attack will start at 6 a.m. tomorrow morning. These just went to join their main force there."

Arriving in our village, we went to our homes and quickly took supper, then gathered in the house of Captain Branko Radevic, which was the headquarters. The patrolling through the village was as usual. About 8 p.m., the order was issued to company captains that tomorrow, on January 20, 1942, they had to muster their men, each in his area, where they would receive new orders and instructions for further work. About the same time, Petar Milosevic let us know that his godsister had come from Jabuka, and she ought to inform George Lasic in person about certain things.

At 9 p.m., this intrepid young lady came in. She told us that yesterday great partisan forces had come to Matesevo. At 2 p.m., when she left her home, their smaller detachments had occupied Jasen and (on Moraca territory) Jabuka. Their patrols were criss-crossing the area up to Uac and Vucetin Kami in our county. Frightened, she told us that the partisans had plundered the homes of the poor. From a woman in the hamlet on the east slope of Jabuka, they plundered last night about 200 pounds of corn, many packhorses of potatoes, and other supplies; they even took her bed necessities, so that the poor lady was left with her small children with nothing. And she told us that tomorrow, on St. John's Day, a general onslaught would take place on Lijeva Rijeka. Though she did not tell us so, she was a courier of Leka Vujsic, and our nationalists from this area of Moraca.

With all this known, at 10 p.m. that night, a new order was given to all companies of the battalion of Lijeva Rijeka that all soldiers were to gather in the church courtyard at Lijeva Rijeka at 1 a.m. The messengers went with the new orders.

This night, a severe cold came, worse than had ever been experienced. The strong north wind had been blowing and beating the firs. The shoes were quickly frozen hard on our feet, and you simply felt that instead of shoes you had two planks for sliding, which would sooner crack than bend. When I was ready, my first care had been to see if our cousin Nikola Lasic would be able to go with us, and I went to see him and to tell him about our unexpected movement. He was lying on the bed with his clothes on. He had already been informed of the situation, and I added: "Get up under any condition; you should go with us." He heaved himself up and bent to take his sock off the right foot to show me the sole of his right foot. When I saw with my own eyes how much the shoe had hurt him, I was frightened: all his heel was in wounds, and the red color spread to the ankle. Smiling as usual, he told me: "As you yourself can see, it is also impossible lately for me to put on my shoe." I greeted my sister-in-law Bozana and my little nephews and left their house. So my most beloved brother Nikola was left in our village, and we never saw each other alive again.

Coming back to my home to take leave with my wife Victoria, my sister-in-law Jelena, and the children, I found two of my brothers there ready to leave. George was already at headquarters. We took leave with all ours in the home, and we three went together to the home of Branko Radevic. Our villagers were gathered there. My youngest uncle Velimir, by the second marriage of my late grandfather, was left because his wife Jela, the sister of Milan Adzic, a teacher, was ill, and for this reason he could not go with us. In the hamlet of Krkor, Scepan Gogic did not go.

In the house of Branko Radevic, I found Vule Dujovic, who already had come with his son Miro Dujovic, assistant in command to George. We left from here in groups somewhat about midnight and set out for Lijeva Rijeka. Soon we began to move down Lijeska, an abrupt slope descending on the west of Lijeva Rijeka. I was together with Miro Dujovic. He told me that he had put on moccassins in order to move easier, and told me that I should have done the same. As long as we were moving on a level path, I did not notice any superiority of his moccassins to the other shoes. I asked him if his feet coverings had started to freeze, and he smilingly answered me: "You know, I feel that my moccassins are getting more rigid, but anyhow I will move easier than you with your lowshoes. Why didn't you put on your military boots?" I answered him jokingly, "Ilija put my boots on, but regardless I will slide less than you. You will see when we start down this steep slope to the left!"

When we had turned to our left, I took hold of tree branches on the right and left to prove my previous assertion, but keeping my glance on Miro. He was much younger than I was; elastic, nimble, and strong as an athlete, and he slid down without falling. We re-grouped on a level path, and continued. Pretty soon we got to a narrow long vale covered with snow. Miro was sure-footed with his moccassins and started through this gulley. This time he slid to the bottom of the depression, because there was ice underneath, and the branches were too far away to catch. I told him: "Keep going, Captain, but I go to the right!" And indeed I went that way, zig-zagging to keep myself up. When we got to the highway, we again went together. We continued joking about his sliding down Lijecka, and he told me: "You cannot imagine how my moccassins got polished, they have simply become glass."

We arrived at Lijeva Rijeka, near the church at 1 a.m. We were waiting to regroup, fearing that our men could have been roused on such short notice. The men were not coming in large groups. It was known only that the First Company would wait for us in the lower Lopate, along with the Zecevics in Verusa and those from Opasanica in Tara. We waited a long time, two hours in full. About 4 o'clock they mustered us in front of the house of Bogdan Kruscic, at the end of Lijeva Rijeka, on the highway heading toward Matesevo. There were 113 soldiers altogether. When we arrived at the lower Lopate, close to the house of Scepan and Mileta Djukic, both partisans, a female would jar the door open to look out; some soldiers told us she was counting us. They were ready to put her house on fire. George Lasic rushed out and prevented them from doing so.

The cold was terrible. Especially here the cold wind was blowing from the hills, cutting our faces. We set off by short cut to get as quickly as possible to the roads at the top of Viliste, where we could possibly be protected from the wind. It took us some twenty minutes. The beaten snow path was hardly recognizable, and we tramped on the deep snow. The snow had already hardened around my ankles, because I had low shoes on my feet. I covered my head with the upper part of my overcoat, looking at someone before me who was moving forward, almost groping at random. With many hardships we finally reached the top of Viliste. Protected somewhat against the icy wind, we were awaiting others and looking at the lit windows of houses in Lopate down on our right. I saw the house of my uncle Mileta Milosevic, where my mother was born and raised until she was 21 years of age.

Our men regrouped here, and we set off to the east, toward Verusa. We were going one by one, or rarely by two, according to the span of the snowbeaten path. When we were nearing the depression at Raskovo Guvno, I looked back and noticed that all our army officers were grouped. I stopped for awhile, and asked Vidak Zecevic, our battalion commander, to warn the other army officers not to go in a group but to separate immediately one by one. I told him frankly: if the fighting starts at the depression ahead, it would be better that the army officers mingle among us and not be wiped out together with some mortar shell or grenade. Vidak went to the others to tell them my opinion, and they started to disperse: he himself later joined me, selected a patrol to go before us, which included Rajko Zecevic, Milicko Lasic and Bajo Boricic . I told Vidak that George is angry whenever I warn him to take care of himself. Cautiously we got through the depression at Raskovo Guvno, and without any trouble we entered the watershed of Verusa.

It was dawn. On the cloudless sky above the mountains on the right, to the east, the stars were scintillating with a wonderful glow. The visibility of the terrain was increased by the large covering of high snow, and we easily noticed a small group of Zecevics and Vesovics who were coming down Suvo Polje to join us on the right. Vidak and I were ahead, and our patrol disappeared from sight behind the burned house of Janjo Dabetic in the glen close to the highway in front of us. All of a sudden, the patrol came back and reported to Vidak: "Captain, we noticed a group of men coming to us; it is not possible to know now how many there are!" Vidak and I then noticed them, way down near the burned house of the late Jovan Djukic: there was a dark line moving forward toward us. Captain Vidak Zecevic immediately ordered one platoon to take position to the left above the highway near the glen, and another to the right below the highway, while our main group halted.

There was perfect silence as we waited. After some minutes, a loud order broke the silence:

"Stop! Who is coming there?

"We, the partisans!" came the answer.

"Which partisans?" asked one from our patrol.

"The partisans of Lijeva Rijeka," answered one of them.

"Stop! Do not move forward," said several from our patrol loudly, and almost simultaneously.

Vidak Zecevic ordered us: do not fire without his strict order. To the partisans, he gave the order: "Come near, one by one!" He then ordered Bajo Boricic, Rajko Zecevic, and Milicko Lasic to disarm the partisans one after another, to search them individually, and to take off their grenades and ammunition, and then to single them out and lead them before us. I watched my brother Milicko, who approached the first partisan, a tall young man. He talked with him, but did not take off the partisan's rifle. Instead he started to come to us as though to ask something. I was angry, and told him: "Do what you are ordered by the commander of the battalion!" Milicko immediately turned back, and began to disarm them. They threw aside their rifles, but probably they did not have any ammunition on them.

Since leaving Lijeva Rijeka I had been very worried because of the small number of our men, but I looked back now to see how many we were. To my astonishment, I was reassured that we were a force: there were now about 400 armed men in our group. Then I continued to watch and count the captured partisans. They were but 14 young men, mostly Milosevics and Djukics from Tuzi: certainly my brother had found some cousins Milosevics among them, and tried to ask for permission not to disarm them, but only to take their ammunition. Their rifles, however, were given to those of our men who were weaponless, and these "prisoners" were put into our ranks to continue with us to the Tara River. I was happy because there had been no fighting, hoping that the deceived men would soon desert the ranks of murderers!

We continued forward and soon arrived at Han-Garandzica, where the Verusa and Opasanica join to create the Tara River. Here our fellows from the village of Opasanica joined us: about 50 armed men with Lieutenant Vojin Gogic at their head. Thereafter, we moved almost in military formation because we could expect to encounter greater partisan forces.

The sun already shone. It was cold, but I did not feel it too much, because of our rapid movement. We crossed over the bridge at Vucetin Kami, and soon reached the Milosevic houses at Uac. On the left, across the Tara, we saw a group of about 60 of our men; these were Milikici from Velje Slacko, with Captain Novak Milikic, as well as Adzic from Siralija with Lieutenant Masan Adzic. They had been going on the left side of the Tara to join us at Jabuka.

At Uac, by the cafe-house on the left side of the highway, a large group of soldiers gathered. They asked to get in to warm themselves a little. Before us a defiant robust young man stood, bareheaded, clad with a blue shirt, the son of a Milosevic widow, the owner of this cafe-house: he would not allow anybody to get in. I heart him shout: "I do not allow anybody to enter my house; this is my property; I will shoot at anybody who tries to enter in by force. This is my right!"

Our men were ready to encircle the house to enter it by force through windows from the other side. But just at that moment George Lasic arrived. When he saw what was the matter, he called Petar Milosevic, the captain of the First Company, to him, and told him calmly and smilingly: "Listen, Peko, these are your close kin: settle this matter with them so that the men can get in to warm themselves a little." Petar separated from the others, and went to talk with his relative: I joined them. Without saying good morning, or welcome, to his close kin, Petar, this young man moved back and began to talk to his relative in a loud voice: "If you are coming to talk with me as a brother, Petar Milosevic, you are welcome; but if you come as the captain of a company of the Lijeva Rijeka battalion, I do not receive you, and get away from me!" Petar went back to George, and asked him to appoint any Boricic or Dujovic, because it was hard for him that he as Milosevic should beat and disarm his kin.

George mused a little, and said: "Let this miserable man alone in peace! Our soldiers may go to Radisav's home." The house of

Radisav was on the other side of the highway some yards away in front; he was an uncle of the young man. (Later we learned that in the Milosevic cafe-house three partisans were hidden: the son of Velisa Milosevic, a Djukic, and another Milosevic. All three were killed in the battle at Matesevo and in Kolasin. It would have been better for them if God had allowed us to disarm them and let them join the other captured partisans!)

Having taken a short rest, either in the house of Radisav, whose wife gave us use of all of the house, or in a spacious nearby barn, and having drunk some coffee, we continued toward Jabuka. The sun was high in the sky. Approaching the bridge at Uac, somewhat on the right ahead of us two rainbows appeared, whose colors were distinctly separated—something I never had seen in my life. Some took off their military caps and made the sign of the cross on their breasts. One of the Radevics from Stup approached me and said: "Look! This is a happy sign!" Another added: "God is leading us!" We arrived at Jabuka about 9:30 a.m., on St. John's Day, 1942.

This is the part of the District of Kolasin; there were only three homes near the highway, and the inhabitants were Vujsics, close relatives of Army Captain Leka Vujsic. The soldiers scattered on both sides to take something to eat from their haversacks. Now it was rather warm, but the foods we took with us were frozen thoroughly hard and icy. My eldest brother brought out a piece of bread and a piece of meat from a recently killed young ox and warned me to warm it somehow by the fireplace; he pulled out the meat and a piece of bread. As a woman had made a large pot of tea, and was frying something like doughnuts in the cafe-house, I told him to put all this back in the haversack. We each took two cups of tea and some doughnuts. There were many ready to take, and many of our men helped themselves. This lady did not ask us to pay, but almost all of us paid her well. At five minutes to 10 p.m., we were ordered to gather to go forward. The soldiers were quickly ready in groups on the highway. I saw that there were unknown men; these must have been Rakocevics and Vujsics, I was not acquainted even with Captain Leka Vujsic.

Here we were mustered by companies. George Lasic addressed one of these new men, tapped him brotherly with his left hand on his right shoulder, and said: "Leka, this is your domain: make your men ready to go before us as vanguard." Leka Vujsic was taller than average, slender, with the vivacious gestures common to Vujsics;

he wore simple home-made clothes with his army officer's cap. He immediately mustered the 110 men who had come with him last night to Lopate and spent the night with their godbrothers or friends in this village.

As the men slowly started to move forward, I turned to Leka Vujsic with these words: "I believe that Moracani will not be trampled by these [Communist] criminals any longer; these people had always been ready to fight against the oppressors, be they Turks or partisans!" Leka looked at me for a little while, and somewhat angrily added: "You do not know Moracani of today; they are waiting to see which side will be the stronger, and then will take sides!" He immediately went to the head of his men.

By company we followed after them at short distance. After Rakocevics and Vujsics, first were Milosevics, Vesovics and Djukics—those of the First Company; then Milikics, Radevics, Lasics-Dabetics, Gogics and Adzics from Siralija—the Second Company; after them Boricics, Dujovics, Lakusics, and from Mocila, Radovics—the Third Company; then Zecevics, Orovics and Tomovics—the Fourth Company; and then Radunovics, Kruscics, Gogics and Dabetics-Lasics from Opasanica—the fifth Company.

When we left Jabuka and reached the part of the road in front of the steep slope close on the left, two rifle-shots were heard; George Lasic ran past the Second Company, and turned to us, ordering: "Second and Third Companies: cut off their retreat up over the peak; You others, follow me!" My company immediately set off to move up the steep range, while the Third Company, on more level terrain, headed almost running up toward the top of the ridge. Before me a young man in a hurry made steps in the hard snow to support himself; I used his steps to my advantage and so was able to keep up.

On our right, at the sawmill of Stijovics, on the eastern end of the ridge, after the first two rifle shots, there was a volley of shots from machine-guns: we heard explosions of grenades, and then all this firing came to a lull. When we looked from our position above, our men had already got through and were quickly advancing toward the houses, seen way down above the highway on the eastern side of the ridge on whose top were our two companies. The army officers ordered us to go down toward the hamlet there. We set off in broken ranks. Some of our soldiers got down quickly.

When I arrived at the first houses, I saw some people carrying a wounded man; three women carried him with the help of our soldiers. A little farther down, we were told into which house the wounded man was brought, and some of us entered that house to see if he was sorely wounded as well as to learn if he was "ours" or "theirs". After we got in, we saw three women and two of our soldiers; the latter were standing on the left side of the small room, and the women were busy setting a pillow under the head of the wounded young man, who was lying on a bed made of two joined benches. The women's eyes were moistened with tears, but none lamented loudly. I approached the bed, and after a short while, I said: "He is already dead! What are you waiting for!" I quickly crossed his hands on his breast, and one of the women shut his eyes, telling us that he surely was dead when they brought him into the room. I took off my cap, saying: "May God forgive him!" All present made the sign of the cross on their breasts, except a little boy who was playing by the window behind the men. I looked with compassion at this victim of the thoughtless "leaders" of the partisan armed forces. This was a young man about 25 years old, medium height, thick in body, even stout, with a small round head on a short vigorous neck. He had a small moustache, that was curled in and away from his upper lip. He was clad in the simple raw wool clothes of our villagers. Probably he had been a good party man, and he did not surrender with the other villagers, but tried to escape toward Jasen, and was wounded when he had been on the highway directly below this hamlet. I learned that he was from a village south of Crkvine in Moraca. The women would inform his parents, but they would bury him alone somewhere in the vicinity. We left.

I was informed that none of our men had been killed or wounded; four of the partisans had been killed including the young man, who died when he was evacuated. In addition there were 68 prisoners. We went down close to the highway, and on a path to the left headed toward a house which was some yards ahead of us. All around were the men of our companies. I was told that George was in the vicinity, somewhere, awaiting a reply from a larger partisan force at Jasen, which, we believed, had about 200 men. George Lasic had asked them by an official letter: "Open the highway, or be ready to fight."

I saw the prisoners when I passed the house; they were confined in a fenced courtyard. Approaching the fence, I saw also some of the "first prisoners" taken in Verusa, but I was more interested in these new prisoners, and began to talk with them. These were mostly young villagers from the district of Kolasin. First I addressed one of them, who looked somewhat intelligent and open-minded, asking him: "Why, for goodness sake, did you join these men who kill even those living in peace in their homes?" Before he had enough time to answer me, several of them approached and started to apologize: "Listen, sir, they used to tell us about the fight against the occupiers, who will attack us from all sides, and they organized us as soldiers and sent us where they wanted to; now we know that this "army" of theirs is more like a gathering of highway robbers than an army defending our country." Another added: "We didn't want to fight a few minutes ago, when we saw our brothers going in peace on their way. You know, if we had had a little more time to talk and come to an understanding, we would have surrendered without a fight, and asked to go home in peace." Then they asked what would happen to them: "Will they kill us," someone asked from the rear rows. I told them: "None of you will be tried or killed until the court thoroughly investigates and determines the guilt of each one. I believe that there is none among you who had committed any crime, and you have nothing to fear."

Ours was not the only fighting. Over Drcka on a small field before the Sunga Gorge, at the north end of Bare Kraljske, a strong partisan force that morning tried to penetrate into the upper Vasojevics over Tresnjevik Mountain. Our forces, led by Army Major Andrija Veskovic, with about 700 men, opposed them. The villagers at first begged the partisans to let their villages remain in peace: "We ask you in the name of God and today's holiday of Saint John to go away from our homes." But a Communist answered them: "And what type of yoke do you use for this St. John? Is he a gray, or does he have a white spot between his horns?" This infuriated the villagers, especially the inhabitants of Bare under the leadership of their school teacher, Dmitar Vukicevic, and their wrath grew farther and faster.

Andrija Veskovic and Dmitar Vukicevic tactfully displayed their main forces at the entrance of the Sunga Gorge and surrounding the hills on both banks of the Drcka Stream. When the partisans tried to penetrate by force into Bare Kraljske, Vasojevics opposed them by force. The fighting set off here began about at 10 a.m., almost simultaneously with the fighting at Jabuka. Here the partisans suffered a heavy blow: on the plain near the Sunga Gorge, mostly on its banks, near the stream, they left 69 dead. Twenty-six were made prisoner. Among the partisan dead was Vukman Kruscic from Bjelojevice Village, Kolasin District, whose ancestors were originally from Vasojevics. After our forces had gone into an offensive and drove the attackers over the bridge in the direction of Matesevo, Kruscic's body had been dragged by the victorious soldiers to the stream and his head was soaked in the water so as not to be covered by the snow. They were eager to show what happened to the traitor who brought armed forces against Vasojevics!

Meanwhile, with our own forces at Jabuka, our First and Fourth Companies were ordered to curb the right wing of the partisans at Jasen. Before I got down from the ridge, we had noticed that they were taking their positions to the extreme end of their right wing. To the demand of George Lasic, the partisans had answered they would fight. We were ready to move forward on the highway as soon as the fighting began on our left wing. During this lull I talked privately with my brother George. We stepped aside, and I asked him to switch our overcoats, giving him as the reason that I could move easier with his short one. He immediately understood my forebodings and quickly answered: "You asked me the same thing in Opasanica! This is very 'wise'; you could be killed and I saved. Let me alone." Then he turned and went. I immediately found our eldest brother Ilija, and we agreed that he and Milicko should at all times be around George in the event of fighting. In addition they should take with them our cousin Spiro, and our close relative Milos Radisavov Dabetic from Opasanica, who were good men and intrepid fighters. These four should, without George's awareness, be around him during any fighting and protect him even with their bodies if necessary. So George would have a secret guard of which he was not aware. Now I felt better.

Unexpectedly we had been ordered to retreat to Stijovic's saw-mill. It appeared to me this was a maneuver to deceive the opponents until I heard George Lasic himself giving orders to send out liaison patrols to inform our First and Fourth Companies to come back unnoticed and to follow. Then we headed toward the bridge over the Tara in front of the saw-mill, and began to cross it to Zuren Potok, on the left bank of the river. There, over the stream, I saw a man leading his wife under his arm toward a nearby house. I was told this was Milan Milosevic, a teacher from the Skoplje high school; the wife was weeping badly. Maybe she had been frightened by seeing so many soldiers. We set off to mount the abrupt slope on the right

bank of Zuren Potok. The snow was so softened that our feet penetrated deeply into it, which greatly impeded our climb. The company
captains were constantly urging us to move quickly. To avoid wading
through the high, soft snow, I went with some fellows to our left and
went to the ridge and moved forward much easier. Already we were
opposite Jasen. Unnoticed, we could see what was going on there,
because we were covered by woods highly frosted on the tree tops, as
this was the north slope side, while the partisans could not see where
we were going. Our two companies, who were left to begin the fighting above Jasen, were gradually disappearing from sight and retreating toward the bridge to follow us. This hurried retreating became
clear to me later: The partisan forces that had intended to attack us
early this very morning in Lijeva Rijeka, was now moving swiftly
after us; if we started to fight at Jasen, and later at the bridge over
the Tara River close to Matesevo, our forces inevitably would have
been put between two fires and possibly destroyed. On the ground of
verified information, more than 1500 of the partisans were coming
behind us—about 600 men moving from Rovca and Moraca, and the
remainder from, or through, Bratonozici and Brskut.

Arriving at the ridge, at a somewhat level path on our left, we
quickly got through the woods to Dolovi Adzica near Matesevo. I
heard somebody calling from the positions over Drcka stream, which
mouths into the Tara below Matesevo: "Who are these men coming
from Komovi; are they our men from Lijeva Rijeka, or partisans?" In
the woods above Dolovi Adzica we met and by-passed three old
villagers; I was told that one of them was Todor Adzic. They looked
as if they were frightened, making the sign of the cross on their
breasts: "May the Lord God help and protect you!" At Dolovi
Adzica our forces were quickly deployed: on the right our Second
and Fourth Companies, and to the left, down the ridge, all other
main forces. The fighting started immediately on the left wing, but
on the right wing we had little pressure for the time-being.

Two weeks ago the Italians had been at Matesevo. For some
months the Italian military forces had fortified all approaches,
particularly the top of the hill above and dominating Matesevo, on
which our forces were attacking on the left. Three days ago, the partisans had subdued our company at Matesevo, forcing most of this
company to retreat, and they now occupied all of the formerly
Italian trenches, and machine-gunning. The fight continued all along
the fighting line on the right to Djurovic's sawmill. In the right

section, the partisan resistance ceased, and they retreated to Mate-sevo; we watched them crossing the bridge over Drcka and fleeing in panic toward Kolasin.

George Lasic had been on the left frontline, where the hardest fighting took place. He was giving instructions to the soldiers in the first lines how to throw the grenades most successfully into the op-ponent's trenches, and he himself threw many of them.

After the resistance of partisans on our left wing had been reduced, George Lasic had been in the middle of the ridge, not far off the first lines on this sector, looking to the north; he wanted to give some new order to Vidak Zecevic, the battalion commander of Lijeva Rijeka, and turned his head to his right, saying: "Where is Vidak?" At that moment two rifle shots were heard from a former Italian machine gun pillbox in the vicinity of the house of Radisav Radevic, some 200 to 300 meters west of our main forces. Neither shot missed: George was wounded in the head, and our younger brother, Milicko, in the left arm. George's wound was grievous; he fell and was unconscious from the start.

Just before darkness set in, the captain of the Second Company, Novak Milikic, who had been posted on the hill separating our two companies to the right, and was watching the fighting called me: "Milija, we ought to retreat; George and Milicko are both wounded!" I was shocked and so grieved that I was unable to move for a while. I was talking to myself: "Woe is me, and I have no bandage!" But, nearby was the house of Milic Adzic. His wife perhaps heard me talking about my having no bandage; she came quickly out of her home and brought me three of them. She said: "These are English bandages; they are very good!" I hurriedly put them into the pockets of my overcoat, and started to run up to join our main forces, which were going to the left above Dolovi Adzica. After a few minutes of walking, my legs stopped moving from the knees down; I was unable to continue, and sat on the snow. Fortunately, some of our men soon came from below and I asked a young man to give me his hand to get up. He gave me his hand and took me under his arm and went with me some steps forward. The thought that I should see my wounded brothers as soon as possible gave me extraordinary strength. I thanked the young man for his kindness, left him behind me, and again began to run, by-passing many soldiers who were in front of me. I met many men who had been on our left wing; they told me: "Milicko's left arm is wounded very sorely, but George has been shot in the left cheek very slightly." I was encouraged, and I continued to speed forward to bandage their wounds.

On the path through the woods above Djurovic's sawmill, I joined a group of soldiers carrying George. At that time he was carried on the shoulders by the son of Dale Vukasinov Vesovic. I approached him, asking him how he felt. "All right," he answered me. We were striving hurriedly to reach the house of Gruja Milosevic, a cousin of our late father. The owner of the house and his wife quickly made a bed ready to put him on. My Milosevics relatives did all they could to make him comfortable, and I began to unbandage his wound and to apply a new bandage. I took off all the previous blook-soaked bandages and woolen shalls, washed the wound and applied the bandage I had. It looked to me as if the projectile had touched him somewhat deeper on the cheek, and that his wound was of a light nature. The house was filled with many people, and I told them: "After two weeks or so, all will be all right," and they rejoiced and were happy. "Thanks to God," they repeated many times.

Soon our eldest brother came; I told him the same as I had to the other men, and added: "You take care of Milicko, and do not worry about George. I will be constantly at his side." My brother told me that all four of them that had agreed this morning to protect George had been around him during the fighting, but they did not expect that somebody would shoot at him specifically from afar.

During all our fighting this day, at Jabuka and at Matesevo, we had had only three casualties: a Labovic from Bare dead, and two Lasic brothers, wounded. The losses of partisans, except those I mentioned earlier, could not have been evaluated exactly by our men. There had been many dead and wounded even during the fighting after noon at Matesevo; especially our men from the right bank of Drcka felled them when they began to retreat from the Sunga Gorge to Matesevo—the partisans could not have any protection from Sunga to Matesevo. All night through they were evacuating their dead and wounded toward Kolasin. Among us it had been known for sure that during the night they managed to take from the battle field an additional number of about 180 dead and wounded. They will well remember Saint John's holyday and Vasojevics . . . .

As darkness set in, the fighting stopped. Some of our men were coming to the house of Gruja Melosevic, and the others were going out, to learn how George was, and to spread the news that he was not sorely wounded. From behind his neck a light stain of blood was appearing again and again; I wondered where this came from. George was now out of his underwear and his blood-soaked clothes and resting in bed. I was told that my youngest brother was all right, although the bone of his arm had been fractured. He was going around without difficulty. In the room there were constantly 20 to 30 men, talking about today's events. About midnight, someone told us that many partisans had come down the Tara to Matesevo, and they were quarrelling among themselves. A soldier of ours had managed to mingle with the newcomers unnoticed, and he knew exactly why they quarrelled. A group of about 450 armed men from Kuci started to grumble as soon as they learned that at Matesevo there had been no Italians. Nikola Vujosevic had told the partisans: "You told us to come to fight against the occupiers at Matesevo; we are here, but where are your occupiers?" Then he turned to his relatives, the Kuci: "Brothers Kuci, we have been shamefully deceived. Instead of fighting against the occupiers, they called us here to fight against Vasojevici. All of you who are Kuci, take your arms in your hands, and come back with me up the Tara River to our homes. The Vasojevics will be able to defend themsleves alone." Immediately after this, all Kuci went back. The partisans did not even try to prevent their leaving. The partisans could intimidate only the cowards, but not the Kuci and other good Serbian people.

Meanwhile all our leading officers urgently met in Dragojevic's cafe-house on the other side of Sunga, at the northern end of Bare Kraljske, where they made plans for defense and undertook all measures to protect this area from a new attack by the partisans. They also immediately appointed Dusan Arsovic, military court judge, to act as liaison and to help me with George, who remained unconscious. Soon Arsovic came to the house of Gruja Milosevic, and told me what we had to do. He had already come in contact with Jevto Djurovic and obtained his sleigh. It was already before the house ready to move. Dusan wanted to clean the wound by himself, and we did it again, and gave some medication, seeking to prevent any worse condition. But neither Dusan nor I were able to explain the appearance of blood on the neck, which did not come from the wound on the cheek. We quickly got to work. As I had previously changed his clothes, and taken to safety all confidential written materials George had with him, we wrapped his head in a woolen shawl, and put a warm military overcoat lined with wool on him. Aunt brought woolen socks for him, which we, on her advice, filled with carded wool to keep his feet warm. Our uncle Gruja Milosevic, with other soldiers, tried to make him comfortable on the sleigh, outside near the house. Gruja had put on two thick wool mattresses and brought two covers. We were all aware of the severe cold on Tresnjevik Mountain in January.

Just when we were about to carry George out, one of the soldiers noticed that a partisan had sneaked among us with a red star on his cap. When it was certain that the unknown was a Kruscic from Bjelojevice, they took him out. Soon they came back, and without any visible emotion told us: "We took him to pay a visit to his close kin Vukman underneath the bridge over Drcka!" We did not hear any shot fired, but I do not believe that they did not beat him to death somewhere nearby, or maybe beneath the bridge: that two Kruscics should be together where Vukman been killed earlier.

The soldiers at hand helped us carry out the wounded. We put George on the bed on the sleigh, covered him with two coverings, which we tacked on all sides, and we 14 men went forward. Akso Arsovic, a 60-year-old man, a veteran, was driving the sleigh and closely watching our wounded, and we were accompanying the sleigh on foot. Three of us were ahead of it as a patrol. When we were approaching the bridge over Drcka, ahead, they showed me the supporting pile at which lay the body of Vukman Kruscic, a notorious Communist murderer and organizer of many killings. Having crossed the bridge, they showed me on the right the killed partisans, more than 60 of them on this small space alone. Their bodies were scattered all over. In the close vicinity of the highway I saw three bodies piled one over the other. The bodies were covered with snow, which a few minutes ago had begun to fall in large, dense flakes. The bodies looked like some crossed lumber. "Look to your left," one fellow told me. There were other dead bodies covered with snow. I was shaken, and began to look at the ground, speedily going forward. One of our companions, on my right, who the large snowflakes falling between us prevented me from seeing clearly—he looked like a living angel—said: "Here, dear brother, on this level space, for two full hours we took off our caps in supplication this morning, asking them in the name of the Lord God and Saint John to go in peace away from our homes. But they blindly were pushed forward like oxen, to get into Bare to plunder and kill us. God has punished them."

CHAPTER SEVEN: THE COMMANDER HOSPITALIZED

Gradually we were leaving behind us this awful plain of the dead, and soon encountered the Sunga Gorge. We arrived at the Dragojevici's cafe-house. Here we waited for some minutes. I checked to see if George was well covered. Some Dragojevics came out; one of them gave me another blanket, saying: "Tresnjevik is ahead of you. We should put another blanket on him. Take care, because of the cold, for my wounded Djojo (George). May God help him to be healed soon, and to come among us to lead us against our foes!"

I told them I intended to lodge George in the house of Ljubo Vuksanovic, or in the cafe-house at Bandovic Bridge, and from there to seek the medical help of Dr. Kaberice. We then continued moving with George up Bare Kraljske in the direction of Tresnjevik. We had done all in our power to sooth his pains and to protect him against the cold which grew severer as we started to climb. George was very restful, never giving any visible sign of pain; sometimes he would take the blanket off his face, which one of us would immediately fix. At Han Drndarski I entered the Popadija's house to change my socks, which were thoroughly wet because of sweat, and asked for some new ones. One of the daughters brought me a pair of new woolen socks. I quickly put them on, put on my shoes, and went in a hurry to join my companions.

Until now we had been going swiftly, but from above the Han Drndarski we slowed down somewhat. The cold was more severe, but I took no notice of it, and we continued forward. When we reached the last ridge this side of Tresnjevik, Dusan Arsovic dispatched three younger soldiers to scout a level area on Tresnjevik. After awhile, just when we were some hundred yards away from a depression on this side, they came back and reported: "In the house on the highway on top of Tresnjevik there is a great fire. Among the men who were sitting around the fire, we recognized two Communists— Keljanovic and another. This was clearly a partisan detachment, but it was impossible to estimate their number." Even while these men were reporting, Akso Arsovic had turned the sleigh back with the other men and disappeared from our sight. These three men quickly followed. Arsovic and I sat on the snow at the left snow bank. "George is now most at ease," said he, heartbroken, After a moment, we two went after them, struggling in huge snow drifts, which were growing so quickly and changing shape almost every minute at the top of Tresnjevik about 1 a.m. As soon as we got through the snow storm, we came to that part of the highway where the north wind was less cutting, and then headed down, speeding our steps. We found our men in the house of Scepan Arsovic at the edge of the highway in the mid Tresnjevik. Here they had taken George off the sleigh, carried him in and put him on a bed in the large room. Akso Arsovic told me that George vomitted a little, which I understood as being a bad sign. I approached him, and, tapping him on the right cheek, asked him if he felt much pain. "I feel no pain. Where are we now?" he asked. I started to explain to him, but he could not follow my answers—he was in a delirium.

George spent all day, January 21, 1942, in such a state. The partisans from the area of the district of Andrijevica held Tresnjevik. We were about three kilometers from them, and all day we watched them coming in patrols over that part of the highway from the top of Tresnjevik to the first house in front of us, hardly a kilometer away; but they did not dare approach us.

Very early the next morning, on January 22, 1942, Dmitar Vukicevic, with the men from Bare had freed the top of Tresnjevik from Communists. We had already set out in this direction. We got through Tresnjevik with the rows of our armed forces on both sides, and continued to Kralje. The day was cloudless and the sun shone, and we descended the highway without great impediments. We arrived at Bandovic Bridge early in the afternoon. Arsovic, who went forward before us, had been informed that Dr. Kaberice could not make any operation, because he was not a surgeon. Dr. Kaberice had advised us to bring the wounded to his ambulance, and he would ask help from his Italian colleague, whom he knew as a good surgeon, and who was his friend. There had been no other solution, and to wait any longer would mean losing a dear life. Dusan Arsovic quickly got permission to bring the wounded into Andrijevica, and this was done immediately. Dr. Kaberice examined the wound in the ambulance cart, shook his head and told us he could not do anything, and, as expected, asked permission to call his Italian colleague. After our consent, he sent his assistant Balsic to find him for us.

Soon the Italian surgeon came, a Captain in rank. He told us that an urgent operation was required, which he could perform only in his operating room, where he had at hand all necessary instruments. "It must be done immediately," he said. We quickly brought the wounded there. The Italian surgeon set to work in my presence.

After about a half hour, the wound had been completely cleansed. When he was pulling out the small bones from the cheek of my brother, I felt as if the surgeon was cutting off the parts of my heart. Only here I learned that the entrance of the projectile had been in the part of the head in proximity to the left ear; the bullet got through the middle ear and smashed the left cheek bone. The surgeon explained to me that the unconsciousness was due to the shaking of the base of the brain. Judging from the present state of the wounded, in his opinion, there was little hope of his living.

Meanwhile, Dr. Kaberice had found a room in a private house near the exit of the town, where he would come often to see him, and we carried George there after the operation was performed. During all of the operation George had been in a coma; he did not give any reaction. Only once he spoke: "Let it; enough!" The surgeon cleansed the wound every 24 hours, usually at 9 in the morning. I had been constantly beside my wounded brother, watching any move of his head or hands, awaiting more his death than his life. At night I never slept all night through, constantly sitting on a wooden chair in the corridor in front of the partly opened door of the room. During the day I was relieved by somebody to sleep for four hours. To prevent his exhaustion from the lack of nourishment, I organized through my relatives and friends the foods for him and all the time I gave him something to eat using a teaspoon as for a little baby, because he hardly could open his mouth. As a rule, I used beaten egg yolks, cream and different jams. He did not get weak in the body anyhow, but for the full 12 days he was completely unconscious. About 5 a.m. of the 13th day he asked me a few times what time it was. I answered him very quickly; 5 minutes to five in the morning. He slightly raised his hand, saying: "All is over! This is awful!" I expected that he would die any moment, and did not take my eye off of him for a second. To our friends and relatives who came to visit him that morning I openly told them to make ready a new civilian suit he had ordered from a tailor's in Andrijevica. I told them to make all preparations for burial.

To my great happiness and extreme surprise, on February 2, 1942, at about 3 p.m., George recovered his consciousness. First he asked me about some common things, and immediately he began to ask me what had happened after he was wounded at Matesevo on January 20. He was absolutely conscious of all events that occurred before he was wounded, but of nothing since. He was unaware even of where we were now. When I told him what we had experienced these last 13 days, he quickly and thoroughly understood the sequence of events, and asked me about the present situation of our forces in Bare Kraljske as well as in the district of Berane. I omitted telling him about the wounding of his classmates, Bozo Joksimovic and Miomir Cemovic, who were also in the hospital in Berane. There was no end to my happiness, but I did not want to tire him; rather I joked with as before. Now I used a nickname we used to call him in his earliest childhood; he told me he had almost forgotten that name, and laughed under his heavy bandages. That morning I was heartbroken and unhappy, but that night I was delighted and rejoicing—my brother had returned from the dead!

During all of these 11 days spent in Andrijevica, the Italian sentinal had been regularly relieved on schedule. We both had been treated as prisoners of war. The Italian military authorities told me we would go first to Skadar and later to Italy. The last days they forbade visits of our relatives from this small town. I was informed our being transported from here had been urged by the Italian commander in Andrijevica under pretext that in Skadar, George could get better medical care. Through our civil authorities I was able to prevent our transportation, giving the reason that I did not believe my brother would live, and I wanted to bury him in our country. Factually I had another idea in my mind: if he survived, it would have been harder for us to escape from Skadar, and more so from Italy. Our medical doctor from Berane, Dr. Vukota Dedovic, the chief of our civil hospital, sided by other of our men in Andrijevica and Berane, was finally able to get permission not to have him deported to Skadar. On February 3, 1942, he came with his private automobile to take us both to his hospital. After many tiring procedures at the exit from Andrijevica and at the entrance to Berane, we were able to bring George to our hospital; we carried him quickly to a large hospital room, where there were already some 20 of our other wounded men.

I myself was now one of these victims. I had been frost-bitten on both feet at Tresnjevik on January 20, 1942. At Andrijevica the doctors cut off the swollen heels ("calotes") and on the toes, but the healing was slow because I was on my feet most of the time to take care of my wounded brother. I had been so preoccupied that I noticed that I was frost-bitten only when my feet "got longer" through the accumulation of liquid between the flesh and the skin on the heel and toes. In this hospital I learned and recognized that I could have been worse; I learned the difference among the degrees of frost-bites. I had avoided the pulling out of the toe-nails, which looked as small black dots, and swelling of some or all joints on the toes; my case being the first degree of frostbite. Thanks to this, I was able to take care of others, or to give some consolation to those around me. Here there were many of our gravely wounded soldiers, as well as partisans separated in the other hospital rooms. In the bed beside mine was a young man named Tomovic from some village around the county Berane. He had been shot above the knee of his right leg, and for some time he was all right. Unfortunately, his wound got worse, and they took him to a smaller room; later the doctors were compelled to amputate his leg to save his life; I can not take his looks out of my memory. A boy of some 15 or 16 years was in the bed in front of mine, and I saw him every day during our two weeks of living in this hospital room. His name was Milorad Cimbaljevic, a brother of the priest Cimbaljevic from the area of the upper Vasojevici. A grenade smashed his left hand to the elbow, wounded his face and put out both of his eyes. They had amputated his hand some time ago, and the stump had healed; they were waiting only for his mother and brother to take him home. These last days he was talking about their coming almost every moment. I often used to come to him tapping him tenderly on his shoulders to make his feel that he was not alone in the desert of darkness, in which he had to spend all of his life. Sometimes he felt pains in his arm and complained of feeling pains in his "fingers", which were not there. Even in the middle of the night he would ask me: "Why haven't mother and brother come to me; is it daytime?" He used to repeat this question during the day or night. Sometimes I asked the hospital personnel to let me feed him by myself and to console him, and he was happy to know that I was beside him; but he was unaware that just at that time I was most shaken and saddened. My heart had already as many scars as his face, which the bomb had disfigured and left with countless small blue spots.

Here I learned about recent fighting in this area. The partisan command in Kolasin had dispatched their "army" of about 500 mer to subdue the lower Vasojevics, where Captain Pavle Djurisic had undertaken to organize the people to defend themselves against the Communist terror. The partisan forces crossed over the mountains, forces penetrating in the direction of Matesevo and Bare

Kraljske. After some small engagements, the battle at Lubnice Village took place on the day of Saint Sava, January 27, 1942. Through skillful maneuvering under the direct command of Djurisic, the national forces from this district defeated the attackers at Lubnice. The partisans left 75 dead on the battlefield, the remainder retreated, surprised by night in the mountains, where severe cold had set in. They tried hard to burn some stacks of hay, but an icy crust prevented the fire from catching on. Then they ran out of matches, and began to dance on the hard snow to save themselves from the freezing. We were told later that this night alone about 200 of them perished, and a few survivors came to Kolasin the next morning. With this, the countryside left of the Lim River from Zaostro to Sahovici in the district of Bijelo Polje, was essentially cleared of Communists, although prior to this there had been frequent fighting.

George's wound was hard to heal. The swelling was still great, and the pus formation continued. His life remained in danger. The doctors visited him many times daily and at night. Dr. Dedovic asked help from his Italian colleague, Dr. Cirollini, in all of the graver cases, especially those of surgery. He was very good to our men. After some days in the large hospital room, we moved George to the room where Joksimovic and Cemovic also were. I saw him many times each day; every night at 11:30, Dr. Dedovic would come to spend one to two hours with us. He would sit near the window between George and Bozo on one side, and Miomir on the other.

Every night Dr. Dedovic brought us the most recent news. About our men in Bare Kraljske, George secretly received regular reports from the commanding army officers. The situation of our forces there was very difficult, and became worse day after day. The partisans were attacking repeatedly from all sides with smaller or greater forces. Some great onslaughts had been successfully fended off. Morale among the fighters was excellent, but they lacked other things. They kept their positions on the front line from Kukoraj Brdo-Sunga-Bukova Poljana. The partisans had tried to attack over the Komovi Mountains, down the Crnja Forest, to arrive in the middle of Bare from the rear. One of their detachments went from Opasanica up Margaritska Rijeka, and another from Uac over Kotic. The first partisan unit was at Margarita, and the other near Jelic Platno, on Komovi Mountain. But unable to recognize each other because of heavy snowstorms, fighting began between the two forces that virtually annihilated them. In addition, the Communists from both our districts had been organized to prevent the food supply from reaching the Andrijevica District. In the Bijelo Polje District, the area from Sahovici to Kovren was changing hands. The national forces under Pavle Djurisic would chase the partisans to Kovren by day, and they would come back to Sahovici at night; the next day would be the same. George pondered these reports but did not comment on them.

During these trying days, the men in Bare showed themselves to be intrepid fighters; Dmitar Vukicevic was their leader. This small area of 99 homes in Bare below Komovi Mountain shared even its last piece of bread with about another 1000 fighters there. They had enough meat, because this is an area of cattle and sheep raising, but bread was diminishing rapidly, so that in the last days the fighters had been satisfied if they got three potatoes a day. For a full month they got a total of only about 1200 kilograms (about 2,700 pounds) of corn through Ljubo Vuksanovic.

One of the fighters in Bare Kraljske, Trifun Vukicevic, told me one day: "My village, for a full month in the beginning of 1942, had been the entire free Yugoslavia, the seat of her entire military forces, and legal government in the country; it alone supplied her army, and together with our brothers defended her freedom!" He did not exaggerate, as far as this part of our country was concerned—from Lovcen Mountain to Komovi and from Niksic to Pljevlja.

If our forces in Bare were subdued, the partisans would have occupied the Upper Vasojevics and imposed their terrorist rule throughout the villages there, and from there sought to rule the District of Berane. Therefore George Lasic, through Dr. Dedovic, and other trustworthy men, had ordered Pavle Djurisic with all the national forces from the District of Berane to come back from the district of Bijelo Polje. George had set the meeting to take place at 2 in the afternoon of February 9, 1942. At 1 o'clock that day, Dr. Dedovic and I took him into the doctor's car for a short "ride". When we came to the other side of the village, we helped him to get out of the automobile and into a house. It was already 2 o'clock. We took George into a small room, and met Pavle, who had been hiding alone in some house to the right. The two alone spent 15 to 20 minutes in conversation. Dr. Dedovic and I then took George under the arms and quickly returned to the waiting automobile.

Thereafter, Pavle Djurisic immediately withdrew all armed forces from the Berane District and returned to this area. From here he gathered all of our organized forces as well as some laggards from the upper district. On February 18, 1942, he had concentrated about 1,200 fighters from the Lower Vasojevici, and about 600 from the Upper Vasojevici, at the village Kralje this side of Tresnjevik, and on February 19, 1942, he crossed Tresnjevik to reinforce our forces in Bare. Those die-hard fighters, who had endured so much, received their brothers with enthusiasm and joy, preparing to continue the fighting. The 114 partisans previously made prisoners also rejoiced; they all were spared and alive, having spent all this hard time in peace in a house near the highway through Bare. Pavle Djurisic had under his command now a fighting force of 3400 soldiers; out of these more than 3,000 fighters had been from the Lower and Upper Vasojevics, and about 400 fighters from Prekobrdje and Recine, district of Kolasin. All were confident and convinced of their eventual victory, and their song went:

> *"Partisans, you black ravens,*
> *Your dark days await you!"*

According to the strategic plan of parting our forces into three columns, on the left wing under the command of Captain Vidak Zecevic, in the middle under the command of Major Andrija Veskovic, and on the right wing under command of Major Milorad Joksimovic, all three under direct command of Captain Pavle Djurisic, the general attack on Kolasin began at night on February 21/22, 1942, against the Red occupiers of Crna Gora and Brda, who were using the fortifications of the invaders of our country at the Matesevo-Planinica line.

The fall of Kolasin really had been the signal for a general revolt. In Brskut and Bratonozici, the people killed the Communist commissars and organized their nationalistic battalions under the guidance of Vlado Djukic, a Staff Army Captain; they went to fight at Stavanj. In Kuci, where the Communists never had any influence, about 1,800 Kucs organized their patriotic units under the command of Lieutenant Colonel Savo Vujosevic, who was immediately joined by Army Major Novica Lazovic, Captain Ilija Ivanovic, and many other leaders from this courgeous Serbian tribe. All of the valley of Zeta near Podgorica was in revolt; here Lieutenant Colonel Relja Piletic and Army Major Dimitrije Boljevic were leaders.

In Bjelopavlici, Colonel Bajo Stanisic, who had managed to survive Communist terror with a small group of men hiding and moving from one place to another, increased his forces with more fighters, and united with the forces of the brothers Mijuskovici in Strasevina near Niksic; their forces rapidly increased, mounting to some thousands. In this area, Stanisic became a central figure to unify our fighters for liberation from the Communist terror. He was joined by Kuci, Zecani, and about 250 Piperi, who with their own leaders, cleaned the partisans out of the whole territory from Medun in Kuci, the valley of Zeta to Planinica near Ostrog, and (crossing to Zupa) of Niksic. This tightened the belt around the partisans, who fearing the wrath of the population, retreated to the District of Savnik, leaving in a hurry even their notorious Radovce, where in the last moment they killed 32 female "comrades" being pregnant and unable to go with them.

Our forces from Kolasin were giving blows to partisans between Lijeva Rijeka and Rovca and all along the low ranges of Sinjajevina to Mojkovac on the Tara River. In all of this area hard fighting continued, while the people behind the partisans' lines gradually were liberated and increased our ranks. In the upper Lipovo Savo Lazarevic, a retired army major, survived with about 60 of his fellows from this locality; Captain Ivan Ruzic with 200 fighters managed to rid an area of partisans and then joined the units of Pavle Djurisic above Polja Kolasinska, reporting to him that about 2,000 men under the leadership of Momcilo Corovic, a circuit court judge, were awaiting our forces at Goransko still within the partisan area. To insure our victory, and to liberate our people from Ustasi in Sandzak under the notorious Croatian killer "Satnik" Jakovljevic, Pavle Djurisic had asked help from our units in Pozega under the command of Army Major Milos Glisic and Captain Vucko Ignjatovic, now at Nova Varos. They crossed the Lim River with some 2,000 fighters, and took their positions from Mojkovac to near Pljevlja. Captain Nikola Bojovic was fighting in this area with about 300 fighting men. The belt tightened more and more about the Communists, so that on June 14, 1942, the area was liberated. In this way Crna Gora with Brda, as well as Sandzak, had been liberated simultaneously from two terrible foes of the Serbian people, and all free men and nations—from Communists and Ustasi.

The wound of my brother George was gradually healing; there had been less pus, and the bandage was changed less frequently. Then the large bandage was taken off, and they put on the gauze, which we fixed in place. The swelling of the left ear was still great, but it would gradually go down by being exposed to the sun's rays. Now I was most concerned because of the inflamation in his left eye, which could get worse.

My cousin, Nikola Lasic, was killed by Communists on April 1, 1942, near Zeleni Vir in Rovca.

Entering my native village for the funeral, I greeted all Radevics in lower village, who were as mournful as we, and hurried to see Nikola's wife, Bozana, and their sons Slobodan and Stevan. She was not yet told that her husband had been killed. Approaching the house, I was thinking how Bozana would take the blow when she learned of her husband's death, for she loved him with the love of a good and honest wife. I entered the room, in which there was already my uncle Jovan with many of our close relatives and friends; my wife Victoria was standing beside Bozana, whom I greeted first, and then with my uncle Jovan and the others, Bozana told me: "You are not the Milija you used to be; you are saddened! What is the matter? There is something you are hiding from me, all of you!" My wife, after a little pause, asked her to give them Nikola's new suit, but she was not willing to let anyone open the wardrobe. Finally my wife took the keys from her hand almost roughly, saying to Bozana: "Are you not ashamed to let our Nikola come back in his old dirty suit?" Bozana pondered a little, and let them open the wardrobe by themselves, and take some underwear and a suit.

After this, I gave a sign to my uncle to leave with me. When we got some distance from the house, I embraced him again, with tears running profusely down my face, and my words choking me. My old uncle looked at me very calmly and without any emotion told me: "Take it easy, Milija; be more courageous! we are not to be afflicted alone; we have many relatives and friends to mourn Nikola and other victims in this great misfortune. Give thanks to God who delivered us from criminals and killers, and saved our George."

This same evening I went to see my good aunt; I found her thoughtful and saddened, but not in tears. She embraced me, as usual, and asked me about her nephew George. She told me: "Tomorrow in the afternoon, I myself will break the news to Bozana; anyhow she must learn this afflicting news, and I will be able to tell her on the way. We ought to spare her even one day less of sorrow."

This is how Nikola had died: At dawn, after we had left our villages on January 20, 1942, the partisans had overran Lijeva Rijeka from three main directions: from Brskut, over Vjeternik Mountain coming from Bratonozici, and from Stavanj coming out of Moraca and Rovca. From Stavanj came about 600 partisans, and from Brskut and Vjeternik about 1,200 others, and maybe more. All these converged on Lijeva Rijeka under the command of Lieutenant Mileta Djukic, a cousin of the notorious murderer Scepan Djukic. This horde, set to impose Communist rule on the rest of the tribe of Vasojevics, set off a systematic plundering of the villagers' homes throughout the surrounding villages, except Malo Slacko where 22 Adzics were living. Within less than a month of their "occupation", the partisans took off with them 960 sheep, and some hundreds of oxen, cows, and calves. In addition, they carried off corn and potatoes almost to the last supplies found in their villagers' homes; besides they took and carried with them the winter supplies of dry meat, bacon and lard, as well as the large containers with cheese, butter and cream—in short, all that the villagers had prepared to feed their families in these hard times. My sister-in-law Jelena told me what they plundered from our home alone: "31 sheep out of 41 we had for winter; they took and carried off almost all of our supply of corn and wheat; I think we could hardly gather around the pantry some 200 kilograms in corn cobs, as they took with them about 800 kilograms on the first day of their rule; of the potatoes they loaded on horseback 15 horsepacks (about 2,500 kilograms). One morning they came to take off all our meat, lard and speck, as well as our cheese and butter. From all of these supplies I managed to save the biggest band of speck by quickly grabbing it and putting it into my curtain cloth; I then ran to the stable and hid it in the hay near the calf. Later they loaded on their horses seven horseloads of hay. When they plundered our corn, the teacher Radovic from Kolasin was sitting on the road above our house and loudly weeping. I asked him why he wept, and he answered me in tears: 'Why should I not weep, it would be better if I killed myself! With your husband, my dear Iko (Ilija), I many times drank and feasted through Kolasin as brothers, and now I come to plunder his house.' Carrying the horsepack load down the village, he stopped at the house of my uncle and unloaded there some corn, asking them to give it back to us later, but not to tell anybody about that." From this point of view some fared better than others. Anyhow, all villagers' homes had been plundered in a similar way on the part of the "authorities." I asked my sister-in-law and my wife what our children had done while our home had been plundered. "The children huddled around the stove and looked helplessly at how these mad men were taking your suits from hangers and piling your shoes." They took the razor, razor blades, soap and toothbrush, putting all in their pockets. Victoria leaned against her bed with little Milica on her lap; in this way she screened a trunk with clothes and some underwear, which she previously had pushed into the corner under the bed, and they did not notice it.

One of the plunderers had been our godbrother Miras Kostov Adzic from Malo Slacko; he looked at his godsister-in-law Victoria, and said as if to himself: "Oh, if we were not related by godships!"

During the period of their occupation of Lijeva Rijeka, the partisans captured only Nikola Lasic, under pretext that he could stir the population in their rear. To take Nikola they sent some armed men with an explicit order to report immediately to their "command" at Lijeva Rijeka. At that moment he was cutting wood for the fire in front of the house, and he smilingly told them to wait a little to finish his job, which was "very important" because of the severe cold. Nikola made ready as far as he could; he put on two woolen socks on his sore feet, took some necessary things, and, half-barefooted, went with them to report to the new authorities. Somewhat before dark, on January 22, 1942, the local commander, Lieutenant Mileta Djukic, questioned him and finally put him in the house of Vojin Orovic. He stayed there under guard until January 27, in the morning, and then with two guards was sent, still half-barefooted, to the headquarters in Kolasin.

It is interesting to note that one of his guards was the young Djukic on whom the Italians had found a bomb in his pocket and intended to shoot him. At that time his parents with about 50 other villagers came to Nikola's wife and asked her to go there with them to save the life of their son, which she did gladly, and by her knowledge of French she greatly contributed to sparing the life of this young man who now led her husband to the executioners. He did not even try to save Nikola, though he could have done so by getting to the right bank of the Tara River and coming to our forces in Bare.

At the partisan headquarters in Kolasin, Nikola Lasic was questioned on January 29, 1942, about the organization of the first national battalion at Lijeva Rijeka by George Lasic. They asked him to denounce his "brothers" and return home in peace, but he answered them: "I do not renounce my brothers and I will never do that. My brothers follow a right and honest way, but you are following a wrong course and causing catastrophic misfortune to our people."

They did not kill him right away, but put him in their lousy prison until February 22. On this day they brought him to the village Crkvine to the west of Kolasin, where he stayed in the house of a Medenica, son-in-law of Milisav Radevic from our village. Afterward they evacuated him farther toward the Monastery of Moraca, and finally they kept him in the house of Vlahovic near Zeleni Vir in Rovca. His custodians had suggested that he flee, but he refused to do that, saying: "I am neither a burglar nor a killer; I do not fear any bad deed of mine, and I would not like you to kill me trying to escape—you or any other I would encounter in this area which is unknown to me."

An entire week, before he was killed, he stayed in the Vlahovic's home. On the eve of April 1, 1942, smiling and radiant, he told the hostess of the house: "Listen, sister, these men will kill me soon somewhere around here, and I ask you to be kind enough to watch where they bury me, so to be able to show my mother where my grave is. Listen, she knows how to lament beautifully, and you help her in weeping together. Also, I want you to tell her this: that my wife Bozana should immediately take our children to her parents in Belgrade." This honorable Serbian lady looked on the tall, skinny, and smiling Nikola, while the tears ran profusely down her face. She managed only to say: "For goodness sake, sir, they will not!" "Yes they will," continued Nikola smiling. "Now stop weeping; you will have enough time to weep. You, my mother, and Bozana!"

The next morning at about 10 a.m., the three executioners came to take him somewhere; Nikola was ready and, without any visible emotion, went before them in some direction indicated. The hostess of the house did not appear, but she had told her 9-year-old boy to go after them unnoticed to see where they led him. The little boy went after them, bouncing to and fro, but never losing them from sight. Soon he came back running at all speed, and, shaking, and trembling in his voice, told his mother: "They killed Uncle Nikola on the top of the ravine above Zeleni Vir!" On this very spot his body lay until April 13, because there had been hard fighting against strong partisan forces in this area who were trying to break the chain of nationalist forces around them.

Also, after our retreat from Lijeva Rijeka, on January 20, 1942, Major Pero Cadjenovic had been "summoned" to report to the "headquarters" in Kolasin. Very probably he had been accused because he joined the resistance against the Communists, and they knew that he had been to see George Lasic twice before we left. In the "Kolasin headquarters", they broke both his legs and arms, and some hot tempered partisan females poured a kettle full of boiling water on him, before they carried him to the "dog cemetery" and threw him into the snow. After the liberation of Kolasin, his wife and his brother with their relatives went there, recognized him among other martyrs in the "dog cemetery", brought his body to Brskut and buried him in the resting place of his ancestors. Pero's younger brother was so heartbroken by this tragedy and preoccupied with revenge that it was difficult to understand his speech.

These are but short accounts of two martyrs whom I knew personally; they can only serve us to give an idea of what the butchery of men in Kolasin was like. But the story of each victim surely has its own particularities.

There was a danger of famine. In the village I met my younger sister Vidra, or "Fairy" as we endearingly used to call her. She had been married in the village Prekobrdje, lower Moraca, where the people had long suffered under the occupation of partisans. "I wonder, Fairy, how you and my brother-in-law Radoje were able to support your seven boys, as I am aware your supplies of corn were meager?" She began her story in detail, how they used to cull the walnut fronds which she boiled in milk and fed their nine members in the family. I thought that they simply had culled the walnut flowers in quantity of some pounds a day, put it into a kettle and boiled it in milk, but she as an "expert" explained to me the whole process: "First we culled the raw walnut flowers, and dried them on the stove. Then, so dried, we would press them between the palms of our hands over a large dish or other receptacle. I estimated how much would be enough for a meal, and this quantity I poured into the kettle with the milk, just when the milk was on the point of boiling. After this I would let it cook for a while, and pour it into the plates of the children, or into a common container, and then we started to eat, starved as wolves! Brother dear, we were nourished in this way for 28 days." I asked her what would she have done after the disappearing of the walnut flowers. "What I would have done when the forest is green and all plants are growing?" continued the Fairy. "There would be the goat-plant, wild spinach, meadow leaves, field grass, and different other green growings. For sure, in summer we would not have to die from starvation. In the same way I nourished my children, most people had done it," she concluded.

They told me about the personal tragedy of Milos Pavicev Adzic from Malo Slacko. He married a Vesovic girl. Their 17-year-old boy went with his "uncle" Mirko, as did all the Adzici from this village; the boy was their only son in their married life. When his father learned that the boy died in fighting at Matesevo, he almost was out of his mind. For many weeks after this, the afflicted man went through the hills around the village loudly lamenting, so that it was hard listening to him all day, and even at night. Very often he would enter someone's house and continue to take off his sorrow, thinking that he was in his own house; then when he got to his senses and recognized other faces in that house, he would leave and continue to weep. He forbade his wife and daughters to eat anything but some bread and water. All of his supplies of any fat he took out of the house, and distributed them to other people. He had been our god-brother of old, and these days, meeting him at Lijeva Rijeka, I tried to console him, but there would be no consolation in his heart until the grave.

Djordje ("George") Lasic, in his uniform as a captain in the Yugoslavian Army prior to the outbreak of war.

CHAPTER EIGHT: REVENGE

Shortly after Kolasin passed into our hands on February 23, 1942, a military court was established which passed sentence on Partisan army officers and some notorious killers. As to those army officers who joined the communists, the people at large had made the best judgment: "You betrayed our country, our King, and our people. Death!" Villagers near Podgorica captured Lieutenant Colonel Radisav Radevic, my cousin on my mother's side, and interrogated him: "Why, Mister Lieutenant Colonel? What was the matter with you to join the 'tailwaggers' [stray dogs] and all-destroyers—you who were so privileged?" His answer is unknown, but subsequently a young Communist woman, the daughter of Mrs. Krisanta Nedic, an elementary school teacher in Berane, was summoned to Kolasin. When the villagers saw this girl, they made a halter out of rope as for a calf, forced it on the neck of the "lieutenant colonel", and told her: "Now, girl, because you seduced Mister Lieutenant Colonel to the all-destroyers, you will have to unmake your deed from here to Kolasin." This girl led him in this way 11 kilometers to the town, and then through the streets of Kolasin, where the villagers delivered him to the military court. He was sentenced to death, and behaved courageously in the court and at the firing place. There he shouted "Shoot; this is the breast of Radisav Radevic. Long-live King Petar II Karadjordjevic!" Blagota Selic and Lieutenant Colonel Andjelic endured similar trials. Around their necks the villagers put bells taken from nanny goats or from the rams that lead flocks of sheep. They ordered them to bend a little forward so that the noise of bells could be heard better, and walked them through the streets to deliver them to the military court. The sentence was death by firing squad.

Captain Batric Zecevic, the Partisans' "war minister," and Army Captain Tomica Jojic were brought to the court martial directly, without the "bell walk," and were sentenced to death by firing squad. Those who appeared before the court martial had those who pleaded for their clients earnestly, but for the army officers there was never mercy. The members of the court martial could hardly have gone before the people, if they had shown any leniency. I talked with Uncle Krsto Radevic, at that time about 80 years old, about the death sentence of our mutual relative. He told me: "Listen Milija, when Radisav Radevic was at Lijeva Rijeka five months ago, I asked you why you did not bring in this miserable 'dog', so that you and I could have killed him beautifully on the very threshold of my house. I would have killed him at that time more earnestly than that court martial." These military court sentences were unlike the "popular sentences" of the disgusted individuals who, in fightings, or on the front line, showed their wrath against some notorious opponent. There were many cases when brothers assailed their "renegades", who had gone with the "tailwaggers" to fight against us. Whenever possible other men intervened if the "brother" was a boy; but for men there was no mercy. In this way on February 22, 1942, Jevrem Mujovic, a wealthy farmer from the village Stup, county of Lijeva Rijeka, was killed by his close relatives.

On May 20, 1942, I got a seat in a truck to Podgorica and then to Niksic to visit my Uncle Radomir. The weather was beautiful, but the scenes were heartbreaking. Many houses were now desolate ruins. On the highway we spotted large stains of gasoline, where last year the Partisans destroyed 52 Italian military trucks, plundered some food supplies and fled; here also they killed Miras Popovic from Han Garandzic as well as some other persons.

The steel bridge over the Moraca River had not been destroyed, but the whole settlement was but a heap of ruins. They told me that here too the "army" of the Partisan Arso Jovanovic fired some "shots at random" at the Italians, who retaliated with total destruction of this beautiful small settlement of our Kuci. Here I learned the heartbreaking story of annihilation of a family. As soon as the Italian punishing expedition the year before had opened their hellish fire, the women left their homes in a hurry with their children, and looked for shelter in the surrounding rocky area. One of these women went to an isolated precipice nearby, and left her cradle with her baby in it. With the older children, she went back home to save some possessions; there they were engulfed in cannon fire and perished. After a few days, the surviving inhabitants found the cradle with the dead baby.

Back again in Berane, I again saw George. The swelling of the left side of his face had greatly diminished. There would be a deep scar to deform the left part of his face, because his cheek bone had been smashed, and many bones were taken out during the operation. Dr. Dedovic was delighted that the left eye had been saved, especially since he feared that the loss of the left eye could imperil the right eye as well. Now he thought that danger no longer existed, but he nevertheless asked for the help of an eye specialist in Podgorica. On

May 29, 1942, our men in Berane completed all steps necessary in connection with obtaining permission of the Italian military authorities to let George go. Thus, after 130 days, wavering between death and life, George Lasic was again able to continue his work.

In Kralje many people had gathered in anticipation of our coming, hoping to see George and to greet him, thanking God for saving him. Crossing Tresnjevik to the other side, all the way down Bare Kraljske, we stopped many times so that George could greet the people who had been waiting a long time only to see him again and to embrace him. At Matesevo we also spent some time; the faces of our men were radiant with happiness. Then George went to Kolasin to see Pavle in the headquarters, and then continued to Lijeva Rijeka. During George's travel to Kolasin and Lijeva Rijeka, without George's awareness, Ljubo Vuksanovic had about 20 soldiers whose duty was to protect his movements.

In Lijeva Rijeka, on the same level space beside the church where we had made our oath, almost five months ago, to defend our lives against the Partisans, many people had gathered to await the arrival of George, knowing he would come to the church. As we arrived and payed tribute at the fresh graves, they told us Captain Novak Milikic was coming with the dead body of his older brother Jovo, who had been killed a few days ago in Crni Do, district of Savnik, where the last hard fighting was going on against the Partisans. All of us remained to attend the religious service and to bury this latest victim of our battalion in driving from this area the killers and bloodthirsty criminals under the leadership of Josip Broz Tito, Arso Jovanovic, Mosa Pijade, Milovan Djilas, and other Communist rabble from all over Yugoslavia.

In the evening of May 30, 1942, we went to our native village, Kami, where it was especially joyous. In the village we heard the children calling one another to let them know the good news: "Uncle George has come!" or "Godbrother George has arrived!" Every 24 hours a platoon was relieved for security reasons. Through our villages, however, complete peace and security reigned. But in the fighting at Drobnjak these past few days, 150 men of our battalion took part.

In the village George was feeling better. The wound seemed to be healing and clearing; every morning I would change the gauze. But the inflamation of the left eye continued.

In June of 1942, I first took a long journey to relay information to our military units, and late in that month started "home" to

Krusevac by train. Passing through the villages along the way, which were well known and dear to me, I was saddened. There was news here of the devastations of pre-Kumanovo Serbia by the German punishing expedition last fall, and of the huge common graves throughout Sumadija, into which the Germans had buried tens of thousands of my brothers from this area. From Kraljevo there were witnesses who described to us in vivid words the horrible massacre of some four thousand, mostly Serbian refugees from the territory occupied by Bulgars and Albanians, as well as about 1,200 railroad workers from the Belgrade railroad line. The farther I went through this Serbian land, the more my sorrow grew. At Kraljevo I had lost some friends. My good friend Jordan Petrovic, a high school principal in Tetovo, South Serbia, now occupied by the Bulgars, had with his two sons escaped the Bulgars, but as soon as they got off the train in Kraljevo, they had been picked by Germans, and all three, the father with his two sons, fell under the German machine gun fire in a group of 200 Serbians.

Nearing Kraljevo, the train moved slowly; a little to the right on a turn, and farther on the left of the railroad tracks, were countless black flags fluttering gently over flowers; there were many women to be seen watering the flowers and lighting the wax tallows for the requiems. This frighteningly large grave was in the shape of the letter "L", but one could notice other smaller ones nearby. This left a sorrowful impression in my heart; one would need iron nerves not to be broken by the sight. The men in my compartment told me that the Germans, early last spring, had ordered this common grave leveled with heavy rollers, because the hands and legs of the massacred were sticking out of the earth with which they had been initially covered.

In Kragujevac, at about 50 kilometers north of Kraljevo, more than 8,000 Serbians lost their lives in a similar way. These had been put by the Nazi-executioners into large dugouts at Sumarice near Kragujevac. The number of our casualties last fall in Sabac and its surroundings reportedly amounted to about 16,000 men, though, I was told, they had not been buried in large dugouts, but were interred in small groups.

I finally arrived at Krusevac after an absence of almost a year, and quickly went to the home of my Godbrother Radivoje Javanovic, an elementary school teacher, and learned the news of this city.

Our main attack on Krusevac, that is, against the German armed forces in this city, had been made September 22, 1941. Our forces

under the command of Major Keserovic had been very strong, estimated at 10,000 to 12,000 men. The Germans at first had only one
battalion, but this was quickly reinforced. The insurgents advanced
from Jastrebac crossing the Rasina River and came to the center of
Krusevac, where the Gremans were strongly fortified; the insurgents'
left wing beat the Germans on the sector Rasadnik-Bagdala at the
southwest side. During the night the Germans brought in substantial
reinforcements, and the insurgents were compeled to withdraw toward
Jastrebac. On the battlefield 34 Germans and 57 Serbians died.

In Krusevac there was panic and fear; it was known that in Kraljevo and Kragujevac tens of thousands of people had been massacred.
According to the German scale, 3,400 Serbian people should be killed
for 34 Germans! No one expected to be spared. Of about 15,000 inhabitants, 3,400 men would have meant almost all grown males
would be killed, considering that many had already been taken as
war-prisoners to Germany in April.

Fortunately, the commander of the German forces in Krusevac
had been a law professor in Hamburg, and was more humane than a
typical Nazi. He lived in the house of Krsta Novakovic, a druggist and
acting member of parliament for the district of Krusevac and known
as a "pro-pact" man. Thanks to this, the bulk of Krusevac's men
were saved. The German commander in Krusevac considered the 57
fallen Serbians as killed in retaliation, and ordered 43 more gathered.
Of these, most were our poor Gypsies, who went to the firing place
sinless as lambs, unaware what was going on.

On July 7, 1942, I went to report on duty in the school, after
almost one year of absence. My collegues were surprised and glad
that I was still alive. As to my re-commencing teaching, this could
not be settled either by the principal Dragi Popovic nor the "inspec-
tor" Nikola Kaconik, but I would have to write a special petition and
bring it to Belgrade. Eventually I made the trip, and was permitted
to teach.

Among the city population there was great emotion and thought-
fullness on how to procure food for the forthcoming winter. Prices
were increasing every day, and the citizens tried hard to assure some
supplies as soon as possible. Corn was now the principal food. Those
who had no linen left used to sell their bed pieces and furniture. My
relatives Javanovics were lucky to get 150 kilograms (about 330 lbs.)
of corn for their dishes (12 deep plates, 12 common plates and other
kitchen utensils); my Godsister Darinka considered this a bargain!

This sale was made by my Godbrother Radivoje and me when we went to the village Kukljin and Bele Vode. Then it was necessary to sell furniture. Prices for corn were about fifteen times higher than before the war, when one was lucky enough to find someone who would sell it. The struggle for survival in the cities, as far as the procuring of supplies was concerned, gradually diminished. The city civil authorities several times delivered 9 kilograms (just under 20 lbs.) of corn, then 6 kilograms, per person per month to those who were unable to procure it alone.

Meanwhile, we prayed to God that our Allies would trap the Italians and Germans in North Africa, and that the Russians would hold at Stalingrad. On the (Orthodox) Christmas Eve we lived in fear, and impatiently awaited news of the result of the battle at Stalingrad; a special proclamation in the Serbian language was about to be published concerning "the brilliant victory" of the German armies over our brothers in Russia, and we sunk into darkness. But we learned somehow that the local German commander had ordered publication postponed, and it occurred to us: our "news" from underground was more accurate! Already many among us were talking (or better, whispering) that this was a crushing defeat of the Axis powers. The majority of us thought that our Yugoslavian military forces would play a brilliant role in crushing the German military machinery in this area at the very moment the Allied forces advanced from the West.

Old houses of this type are still fairly widespread in the Šumadija and Morava regions of north Serbia. The square plan and the veranda have survived as typical features of the modern houses, but the wooden framework and walls have been abandoned in favour of bricks. The peculiar chimney, which was characteristic of the Šumadija houses, is now seen only in old houses.

CHAPTER NINE: A PRISONER OF WAR

On January 27, 1943, St. Sava's Day, I entered the house. The kitchen door opened wide, and my Godsister Darinka appeared, tearful and pale, followed by a German under-officer, and then my Godbrother and all three Godchildren. My Godsister, very frightened, shouted: "Godbrother, the Germans are looking for you!", to which I smilingly replied: "All right; for God's sake, what is the matter with you! Don't be afraid; this is nothing; they will take me to their local command and I will be back soon." Later I learned this German under-officer had come to "capture" me at 10 in the morning; a full four hours and a half he had kept all members of the Jovanovics family in the kitchen, not allowing even the children to leave.

The German asked me immediately if I had my lunch, and when I answered him affirmatively, he ordered me to put on my overcoat and go with him. Smiling and radiant, I took leave of my Godbrother, Godsister and Godchildren, and left for the city.

On the way I asked him if we were going to the "district command" but he answered: "first we have to go to my command." At that moment I did not understand what he meant by "my command," and when we got near the district command, I asked him again: "Are we going there?" But the German insisted on "my command." We bypassed the circuit court building, then the high school in the direction to the upper market place, going through Milos Street, when he told me that we were near "his" command. On this house I saw a board with a sign in the German language and some other signs, which I had never seen before. In front of the Priest Vesic's house, the German told me: "Here", then he took me through the gate and into the house.

I was very recollected and almost indifferent of what was happening, and what was awaiting me. My main preoccupation was to develop a defense to the immediate situation.

Exactly at 3:15 the German under-officer took me to the office of "his commander." He was a rather young German army captain. He pointed me to a chair in front of him across from his desk, on which I unhurriedly sat. Immediately he asked if I knew anything about their "field gendamerie". I answered him, "Yes, I know that in the German army there is a field gendarmerie, and that they serve in the occupied countries, but I have no closer knowledge about it nor am I in the least interested." He started to get more excited, and proudly put his hand at his breast, telling me: "That is what we are!" Not knowing how to answer him, I simply said: "Thank you!" He continued: "You are arrested!" and quickly got up; and I instinctively also got up. Coming toward me, the Captain began: "You are in liaison with the men in the mountains, specifically with Keserovic!" I calmly told him: "That is not true". My calmness infuriated him, and he repeatedly shouted "It is true!" I answered each time more loudly: "It is not true," looking him straight in the eyes and following his movements. After awhile he stopped shouting and went to a cupboard to his left, and started to read a small slip of printed paper with three and a half lines, keeping it a little aslant, from which I easily noticed in the middle "D.M.". Now it was clear to me that this was a denunciation from Belgrade, and I was greatly reassured.

The German Captain started again to charge me with being in liason with the men in the mountains, but I again categorically answered him "It is not true". Finally, he charged that I was in contact with my brother George Lasic, army staff major, to which I answered him: "This also is not true; my brother was gravely wounded by Communists almost a year ago, but unfortunately I am not in contact with him, nor do I know if he is still alive!"

The Captain began to pace the room nervously thinking, then stopped in front of me and said: "Who is talking here, you or me?" Emotionlessly I answered: "You are talking, but all that you have said is not true!" Again he started to pace the room nervously, then he approached the door, opened it, and called in the same under-officer who had brought me sometime earlier, and he ordered me to go with him.

In the next room, where I been before, the under-officer had set up his typewritter, and began to interrogate me. He asked where I attended school, what languages I spoke, where had I been at war— the place, company, battalion, regiment where I had been last year, when I came back. He asked these questions slowly, so that I was able to understand him very well, and he wrote down my answers. When he finished typing, he asked me if I wished him to read it before I signed. This having been done, he took all this to his commander, while another German under-officer came in to take charge of me.

From the house of the Priest Vesic we went toward the building of the high school, and then to the main street. I was between the two German under-officers, to my left my "guide" and investigater and to my right the new one. Going through the street, I met many known faces, students and other acquaintances. All of them bent their heads slightly and nervously brought their right hand to their chests, but I was serene and smiling; I greeted each by raising my hand, but I did not utter a word, fearing that I would cause them some trouble.

It was about 6 in the evening when I entered the courtyard of the police prison in Krusevac. The gendarme delivered me to one of our gendamerie sergeants. He took all of my money, my tie, a small knife, and other things of small value. Then he opened the door of a cell to the extreme end at left of the entrance to the prison, and shut the door behind me. Inside, almost all were known faces: Dragomir Markovic, my son's teacher when he was in the elementary school; Djordjevic, owner of the "Serbian King" cafe-house; two university students, formerly pupils in the Krusevac high school; and a business-man from Krusevac. They all were surprised and sorry that I got "in this trouble". Dragi Markovic warned me to sit on the table in the middle of the cell, because everyone was "overloaded" with lice. He told me also to hang my overcoat on a hanger at the door. The teacher had been in this cell more than three months. They had put him into prison some time ago, let him free, then imprisoned him again. Djordjevic and the businessman had been imprisoned only yes-terday, and the two students 15 days ago.

Our cell was a small room with a large window at the wall looking west: inside the inner wings of the window there were low spaced iron bars linked by others. The window was filled with rectan-gular pieces of corn bread, which nobody would eat because their families regularly brought meals from their homes. The eastern end of the cell had a long, small empty space, at the beginning of which was a well-heated stove; Dragi Markovic had his bed on the floor left of the stove, and near him was a common bed for Djordjevic and his fellow businessman. Along the window, near the door, the two stu-dents were lying, separated from the other fellows by the table on which now I was sitting.

Somewhat after 7 in the morning, on January 28, 1943, in the corridor of our cell, some conversation and the ringing of the iron bars was heard. The door was opened briskly. A guard stuck his head in and called: "Milija Lasic must come out quickly with all his belong-ings!" Immediately I came down from the table, and while putting on my overcoat I started to joke: "Do not fear . . . I will not be a coward on the shooting grounds; I am not Blagoje Atanackovic to faint!" All of my fellows in the cell were on their feet and gathered around me, I embraced them quickly one after the other. Markovic told me: "You will not be shot here, at least this time. You will be taken to Belgrade." Once again I loudly greeted them: "Farewell, brothers! May Lord God save you all," and I went through the cell door. First they took me to the guard headquarters, where they gave me all my belongings that they had taken last evening.

Outside, visibility was not yet good; it was cloudy and foggy. The guard told me to hurry, and pointed me in the direction to the courtyard. There were six men and three women. I came closer to the group of men, mostly clad in the villager woolen clothes; some even had our military blouses or socks. The three women were our villagers. A gendarmerie sergeant told me with gestures to cross my hands to put me in chains, which he was holding in his hands. I refused, telling him that I was neither a burglar nor a highwayman to be put in chains. He whispered answering me: "This is the order; all of these are in chains. You also ought to be." I turned to my left, and noticed that all six men were in chains; the first pair lifted their hands to convince me. They put me in chains also.

It was nearly 8 in the morning. The gate on the fence of the courtyard was opened. First the three village women, who had not been chained, went out; then we seven chained. Nobody knew where they were leading us. But we were moving in the direction of the "Hotel Europe"; surely we would be shot on the airfield. Our guards were seven soldiers of the "Serbian State Guard", the Nazi auxiliary force under the control of the German commander-in-chief in Belgrade. When we got out of Colak-Antina Street, we turned to the right, and went along the street leading to the 12th Regiment Barracks, then to the left through the short street leading to the railroad station. The prediction of teacher Markovic was correct: they would take us to Belgrade.

Now visibility was greatly increased. Having been chained alone, I could move more freely, and got in between the rows of our men in pairs. They were silent and rarely spoke, except for a small bearded man in a coat of the most coarse village cloth. He was in the first row with his chained fellow. As soon as I got between these two and the pair behind them, he addressed me with these words: "Mr. Lasic, I am an Air Force officer; we must flee. Otherwise we surely will be shot at Jajinci near Belgrade!" Then he put his hand into the left pocket of his coat, and offered me a drink of brandy from a two-pint bottle of a dark color. I thanked him, telling him that I did not drink alcohol, and he alone drank. I warned him that from Krusevac to Stalac we had but 13 kilometers, and in this part it would be hard to try to escape. On the left side of the street, when we were past the house of Misic, a hardware dealer, we saw his wife with a broom cleaning the entrance stairway; I lifted up my hands over my head, telling her: "Good morning, Mrs. Misic!" She had looked, obliquely while we were approaching, but now she stopped cleaning, stared at us frightened, let go of her broom, and turned on the stairs, unable to utter a single word. With her husband and her I had been friendly for many years.

We were going forward quickly and pretty soon we were near the railroad station. On the way, I learned who my co-sufferers were: Lieutenant Matic, Air Force pilot; five of our Army underofficers, and me—all belonging to the Yugoslav armed forces in the country under the command of General Draza Mihailovic. As of now, we were spiritually strong, and began to talk to each open-heartedly. Except for Matic, we were all calm and talking in low tones. Matic was greatly under the influence of alcohol; very often he would take his two-pint bottle and gulp a drink. He had been captured treacherously; an Army officer who had been in the ranks of the pro-Nazi "Zbor", or "state guard", had given him "his word of honor" to let him free if Matic surrendered to him. His group had been surrounded, and Matic thought he would save his men if he alone surrendered to his known friend, and now he deeply regretted it. He told me that the treacherous Army officer would be punished sooner or later by losing his head.

After arriving at the railroad station, we waited outside, to the left of the entrance. Lieutenant Matic became more and more impatient and excited. He drank more often from his two-pint bottle and would turn to me frequently, saying that we must escape; it was better to escape than to perish in chains. As though I did not believe him to be an army officer, he repeatedly told me: "Mr. Lasic, I am a military officer; do you believe me?" I answered him most categorically that I did not doubt it in the least, but that under today's circumstances this had no significance: "All of us are fighters for freedom for our people, and if our fate is to perish and lose our lives, we will all become shining members of the new cycle of our heroes and martyrs in this awful world holocaust."

I pointed to three poor farm women, and told him they also will be counted among the holy sacrifices of our people. One of them was about 40 years old, the other two about 20 and 25. I asked them why they were taken, and the oldest answered: "Some days ago the news spread that our village would be surrounded by German and Bulgarian armed forces, and all of our villagers fled to the forests; but we three were charged to remain in the village to watch our homes and the houses of our neighbors to prevent plundering. When these forces occupied our village, all three of us were caught and brought to Krusevac. Our village surely has been destroyed completely, but we trust God to have saved our men, children and other women."

Lieutenant Matic was more emotional, telling me time and again: "We must escape, Mr. Lasic! I am a military officer, do you not believe me?" Then he took out of his pocket a wedding photograph, which he showed to me: a handsome young man in an Air Force uniform and a beautiful Serbian girl in white wedding clothes. I repeated to him my previous opinion about the shortness of time and the distance to Stalac; this could be tried, probably, on the way to Belgrade, and only with the help of our guards. By now, they took us to the platform, where we did not wait for long. The guards took us together to a carriage. I sat beside Matic and his "pair". I pointed out to him the "floor" of our compartment, and smiling whispered to him that bare-handed here nothing could be done. He was thoroughly preoccupied with the idea of fleeing. His situation was extremely dangerous: a military officer captured in fighting—the death sentence was presumed absolutely. He still was under the influence of alcohol, though he had already thrown away his empty two-pint bottle. About noon we arrived at Stalac.

Our guards took us immediately to the platform to wait for the express train Nis-Belgrade, which was to arrive at Stalac about 1 in the afternoon. The weather was rather cold. Somewhat because of the cold and also because of the chains tightened around my wrists, my fingers became blue, but the rest of my body was not cold. I looked at the men moving on the platform.

The train for Belgrade was still late. It was near 4 in the afternoon. The weather was cloudy and it was becoming colder. The German army officer was still in sight. All of a sudden, somebody approached me from aside and quickly started to put warm woolen gloves on my hands. This was my Godson, Predrag Cemovic, a high school student; how he had come here I had no idea. As soon as he had put the gloves on my fingers stiffened by cold, the German army officer approached our group and our guards, and furiously began to speak, pointing at us in chains, and saying loudly: "These ones had been shooting at German soldiers today!" Now I was most concerned what would happen to my godson; Bulgarian soldiers took him quickly away from the station. Later I learned that this boy had paid for his courageous deed with 15 days in a prison in Krusevac.

Our train at last arrived, a few minutes after 4 p.m. The guards took us in a hurrry to a carriage. Inside there were people to its full capacity; we barely got room to stand in a corridor before the first class compartments. From one compartment a young man stuck out his head and immediately greeted me: "Good afternoon, Mr. Lasic!" I returned the greeting and wondered how he knew me. He answered that he was a teacher by profession and that I had taught him in the teacher's college, probably in Kragujevac. At once, he offered me his seat in the compartment, which was filled with all sorts of people; he was standing up to Jagodina. The conversation in the compartment was lively. I told all of them that I had been arrested without any guilt; I was not interested in politics at all, and still less with the fight against the invading powers. I fitted my words to the listeners, as it was unwise to be open-hearted. My former pupil understood me correctly. I did not know what was going on in the corridor; here it was warm and I was comfortable sitting on a seat of the first class carriage. The travelers looked at me with wonder and sympathy.

My former student got off at Jagodina. It was getting dark, and the train was still creeping on. Suddenly it stopped about two kilometers out of Jagodina. In the corridor there was a stir. They told me that Lieutenant Matic had escaped! I learned that at Jagodina he had asked the sergeant to be unchained from his pair to go to the toilet, which was on the south end of our carriage. There he remained while the train was at Jagodina, and when the train started to move, he broke the window with bare hands and slipped out. Our sergeant was furious; he let two guards go after the fugitive, and the train continued, taking more speed. In the corridor the men told me that Matic had cut his hands breaking the window, as blood had dripped inside and outside the window. We were happy, however, and hoped the two Serbian guards would desert!

About 9 in the evening we arrived in Belgrade. Our guards, now being but five, were frightened: they feared German Gestapo authorities for the reduced number of "slaves" to bring them. They had been told to deliver us to the Gestapo headquarters in King Alexander Street No. 5. We headed to Balkan Street, passed the Hotel "Moscow", crossed Terazije, and through the gate to a small courtyard. The sergeant went to the Gestapo quarters. After a few minutes there appeared German guards—Gestapo! The Serbian guards we never saw again.

The German Gestapo guards took us to the main building, and ordered us to stand up in a corridor left of an office with our hands up, facing the wall. Our former guards had taken off our chains before they handed us to the Germans. At right were the three farm women; I was the third in the file of the soldiers. A German in complete military attire, except for his haversack, was standing guard, pacing the floor behind us in his heavy boots. Farther to the left I saw a group of 16 men in villager clothes; these were our captured soldiers from the village of Mirijevo near Belgrade. A small group of the organization of Draza Mihailovic must have been discovered. I saw, or heard, how they took one after another, leading them behind our backs to some room to the extreme right. Each was retained there for some minutes, and then another German guard would take him somewhere. In this position we waited for long. The oldest farm woman suddenly dropped to the floor. I shouted in German, without turning my head: "Sie ist krank! Sie ist krank!" [She is sick!] The Gestapo guard approached her and told us to let her lie on the floor; they let her know that she would be permitted to sit down.

Finally, the poor fellows from Mirijevo disappeared from sight one after another. The turn came for my group. First they took the oldest farm woman, and then the other two, one after the other. I imagined all the worst things: probably they would take us to a torturing place where they would beat us, or to some humid and dirty room where the days of life for us were numbered.

The Gestapo guard pointed me to a large stairway leading up. Then, in the corridor of the second floor, we passed two doors and stopped in front of cell number 10. The guard unlocked the chains, took a heavy iron bar off from across the cell door, turned the electric switch from the outside to the right, opened the door and let me in. I heard him putting the bar on again. It was 25 minutes to midnight. Inside, I stopped, took off my hat, and started to laugh loudly—I was surprised there was no humid floor, dirt or beating on the back! To the left against the wall I saw nine human creatures lying on the floor piled like sardines on each other, some of them having a miserable blanket, and the others not even that.

From beneath a military blanket a small head stuck up looking at me, and said: "Where are you coming from, Mr. Lasic? Why do you laugh?" I answered him: "I could ask you the same! Who are you?" "I am Dusan Sedlar, gendarmerie captain, your former student," he continued.

I told him: "Well, Dusko, we met at a good place; but, I beg your pardon! I cannot remember your name nor where I taught you, and still less can I remember your appearance, because many years have passed, and looks change greatly when pupils grow up."

"Do you remember the smallest student in the first form of the third year on the teachers' college in Sombor 1925/26?", continued he.

"Oh that small brat, whose father was a customs officer, in Sombor?", I said jokingly.

"I am he," Dusan answered laughingly. I asked him if he was now twice as tall as at that time, and he replied: "Not twice, but I am taller anyhow." He told me to take off my overcoat and hat and lie down beside him before they put the light off. Meanwhile he started to move another fellow with his elbow to make some room for me. I crept under the blanket with my clothes on. Dusko had a thin cover on the floor, because he had been a Gestapo inmate more than three months, and so I did not lie down on the bare floor.

The light in our cell went off; now it was midnight; all "slaves" were asleep, except Dusan Sedlar and me. Whispering, I told him my experiences since the beginning of the war, and he acquainted me with his "case". He had been a "loyal" gendarmerie officer in the "Serbian Guard", but had been from the start included in the patriotic organization of Draza Mihailovic; many times he had been investigated by the Gestapo functionaries, but he never admitted anything, nor had they been able to find any real evidence. He hoped that he would not be shot.

About 7 a.m. they opened our cell; the "pail" was quickly taken out by two of the men. We went to our right to the toilet rooms, where we could remain for 10 minutes under the watch of the reinforced guard. The two appointed fellows washed the pail, and prepared clean water to wash the floor of our cell when we got back. We others quickly washed our faces and made ready to endure another 24 hours. After 10 minutes we were back, and the two fellows on duty started to wash the cell floor with the water they had brought. The order to keep the cell clean was set by the inmates themselves, and had been regularly done every morning. They told me it would be my turn after a few days.

At 11 a.m. they brought in our rations, 200 grams of corn bread per person for 24 hours. Immediately I parted my ration in three parts, and I ate one piece at once as my breakfast. At noon they brought us our "cooked meal"; actually, this was a thin broth, in which you could not spot a single trace of meat. It looked to me that they had cooked some meat with cabbage but the "free" kitchen workers had taken the meat and thick stuff, while they left to us the broth. Regularly, they poured only one ladle into our plate. The only worth of the "meal" was its warmth. I crumbled some corn bread into the plate, and I ate it to my satisfaction, and the others did the same.

The "oldest inmate" in our cell was a young man named Cuda-nov, from Srem, who was merely 23 years old, and who had been captured nine months ago and brought to Belgrade. The charge was that a rifle had been found in the cornfield, which he said he knew with certainty had been left there to destroy his household. Because of frequent and long investigations, as well as the uncertainty of what would happen to him, this tortured Serbian boy became very nervous, but had retained his spiritual and physical strength; when you talked to him, he looked at you as an angel with green eyes, whose look is deep and veiled with sorrow.

Other fellows had been jailed because of the blackmarket, it was believed, but they were somewhat taciturn. I was interested in a boy about 16, with rich, slightly curly hair, very skinny in the face, who was sitting in the corner to the right of the cell door. He was the son of a colonel or general, now a war-prisoner in Germany. I asked him: "For goodness' sake, Dimitrijevic, how did you get here?" The boy answered me in a tone of anger: "I listened to the London radio, Mr. Lasic; my mother, my younger sister, and I were put in jail 20 days ago, and brought here; Mother and Sister are in cells for women down there."

Life in our cell was not spent only in cleaning the cell floor and in idle conversations, for we possessed many periscopes made from broken mirrors, and every day the moves of our Gestapo guards were closely watched. One periscope was used at the round small hole of the cell door, turned by hand according to the need. The sentinel at the cell door regularly reported; "The guard is now to the right in the corridor, walking slowly; now turns and is coming back. He is here, almost in front of our cell. It's all right, he went to our left. Be cautious: they are bringing a fellow of ours, maybe they will put him into our cell. Do not worry, they by-passed our cell. Get down from the window, quickly, there is Richter coming!"

Every day about 9 in the morning, and sometimes all day through, our men tried to learn how many Serbians had been brought into this prison or had been taken out to be led to the shooting grounds in Jajinci or elsewhere. This information two of our fellows would get by perching at the window, convulsively holding the iron window bars, and looking down at a small space of the courtyard which could be seen from our cell. From outside, the window was shielded by large planks, or boards, so that it was not possible to see the entire courtyard. But the men at the window would quickly count those men taken out of the prison, while the other fellows were watching at the cell door so as not to be surprised by some sudden opening of the door of our cell. The sentinel at the door, with the periscope in his hand, would say: "All is all right; and the other two would quickly perch themselves at the window and rather loudly give us information: "One, two, three, four, five, six: all with their belongings and without guards, freed, they go home, thanks to God!" And among us there was great rejoicing.

On some other occasions the window sentinel would let us know: ". . . eight, nine; all with their belongings and accompanied by guards—they are going to another camp, to Banjica or Sajmiste, or maybe taken to captivity as war prisoners."

The most sorrowful report from the cell window, however, would be when the watchman started to let us know: "Oh, it is heart-breaking! There are many Gestapo guards under arms; they take them without their belongings: One, two, three, four, five, six, seven, eight, nine, ten, eleven, twelve, thirteen, fourteen, fifteen, sixteen, seventeen—they take them to the shooting grounds!" Among us there would set in a silence for some minutes, and then we would begin to guess the names of our martyrs who would today give up their lives. At Banjica their number would be increased by many hundreds, and very often over a thousand, who would die together.

After 19 days at King Alexander Street No. 5, on February 15, 1943, the Gestapo guards took Sedlar and myself down the large stairway to the corridor on the first floor where 19 days ago I stood hands up against the wall. From this corridor we went out into the courtyard where the black "Marica" Gestapo wagon for transporting prisoners stood. I watched the unlocking of the big chains, the taking off of the iron bars, and the opening of the door at the back of the black car. We were ordered in, going there between two rows of the German Gestapo guards. Inside there were benches on both sides. We put our belongings in the upper space, and sat two by two facing one another. The door shut quickly behind us; I heard the slamming of the iron bar, the putting on of the chains and the clanging of keys. It was dark inside for a moment. All of a sudden the vehicle began to move, and at the same time a tiny lamp lighted on the ceiling. We all tried to determine by feeling the turnings where they were transporting us. From the first turn to the right on Terazije, it was clear that they were not transporting us to Banjica. "Maybe Sajmiste", somebody among us said. At that moment, through a square hole in a partition, a human finger was seen, and in a subdued tone somebody said: "Hail, men! Hail to you, Risto!" We were all astonished. Risto Cukovic and Sedlar asked him who he was. The unknown man continued: "I am, brothers, Army Captain Dragoljub Ivanovic, nicknamed Krnja." He told us that they were not transporting us to Sajmiste, as he had just been taken out from this horrible camp of Serbian martyrdom. He knew me before the war; he had been an army lieutenant in the 24th Regiment while I had been a high school principal there. All of us greated "Krnja" by touching his fingers through the small opening on the wall.

When the "Marica" stopped, we were ordered to come down one by one. We found ourselves in the courtyard of the infamous "Glavnjaca", a well-known prison in Belgrade. A tall, blond German sergeant explained our new status, not as "police" prisoners, but as prisoners of war.

It was now clear to us that turning to the right on Terazije some hours ago meant we were away from the death, at least for the time-being. But we were conscious that many of our Serbian brothers would turn left at Terazije to go to Banjica to wait there for their "turn" to be taken to the shooting grounds in Jajince, where about 100,000 Serbians perished under the German machine guns.

On February 18, 1943, they mustered all our army officers in front of the main building. We from the Gestapo stood somewhat aside, to the right. The Germans had brought here yesterday and today 93 of our army officers. After counting us, a German under-officer pulled out of his coat pocket some paper, stood in the middle of the ranks, and in good Serbian read: "Gentlemen army officers, you were brought here not by the will of the German armed forces, but by the wish of the Serbian Government in Belgrade." We were extremely surprised by such a declaration; after the breaking of our ranks there was laughter about the illogic of this declaration. It especially offended our army officers, because they had almost all been in some secret liaison with our armed forces under the command of General Draza Mihailovic.

At night, about 11, a German military official hurriedly entered and asked: "And Lasic, Milija, professor, what rank in the army has he?" From all corners of the room there were answers: "Captain, 1st class captain, captain, captain!" The German left hurriedly, and I started to explain that this was not good; that there could be complications. To this the real captains shouted from all corners: "Please forget that! Don't you realize in what peril you could have been put yourself? If you were left as a civilian tomorrow here alone, Mauthausen would be certain for you! Are you out of your senses?" That night, we learned that early the next morning all of us would be transported as war prisoners to Germany, by train.

Our train was covered with barbed wire; at the windows and the ends of the carriages the rows of barbed wire were dense and firmly fixed. The train moved; after some minutes, cautiously and slowly, it crossed the Sava River.

In this early morning, one could hardly see through the barbed wire on the windows, and it was cloudy, making visibility even worse. At the Zemun station our train stopped a little. Henceforth, we had to move through "Independent Ustasi Croatia"! The farther we went, the better visibility became. The train stopped again at Stara Pazova, I think. Our men got the opportunity through the door to dispute with a Ustasi army officer they identified as a classmate of theirs from our military academy in Belgrade. I heard them telling him that after the war he would be shot in his forehead, while others put their hand across their throats, showing their "classmate" that a butcher knife was ready for him. The "Ustasi army officer" got somewhat excited and courageous, and seemed ready to get into our train, but the German soldiers, standing along the train, warned him sternly, and he cowered and went back.

The train crept through Slavonija toward Zagreb, and I noticed the expressions of travelers on other trains. The people looked very depressed; there was nowhere cheerfulness as there had been at these stations before; the travelers were sitting at windows as mummies, furtively looking at our train covered with barbed wire, giving no expression either of like or dislike in our regard. One could conclude that they subdued their sympathies, or were afraid.

Getting through small localities, especially in Srem, it was easy to notice that the Ustasi had ruined many Serbian homes. At many places one could see ruins. We traveled all night, and when we approached Zagreb, it began to darken. All of a sudden the sirens began to sound in full force, and before long anti-aircraft was heard. Our train stopped. The German soldiers got out of the train, and were seen pacing alongside. We remained here almost an hour, and then moved on. At a Zagreb railroad station we remained a long while. There were few people to be seen.

We got through Slovenija when it was almost daylight. It was now sunny, and we could see without difficulty. The train continued on; we got through the anti-tank fortifications and impediments at the borders of our country with Austria, where hard fighting took place in the first days of the war. Being now on the territory of Germany, I lost interest in looking at the country, which appeared in my mind bloody, thinking about the awful massacres perpetrated by Germans in Yugoslavia, principally in the areas of the pre-Kumanovo Serbia. However, I could not stop my common human curiosity to study these "monsters" of Europe; here at home they were stern-looking, more frustrated, and devotedly pre-occupied; probably this change in attitude had recently occurred, after their defeat at Stalingrad. On the wall at the railroad stations you could still see large placards with the legend: "Alle Räder müssen für den Sieg rollen!" —all wheels must turn for victory.

The first night on German (now Austrian) soil we spent in a railroad station, and on February 21, 1943, we approached Vienna. The destruction of many houses were strikingly visible. We learned, however, that the city of Vienna proper up to now did not suffer greatly, but Neustatt and some smaller localities where there had been more factories had been heavily damaged. From Vienna we continued past many towns unknown to us, and we had difficulty determining where they were taking us. The next morning, on February 22, 1943, we approached a great city on our right, in which, judging by the many towers and smokestacks, there were many factories and chemical plants. We read a sign: "Oppeln", in the upper Silesia. In this area there were no ruins to be seen, and this greatly surprised us; in Yugoslavia we believed that Germany was all in ruins, and now here we saw that all was intact and that "all wheels" were still rolling for the "victory"!

Our train went on to the northwest; darkness set in before long, and we did not know where they were taking us. Finally the train stopped at 12:25 a.m. on a side track. Some fellows immediately read: "Neuhoff", or something similar to that, and in whispers the news spread that we were now some hundred and twenty kilometers southeast of Berlin. Here we spent many hours under the guard of German soldiers.

Early in the morning, on February 3, 1943, we were ordered to get out of the carriages and to be ready to move on foot. The guards mustered us, and the head of the column set off to the northeast. It was mostly cloudy but from time to time the sun shone. The walk, however, was pleasant after these four full days of living as in a pen. About 10 in the morning we got to a town whose name we read at the entrance: Waldstatt; before long we came before a great building surrounded by dense barbed wire and high sentinel towers. The word spread among us that this building had been the military academy, which had been converted into a prison camp.

Our life in this camp was monotonous, especially for those who could not find any recreation in reading. After a temporary stay in one wing, they moved us into a room in which there were five double-deck beds and a rather large table with some chairs. Here were all of us "Gestapo prisoners" from Belgrade, except Lieutenant Colonel Kovacic, who was with the generals in another room. Here we used to get our food for the whole day, that is bread and margarine, at a set time. Either Dusan Sedlar or I usually broke the bread and margarine in equal pieces and then waited until the others had taken their parts. Before long the Germans began to distribute to each one each week 40 cigarettes, "Gauloise", I think, and Sedlar and I as nonsmokers would divide ours in eight parts, so that the fellows who smoked would have more. In our room the order was perfect. We spent our time playing cards, reading, or talking. Sometimes we visited our friends in the other rooms.

Captain Velja Avejic used to visit our room often, and he told us, besides his tortures in Belgrade, what he had experienced in the concentration camp at Mauthausen. "With food supplies I had been all right. In the beginning I was still strong, and they selected me to take out those who had died during the night. There had been many days when I alone would take out more than 40 dead men. Because of their previous starving the bodies were very light to carry; I would put them on my shoulders, take them out of the barracks, and put them on a heap of others in a large truck in front of the camp; then I would return for more. This job lasted two or more hours every morning."

On May 11, 1943, early in the morning, we left Waldstatt. Leaving our camp, we were escorted by a strong armed force—a large group of German soldiers at the head, another in the rear, while at each 15 to 20 strides on our left and right other German soldiers were guarding us. At the railroad station the carriages were ready. We were quickly loaded in groups assigned to different carriages, and the news started to circulate among us: "They are taking us to Galicia!" Before long our train began to move through the Lower Silesia and then Upper Silesia. We began to pass near known places, and concluded they were taking us toward Poland. We saw countless factories where "all wheels were still turning". We stopped on Polish territory en route to Stanislawów. Some of our fellows had received their food packages from Serbia just before our yesterday's move, and they gladly handed at the stations cookies or other foods to the Polish children, and to men cigarettes; the others only shouted greetings to them in the little Polish they knew. The grown-ups looked exhausted and thoughtful, but our greetings would quickly revive happiness on their faces. Closer to Stanislawów, as well as in the city proper, there were houses in ruins and evidence of devastation everywhere.

In the course of this travel nothing important happened except for the attempt of two younger army officers to escape. They hid in a coal tender and were easily discovered by the German soldiers. In the evening on May 13, 1943, we arrived at Stryj, about 80 kilometers to the south of Lwow.

At the Stryj station we spent the night in our carriages, and very early the next morning we were ordered to continue on foot to the camp some kilometers south of Stryj. In the daylight we noticed that this city had suffered very much in the first days of the war; all around were homes in ruin.

CHAPTER TEN: ESCAPE ATTEMPTS AND FINALLY FREEDOM

From the very start of our living at the camp near Stryj, there were attempts to escape. The most important occurred on September 18, 1943. Twenty-two of our army officers, including Major Pavle Djurisic, and some under-officers who had been brought to this camp several weeks before, managed to get out of the camp.

Djurisic had previously sought to escape. First he had had "an attack of appendicitis" and had asked to be transferred to the local hospital is Stryj. He was granted permission, and they quickly took him to the hospital. There he remained only a week and came back to our room. He told me in whispers: "It was impossible to escape from the hospital; though I tried by all means through Dr. Muska-tirovic to bribe some of the night guards there."

On the day of the escape, Sunday afternoon, there was a match between the two camp football teams on the playing grounds. After the match had ended, as usual we remained on the grounds until 5:30 to walk around. At that time we were ordered back to the bar-racks because of the impending muster. Near the gate between the playing grounds and the barracks I met Djurisic, who wore his winter overcoat, and I jokingly told him: "It looks as if you have lost your calendar! Why did you put that damn military overcoat on in such hot weather?" He furtively shook hands with me, and continued in whispers: "Say nothing to anybody; we shall try to escape tonight." I asked him: "And Rajo and Mitar?" He answered: "Rajo is sick; Mitar will not. Goodbye!"

Our men were coming back in groups to the courtyard in front of the main buildings; on the appointed space for mustering the gradual forming of the ranks was in process. At 6 p.m. the German Army Captain Reis mustered our group at the end close to the main building and the German military personnel crossed to the space between the left and central barracks, checking the first and second rows standing there, and finally headed around to the separate rows mustered between the second and the barracks on the right. While the Germans were going in that direction, many fellows already num-bered began to get through the middle barracks to fill in the rows for the missing officers. The Germans counted the rows of the last column several times, compared their figures, and were discussing something among themselves. Again, they counted our rows in front of the main buildings, and then all others. This time, the number of officers who managed to slip through the middle barracks was much smaller. Later we learned that on the first check there had been but two apparently missing, and the second time about 12! At this, the German Captain began to blow his whistle at full force; within a few minutes, our camp was surrounded by a large number of German soldiers.

They ordered us to wait by groups to be checked individually. This job was done slowly and with great care by the Germans: each prisoner was called separately and approached to compare him with his file photograph; the photograph of a missing prisoner would be taken out and handed to the German commander, Army Captain Reis. The process of verifying and separating the files lasted until 11:30 p.m.

About the end of September, we learned that three army officers from the "fugitive group" were in custody under special guards. Our representatives threatened to complain to "Geneva". We were war prisoners with the right to attempt escape. Finally, in the first days of October, they brought to the camp the three newly captured army officers of ours. We were impatient to hear all the details up to their recapture in northern Hungary.

In the evening of September 18, during the alarm in the camp, the officers and under-officers who had decided to escape were in the latrine buildings on the playing grounds. As the others had returned to the inner part of the camp for the muster, they had been slipping through a prepared hole in the floor of the latrine building one by one to a space not yet covered with dirt and still pretty dry, in the pit of the latrines. Standing as mummies, they heard the alarm in the camp and even felt the steps of the German soldiers over their heads when they were checking the buildings. For six full hours there hadn't been even the slightest whisper among them, still less a single word uttered.

When the tumult in the camp had subsided and they felt the Germans were leaving, which they judged by the noise of their vehicles, there was whispering among them, and they decided to try to cross the barbed-wire rows on the western side of the football playing grounds. Two of them were sent to find the most propitious spot for this purpose. As soon as the "patrol" came back, they learned that on the northern end of the playing grounds there was some light and some German soldiers under arms. Being aware of danger from that side, another patrol reconnoitered the space between the soldiers and the gate in the direction to the city at the end of the playing grounds, which at night was never guarded. (It was functioning only when we were on the football grounds.) Immediately they agreed to try to escape by this way. They formed different groups—two, three, or four, but not larger than four, according to the wishes of the individuals.

About 1 a.m. on September 19, 1943, the groups started to leave their hideout separately with the greatest caution, crawling on their bellies along a zig-zag trench, getting into the trench and disappearing through the gate, without knowing what was happening to the others and where the other groups had gone. These three recaptured fugitives did not even know which direction any other group had gone.

They three had escaped mostly through forests, as far as possible from the highway, heading south through this section of Poland toward the Carpathian Mountains, through eastern Czechoslovakia to Hungary, and then, hopefully, to Yugoslavia. From our camp to the highest ranges of the Carpathian Mountains there was more than 70 kilometers. They covered this without any trouble. Having crossed the mountain crest at a minor gap, they started to descend the range on the other side, encountering some small scattered settlements.

Travelling this way they spent over three full days; they were exhausted. They wanted to get some rest here, hoping that they reached some Slavonic population, probably Ruthenes, who would help them to continue. Cautiously, one of them first, they entered an isolated house. With the members of the household they easily came to an understanding, and got some food, and they were allowed to spend the night sleeping in some hay stacks near that house. Unfortunately, the next morning a local "official" came who had reported them to the Hungarian authorities; they were delivered to the German military forces and brought to Stryj. After long interrogation by the German military authorities, they were brought to our camp and continued their captivity with us.

At the end of 1943, the Germans brought here, individually or in small groups, new war prisoners from Yugoslavia, mostly army officers. Among these there were Captain Nikola Bojovic and Lieutenant Dmitar Ostojic, who had been at Banjica for several months. Bojovic's report told us of martyrdom of our people in this sinister camp, through which legions of fighters under Draza Mihailovic had gone daily to the slaughtering grounds at Jajince: they had been led in groups of 50, 100, 120, 200, and even 1,200 men, who sang on their way to their deaths. He told us that the last group of 400 fighters had been shot to death on October 4, 1943, and up to that date there had been killed more than 63,000 Serbian soldiers, plus more than 8,000 of our Jews, killed there in 1941.

Many of us inquired about our close friends and acquaintances, and often learned tearfully of their being led to the shooting grounds in Jajince. Bojovic told me that Captain Momcilo Mirkovic, an invalid, whom I had left in the Gestapo Cell No. 10 in the King Alexander Street Number 5 prison in Belgrade, had been shot in one of these groups; he had been in the Banjica concentration camp almost 8 months, becoming nervous and exhausted in the extreme. In this way his life was ended, but he was only one of almost 2,000,000 killed within the borders of Yugoslavia!

On January 10, 1944, we were informed that the camp would be moved. This touched off immediate preparation to take with us either some food or other things. Food supplies are the most precious things in captivity. Those who got substantial food packages from Serbia had some spare food stored in safes in the camp general store, or in their rooms; many exchanged their supplies for canned foods to carry more easily, or they gave instructions to the camp store to send the food to the new, still unknown camp.

These days in this area of Galicia (southeastern Poland) there was extreme cold, ranging from 10 to 40 below freezing, centigrade. A high snow had covered all of this area. In all of our rooms there was a hasty breaking of chairs to make small sleighs so that we could more easily take our belongings to the railroad station at Stryj. There was a general tearing of bed sheets and blankets to make sacks or bands; out of blankets some made below-knee "roundings" or shoe-linings, or even bandages for the ears to protect against the bitter cold, for the men were aware there would be long waiting during the counting of our rows in the open field. When there was a distribution of new shoes, I got a pair size 15 or 16, and put into them enough linings, and put on two pairs of woolen socks, so that I had "insured" feet; in addition, I made "beautiful" ear-coverings from small pieces of a blanket, which I had "artistically" fixed together and joined with a bandage. Similar protective covering was made by others.

Our camp was evacuated in two train groups. The first on January 13, 1944; these had been mostly the "partisans". The rest of us left by freight car the next day.

Through the small window of the freight car the fellows were taking turns looking outside. A high snow mantle covered the Polish landscapes, probably our original Serbian homeland Bojka, or surroundings in this vicinity; rarely could one spot any human being. Travelling west through Germany our interest was revived to see the awful sight of Meinheim in ruins.

At night on January 15, 1944, some among us broke the barbed wire on a small window and began to probe if a man could get through while the train was in motion. According to a map, at that time we were some 120 miles north of Switzerland, and the men took to the job: first Dusan Sedlar was helped to get through the window, then Lieutenant Bozidar Jovic, and after them Captain Budimir Reljic; their belongings had been thrown immediately after them. Now, it was the turn of Draguljub Ivanovic ("Krnja") to be lowered down through the window. Unfortunately, the train suddenly stopped in the open, and the shouting of guards was heard, followed by some firings of rifles. The train did not move forward for a long while; we heard running steps of German soldiers alongside the tracks. We learned that Sedlar and Reljic were re-captured and taken somewhere; they managed to let us know by shouting that they had been unhurt, but we knew then nothing about Jovic—he was still at large. He was in possession of a sketch of this territory, and he immediately headed toward the Swiss border. Unfortunately, the Germans recaptured him later and tortured him very much.

We wondered why our train did not move. Penned in our freight car, we remained so till dawn. At daylight they opened the door to let us out, and we saw that we were in the vicinity of some war prisoner camp at the right bank of the Rhine River, on the French border about 20 kilometers upstream from Strasbourg. This was a kind of transit camp; we learned that the first transport of our men coming from Stryj had been kept here and undergone the disinfection procedure. They took us also to this camp, where we remained for two days.

On January 22, 1944, the Germans loaded us again in freight cars which took us to Strasbourg. They unloaded us on the bank of the Rhine near Strasbourg, and escorted us on foot through a suburb of this city. Going through the streets, we immediately felt that we were in another world: the looks of the men, women and children we encountered showed the warmth of their feelings, or better their compassion. From many windows we noticed the friendly waving of hands. Our men, in spite of the rows of guards on both sides of our column, became more animated. On all sides one could hear shouting: "Bonjour, Monsieur! Bonjour Madame! Bonjour mon enfant! Bonjour mon ami!" Very often from among them was heard: "Vive la France! Vivent nos amis Francais! Abas Hitler!" Young French boys in the streets answered our greetings and shouts with the same enthusiasm.

We left the last suburbs of the city and arrived at an old fortress, now called the "Bismarck", surrounded by ramparts, iron gates and barbed-wire. In the courtyard our guards again counted us, and our men began to enter the fort at the main entrance, one group after another. We went to the right through a long narrow corridor sparsely lighted by electric bulbs along which signs were hung to show us the direction to move. On the room doors and the adjacent walls there was writing in English; on the inside walls of many rooms there were many scribblings and inscriptions left by former occupants, apparently by Indian war-prisoners in English service during the war. With my friends I took room number 37, not far from the main entrance to the fort. Alone we chose our beds and immediately set off to work to bring order to our room; we cleaned and washed the floor, and lighted the fire in the stove with wood taken from the unoccupied beds.

One had the impression of coming out of hell. We were able to see the countryside, with men and animals working in the fields, and all this reminded us that life was not extinct.

But a few days later some of us were moved six kilometers on foot to another fort, the "Kronprinz", which was also on a hill. Approaching the gate, one could see the parts of the fortress, similar to the one we had left behind some two hours earlier; to our left there was a small barracks in front of which many German soldiers were to be seen. We were striving to use these last moments, before we got in, to inhale more fresh air and get more refreshing impressions of the pleasing countryside. The iron gate soon was opened to let us in, and quickly shut behind us. Our group was mustered in the courtyard, where we were greeted by our highest ranking army officer, Colonel Brana Pantic, who told us his orders about the military discipline to be observed.

Here I learned about the falling of my brother, Staff Army

Major George Lasic, as well as many other friends and relatives, who were killed in Podgorica on May 5, 1944.

My colleague, Milivoje Knezevic, a high school principal, received even worse news. Knezevic had at home his wife and two sons, seventeen and nineteen years old respectively. His wife had been a high school teacher in Belgrade where she lived with the children during the occupation. As thousands of other Serbian people in our capital city, Knezevic's wife and both their sons had been delighted to be able to greet the oncoming Allied airplanes, and she was on the balcony of the house together with their two sons. They had just begun to shout enthusiastically to greet the Allied airplanes. Suddenly the bombs began to fall and explode as lightning over the roofs of Belgrade. One of these bombs pulverized the whole family of my colleague Knezevic. After we had read the letter addressed to him by his uncle we learned that of his entire family, the neighbors had been able to find only the left foot of his wife in the shoe; the bodies of all his dear ones had been pulverized by a direct hit of bombs and went into the air, so that it had been impossible to perform any burial.

Even here we were enduring day in and day out alarms and listening to the roars of airplanes above our heads, and in daylight very often we were looking at the numerous aircraft formations of our Allies' bombers in the sky as they were moving east. Sometimes we even witnessed the bombing of the city of Strasbourg, or military objectives in the vicinity. Planes were hit by German anti-aircraft fire, and we would be happy to see if the pilot's parachute opened on time.

The greatest joy of ours in these moments was the news in June of 1944 that our Allies had landed somewhere west of us. The men were beside themselves with joy; our rooms, badly lighted corridors and later even the courtyard, were filled with thoroughly changed men, even though the iron gates were not opened!

By mid-September, Paris had fallen, and we learned that our Allies were but 50 miles to the east; we were counting the hours to be liberated. The swarms of Allied airplanes flying above our heads, night and even in daylight, had become more frequent. There were none among us who had thought that our German guards would be able to transfer us from here. Nevertheless, we learned that the prisoners in the fort "Bismarck" would be moved, and we then believed we would be next.

On September 12, 1944, when the sun had just risen, the large iron gate was opened before us, and we left under German guard. As we went out, the freshness of the air and the green all around us revived us; a delight penetrated our bodies and gave serenity to the faces all around.

We were going forward through the endless green; on both sides of the road there were vineyards in which the grapes were already ripening; near the road the apple and pear trees were bent because of the weight of fruit hanging down, and under them were plenty of fallen apples and pears. Our men furtively tried to snatch some apples or pears quickly, while they were assailed by rude shouts of German guards from all sides, threatening that they would shoot them. During our march we stopped frequently before we reached the city of Strasbourg. Everywhere there were large or small groups of German military forces variously armed; here and there they were resting, carrying and piling cases of ammunition; they looked as if they were taking this into prepared dugouts. The work in the fields, however, was going on all around: one could see men and women working on their plots, loading their carts with potatoes or gathering the fallen apples from under the trees.

In Strasbourg, we were led to a side track railroad station, at which some white powdery material apparently normally was loaded. We were loaded into freight cars. The door of our part of the car was immediately shut, and seven German soldiers under arms entered the other half of the car. Through the net of barbed wire we looked at them: these were the dregs of the military; some old men, or young ones with striking defects, myopic, one-eyed, or otherwise noticeably unfit. The loading lasted until about 3 p.m. and then the train set off; before long it stopped at a small side station, and we remained there to the dark hours.

At about 7 p.m. our train started to creep cautiously as it was moving over some dangerous terrain; we did not know where they were taking us. Inside, our men were sitting on the straw or lying in corners. When all were lying down the lack was felt less. Before long we heard a noise of airplanes in the sky; we saw them first dropping some flare balloons of many colors, especially red and blue. They were striking some large city before us. The thundering explosions of bombs in the air looked as if our train was in the midst of this hell. There were some among us with strained nerves, and they urged our guards to take us out to protect us in the ditch along the train; the guards did not pay any attention to this, because they already were in the ditch in front of our freight car. For a long while, even after the silencing of the explosions and the blowing of sirens to announce the danger was past, our train remained in the same spot. In the first morning hours, looking through the small windows of the car we realized we were in the vicinity of a large city which was completely in ruins. The train did not move for a long time, and then began to creep forward over a long iron bridge, evidently over the Rhine; to our right we caught but a glimpse of a small part of the ruined city. We noticed some people moving in a hurry through the streets left in rubble. Our train continued forward rather slowly, going through some smaller localities in the valley of the Rhine, often stopping at stations. The guards today were somewhat more "tame", and one fellow managed to get an opportunity to barter some chocolate or cigarettes for fruit or bread. The local population had been astonished to see chocolate in our hands, which we had gotten in American Red Cross packages. For me, this was the first time I saw fresh fruits in captivity.

On September 17, 1944, we managed somehow to learn from our guards that we were "rushing" on Berlin! Our train was creeping down the slopes. Soon we were able to see, on our left, a part of Hitler's capital city; one got the impression that we were looking at some large quarry, with the difference that this heap of ruins had the color of broken tiles and bricks. In the distance one could see entire streets in ruins, with heaps of rubble to the right and left, and nearby the sorrowful aspects of tall buildings in ruins. Nevertheless, one could still see living persons; you could see them in the windows of the carriages of the trains leaving Berlin, or at the railroad stations at which our train stopped. The men at the railroad stations were moving in a hurry without looking to either side, and disappeared into some underground passage. All of this looked to me like a lacerated and cut-off organism, some parts of which still gave signs of life.

Our freight train left these ruins of Berlin and moved across sandy plains to the northeast. Until darkness we watched men, women, and children working, helped by war prisoners, to get the harvest from the plots of land; on both sides you could see horses hauling carts filled with potatoes, while some persons were readying sacks to be hauled.

Just before dark, our train stopped at a village. From this point, grouped to the last in colums under the watchful guard of our "masters", we went toward the new camp of Barkenburge whose watch towers and lines of barbed wire appeared suddenly on the horizon. The camp was built on a large plain. Left of the entrance there were some larger barracks, and on the right were blocks of small barracks and some empty space before the next block of similar barracks. In the first block were lodged our camp "partisans", our old "acquaintances" from Stryj and Fort Bismarck near Strasbourg; some of them we met immediately; they were looking at us with their cynical glances without compassion. The guards took us farther to the next block of barracks where we were separated into small groups; about twenty of us went to the Barracks No. 25, Room 21, while the others were disposed near us. Here I was in a room with some of my friends from the fort "Kronprinz". As usual in similar circumstances, we settled on our beds, and started to arrange our room; this time we spread our blankets on the wooden planks, because we were told that we would get straw the next day.

Our life here started to proceed as usual; we got a straw mattress and other belongings which were due to us. The food was almost as in the other camps; however, we had still much of reserve food, from American parcels and from Serbia, and had no lack at this point. About the middle of October, our food reserve became less, and we had only the miserable food we got from the Germans.

Our Serbian loyalist battalion, about 750 men, was holding as a living fortress against the greater and greater gathering of Communist "partisans" and their sympathizers. The number of adversaries was increased to reach about 2200. But on January 10, 1945, myself, Milos Popovic and Rade Stafanovic of our Serbian group, plus others from other groups were taken by train about 40 kilometers to a camp named IIb, not far from Hammerstein. Earlier war prisoners told me that in this soldier's Camp IIb there were some 27,000 Frenchmen, 2,600 Yugoslavs, about 150 Belgians—almost all of them under-officers of the Belgian army; and about 2,000 or 3,000 and maybe more Americans. The latter were added to by new groups that the Germans were taking from southern Italy.

Despite the rigorous cold outside, life in the camp was very lively. The barracks were full of soldiers. At the tables in the inner barrack compartments men were playing cards, and gambling American cigarettes, very often by packages. In addition, all around us one could hear and watch small business propositions by barter: the buying or selling or uniforms in whole or part, plus shoes, caps and linen. All this was paid for with American cigarettes. One pack of 20 American cigarettes was the basic unit of value, adjusted according to the brand; I think Chesterfield was of greatest value. The whole American Red Cross Parcel was "valued" at 25 packages of American cigarettes!

For buying fresh foods through the German guards, the American cigarettes were also used; a loaf of bread, almost two kilograms (about 4.4 lbs.) in weight, could be bought with just one pack of cigarettes, and so each day bread was brought into the camp by the German guards in profusion, although those who received it directly were only the privileged "businessmen" among the camp inmates. The items from the American Red Cross Parcel were specifically valued: one chocolate bar was worth two packs of cigarettes; a box of powdered milk was worth three packages of cigarettes, and sometimes less. Every time there was buying and selling in the barracks, the tailors, of all our craftsmen, profitted best in this bartering; they were busy making or altering clothes. Our Serbian military cap was sold for five packages of cigarettes, and other items accordingly more expensive.

The spirit did not die in this camp. There were many different shows made—each national group putting on different ones. I was present at the show which the Belgian under-officers arranged. The French camp shows were the best organized. At our shows, our allies were pleased most by Serbian "kolos" (round dances), and other amusements that they did not fully understand, although explanations were made in French and English for each point of the program.

The camp's libraries, especially the French ones, were furnished with excellent books. In ours there were a few good books and some of lesser value. Our library particularly had been used to form "jobs" for the members of the Communist headquarters, and less to unite our soldiers.

But we didn't stay long, either. The camp was to be evacuated. The first column left on January 28, late in the afternoon. This was a group of a thousand Americans. January 30, 1945 was again a cold day, and crowds of German refugees, with carts, were surging past to the west. Then we too left, about 4 p.m. At the head of our column marched about 800 Frenchmen, then we 115 Serbians, and the rear about 80 Belgians.

Darkness gradually came; the cold was rigorous, but we did not feel it too much, because there was no wind and we were in constant motion. To our left we could recognize the main road, but they took us by some short cuts on the back roads. In the snow we noticed the boxes which the American group had been forced to discard.

We eventually found ourselves on a plateau in generally hilly terrain. The wind started to blow harder, the snow was hitting our faces and we hardly could see the fellows ahead of us. The storm was getting worse and worse, and because of this the men were hindered in advancing. With great hardship, all soaked with sweat, we crossed this terrain with no roads and reached the other side of this plateau, tramping the high layers of snow. We went up a small slope and reached a road which was leading through a high woods; there were some houses or huts to the left of the road. We hoped that it would now be easier for us, but the advance along the road was still harder because it was deeply rutted before it was covered with a high layer of snow, and our legs would slide into crevices. Finally, we decided to leave our makeshift "sleds" and everything on them; we took with us some necessary and easier things to carry on our backs. We did this regretfully because in this way we were deprived of the supply of reserve food, but we thought this could help hungry persons who would pass through after us. We continued to travel by untrodden paths, and encountered artillery in camouflage with soldiers all in white uniforms; huge cannon barrels stuck into the air.

Daily we would cover twenty-five to thirty and more kilometers, spending the night in barns. Here we used to get some food, mostly potatoes, which were distributed boiled. Every day, while moving through Pomerania, crowds of refugees with carts were seen, joining us or passing. These people looked at us with fear in their eyes. Some were small children or exhausted old men or women.

We left behind Boren Walde, south of Shivelbine. We were told that we would camp around Shivelbine and stay in the camp. We went through a rather mountainous region and it was very cold and snow-covered. I was thinking about the events within Hitler's "fortress". In my imagination I saw huge armies of our allies from the west as they were destroying entrenched places in western Germany. I imagined that all French were united against the invaders, and that they were already wallowing in freedom. We almost felt the huge waves of Russian military forces approaching, under whose blows the last German defenses in the east not so far from us were disappearing.

After days more of walking we were nearing the Elbe River, at night. The news was spread by whispers that we would soon cross this river at Boizenburg. The weather was rather cold, but we did not feel it too much because of our quick moving. Our column stopped in a small settlement some kilometers east of Magdeburg, mostly in barns. It was hard to get some food because the men had spent all the reserves they had gotten from the Americans. The French, aided by Americans with us, had been fortunate enough to get some supplies from the American Red Cross in Magdeburg. This helped us very much and made us able to sustain the march which followed after a few days.

When we resumed marching, it was really backward, along a canal. We crossed the outskirts of Ultzen which very recently, possibly the day before, had been bombarded and was awfully ruined. Our German guards took us to a large building on the edge of the city; this was a racetrack before the war, and the building was very cramped. The Germans gave us three days of supplies in bread, margarine, and raw potatoes. But boiling the potatoes was almost impossible because of the lack of fuel. Here I tried to use some tickets for bread which I had bought in Demmin: I gave a chocolate to a boy so that he could buy for me four kilograms of bread. The boy came quickly back with one kilogram of bread, excusing himself that three other tickets had no worth; he handed me the bread over the fence. Thus this honest boy supplied me with bread for one or two days more. This was a beautiful instance of inborn honesty not corrupted by older men!

We stayed three days. Fortunately, Ultzen was not bombarded again these days, although swarms of Allied bombers could be heard steadily over our heads.

For unknown reasons, the Germans took us next to the southwest from Ultzen. The weather was clear and beautiful, and we were generally cheerful. After walking only a few kilometers, we stopped in a village, spent the day, and then continued into a wooded area. Here five Americans fled from our column unseen.

From this wooded terrain very soon we found ourselves in the open, and we went south, then straight west. The road we encountered stretched over a large plain. Many Polish war prisoners were joined with us.

Eventually we passed the well-known military airfield at Luneburg, and crossed the Luneburg bridge in daylight. At this bridge I learned from our countrymen that Zarko Vukadinovic had slowed and disappeared alone in the woods behind us.

About midnight we crossed another bridge. By whispering the news spread that we were recrossing the Elbe River. On the other end of the bridge some of our fellows read the inscription Donitz. The next morning by the map we learned that this town Donitz was about 148 kilometers upstream from Hamburg. It meant that we had crossed the Elbe twice; such foolishness of circling we were unable to understand.

The next day we were going to the north, again from barn to barn. Sometimes we used to go kilometers out of our way to find barns. But the weather was almost beautiful, and we enjoyed looking at the swarms of bombers as they moved towards the east. There had been many days when we were able to count more than 500 bombers as they were flying in formation. The German airplanes had almost disappeared. Sometimes two or three German airplanes would appear above some woods, and then flying very low would disappear. Sometimes English Spitfires would appear low above us. One day two English airplanes killed German guards before and behind us. When we were marching we feared that the Englishmen would fire on us by mistake, and we immediately scattered on the fields to the left of the road and we started to wave with handkerchiefs or shirts. Fortunately, the English aviators did not make this mistake with us, although there were many examples among other columns. A separate French column lost twelve of our co-sufferers in this way.

One day our column stopped to spend the night in a village named Civitz, a few kilometers east of the village Platte, where we had been settled for some days in the middle of the previous month, from the 12th to the 16th of March. In Civitz we settled in barns or in some empty rooms. This settlement was 14 kilometers from Schwerin in Mecklenburg.

The men were exhausted. Here we got some ordinary German rations as supplies, but we also got food from the villagers. Some of us bought by bartering, especially potatoes, though very often it was given for free. Some bought bread and other necessities for cooking. The German population was living in fear; they felt more the danger than we war prisoners, because they knew better what was happening in the east.

The last day of the month of April was approaching. Our guards were in less contact with us. Our men had recovered; among us there was more conversation, jokes and laughter. The weather was bright and pleasant. We were talking of the possibility that our allies would liberate us here, but we feared getting between two fires in the last moments, although for the time-being there was no evidence of fighting either to the east or west of us.

On May 2, 1945, about 2:00 p.m. I was strolling with some of my countrymen near the village on the north side. Three of our countrymen who met us started to shout: "Freedom! Freedom!" The German guards had disappeared unnoticed. We made a tour around the region and you could not see even one German. Within some minutes all of our settlement was filled with great emotion and joy—Yugoslavs, French and Belgians. The Americans left and went to report to military units in this sector. We Serbians, French, and Belgians stayed in the same place, but without German guards. "Freedom! Freedom!" was heard on all sides!

Serbia — This view is typical of many streets in villages. The houses are mainly composed of wood, but walls may be covered with plaster, or less frequently, composed of dried mud or sundried bricks. Note the absence of chimneys, whose place is taken by louvres in the roof. The house on the extreme left is typical of the houses built between 1918 and 1940.

CHAPTER ELEVEN: JAILED BY THE ENGLISH
WHILE YUGOSLAVIA SUFFERS

We learned later that Allied military forces, even in the night be-tween May 1 and 2, had passed north of us, and that these military units, very possibly tank columns, already were about twenty-five miles east of us! By the end of the day, May 2, American military authorities and the American Red Cross had supplied each of us with four large Red Cross food packages.

The leadership of the whole group of us ex-prisoners of war passed to our French co-sufferers under the command of Pierron. We learned quickly that the demarcation line between the Americans and the Russians would be set near us. It seemed that our village could pass to the Russians. The French leader of this group let us know the situation. All of us were willing to cross where we would be sure to be west of the demarcation line in this sector. Early in the morning on May 6, our group was ready to move, and we went to the northwest from here. After some hours of walking, we arrived at a larger village on the right side of the road, through which masses of former war prisoners were storming past each other—Russians from the west going east and others from east to west. Among us Serbians, there appeared some Yugoslavians who urged us: "You know, comrades, our comrades in the country have come to power; they have brought new laws which we ought to respect and to live by. They have altered our military oath, and we are compelled to hoist the (Red) flag even here." I was listening to all of this, but I did not immediately reply. One of them advanced toward me with the words: "Isn't this so, 'Uncle Professor'?" I could not stand it anymore, and I told him slowly: "Young man, do not babble; the national flag can be altered only by a free national parliament in Belgrade. Cloths and rags which the Communists proclaimed in Jajce, or elsewhere, to be a national flag, cannot be the flag for honest men, because all this has been done under occupiers, very possibly on their recommendation to destroy Yugoslavia. Hitler and Mussolini are already dead, and we will soon come to the end of the ludicrous play of Communists in our country!" All this could not dissuade such Communists among us: they had already made a "new Yugoslavian flag" with a red star in the middle. The men in our group, about sixty of us, largely ignored them.

Later we were moved to a camp at Hagenau, where the struggle of the loyalists versus Reds continued. On July 2, about eight in the morning, an English captain with some of his soldiers in full battle dress entered rooms in the camp and started to take our men, one by one, according to the list handed to him by Tito's representatives. When the Englishmen took me to the assigned office, I found there three of the Communist representatives and both of our army officers, who had previously rejected Communist orders. The English captain turned to our men: "I have the order to deprive you of liberty on behalf of these three men according to the political temporary course . . ." The English Captain and soldiers brought us down to a cellar beneath the English headquarters and took us to some cells. In the cell with me were put Momcilo Kostic, Dusan Arsekic, and Milun Savic—two of Draza Mihailovic's Chetniks and prisoners from April, 1941, now reunited. Six fellows were put in other cells. After exactly two months of living in freedom, I found myself again in a prison cell, placed there by the English. The day July 2, 1945 will stay in my memory forever; it helps me to better comprehend the martyrdom of my people and to better understand the injustice done by our allies in the Second World War.

After about a week, the English loaded us in a military truck and drove us through the streets of Lubeck to an unknown direction. Behind us there was an English tank with machine guns pointed at us; in front was another tank. When they unloaded us in front of a tall building, we noticed we were in front of a prison for criminals, and loudly started to protest and resist. The English Army captain ordered his men, fully dressed for battle, to surround us from three sides: the doors of the prison were before us. They started to call our names and identified us as "war criminals". When this was done, they took us by armed guards into the prison, leading us to the top floor of the prison (I think, it was the fourth), along a narrow corridor, then into small cells, shutting the doors behind us. I was in cell Number 6. On the window there were thick iron bars. There were two beds; one was an iron bed with chains, handcuffs, and leg locks at the four corners. Our men in their cells started to sing loudly. By calling out, we learned where each one was; Dusan Arsekic was in cell Number 1, and then followed the names of other fellows up till cell Number 9, in which were both of our army officers, Markovic and Deroko.

Until ten at night our singing was incessant: at that time, a knocking on the door began from the corridor. The doors of some "singers" were opened and the prison guards warned: "Singen verboten nach zehn Uhr". (Singing forbidden after ten o'clock.) This angered us still more, so that this night the singing did not stop until morning.

Imprisonment was especially hard for the smokers. Although we initially had plenty of cigarettes in our haversacks, we had no matches or cigarette lighters. But necessity is the mother of invention. Sergeant Djokic, in the second cell, solemnly declared that he had a cigarette lighter. Now it was necessary to devise some way the others could use it. The problem was solved by Dusan Arsekic, in the first cell, who had a string wound around something in his haversack. He threw this balled string in front of the cells until we had a loop of string passing all of them. As soon as the order had been given for smoking, Djokic would light his own cigarette, quickly tie it on the string, and gave the order to "Pull", "Pull", "Pull on"! His lighted cigarette would stop at each cell, while the men who were interested would light their own cigarette, and say "Pull on". In this way Djokic's cigarette would be extinguished before he could smoke it, but this was not so bad; he had the cigarette lighter!

We ten stayed in the prison until September 2, when we were loaded on a rather large military truck guarded by English soldiers and delivered after an all-day trip to Camp Eversheide near Osnabrück. It looked as though the camp had been informed about our coming: personal acquaintances were waiting at the gate. I heard the words of my kin, Lieutenant Milo Radevic: "You are to stay in my barracks!" Here there were about three thousand of our army officers and soldiers. Most of them had passed four full years in captivity: the difference had been only in the name "ex-war prisoners" and in better food supplies. For us Yugoslavs it would be better to say "not yet liberated war prisoners."

Before we scattered to the barracks, we asked the commander of the camp to tell us why we spent a full two months in prison; his assistant commander answered us: ". . . the men in question were put in prison on behalf of the official representatives of Yugoslavia in Lubeck because of spreading propaganda among the ex-war prisoners of Yugoslavian origin." Several months earlier all countries in Europe were enjoying the return of their sons from captivity, while we Serbians were not able to go anywhere: Fascism and Nazism had destroyed our country; the Allies had handed us over to Communists whose getting into power in Yugoslavia they had greatly helped from 1943 through 1945. This injustice was killing us.

After some time, the barbed wire around the camp was cut. It is interesting to note that our men, after the "breaking of the barbed wire", never, or very rarely, committed any crime or act of violence. In the vicinity of the camp there was a large German village. As soon as the barbed wire had been broken, our men spread to village cafes, or simply walked through the streets. The villagers of Eversheide, who had been taught to fear us greatly, had been surprised when they saw us "barbarians" from the Balkans, for they saw us embracing German children, offering them candies, chocolates, and other things which they saw we had.

The visit of our young king on September 27, 1945, excited our camp. At the mustering place we gathered early in squares, many hours before his arrival. He came in the company of English soldiers, and was greeted at the camp gate by Bishop Nikolaj Velimirovic, who had spent the war in a concentration camp, and some of our highest-ranking army officers. When he arrived at the mustering place, he separated from the group of English soldiers and accompanied by our army officers, Colonel Dunjic and Bishop Nikolaj, went forward and stood in the middle of the review, according to our military order. He called: "May God help you, soldiers!" To this we answered unanimously (about three thousand men): "May God save you!"

On the platform in front he finished his speech with these words: "I firmly believe that the situation will soon improve, and that the day is not far off when you will return to your homes and again, after so long a separation, you will embrace your mothers, your wives and your children. You will return to your country again as you deserve it in full dignity, honor and freedom. I salute you, my army officers, under-officers, and soldiers. Long live our Yugoslavia!"

By the middle of October news started to come about the conditions in our country, expecially news of the great tragedy of Chetniks in the territory of Montenegro and Sandzak who had retreated under Pavle Djurisic. My Godbrother Lieutenant Milo Radevic got a long letter from Branko Radevic, written on October 9, 1945. This letter is of great importance and I cite it at length as follows:

Dear Milo,

I cannot inform you of anything good about our Chetnik

units from Crna Gora, Boka and Sandzak as well as the great number of civilians who retreated with them. Nearly all have been destroyed by Ustasi, and the greatest number captured by Communists in Slovenia and immediately killed. Of those groups who had numbered over 15,000 souls, one can number but two hundred men.

My wife with two small children had been left with civilians not far from Dravograd; about their fate I know nothing, and I can not expect anything good. Besides this group which had been in Dravograd, one group was captured near Ljubljana, another in Celje and at other places. Milinko and Pero, Mihailo (sons of Nika) and Milan (son of Stoja Kojic) were in the group captured in Ljubjana. We were captured by the Ustasi and scattered in groups, with no contact among us. I was disguised, so that they would not discover that I was an army officer, otherwise I would have lost my life. Many of the intellectuals and army officers were separated in Bosanska Gradiska and killed there. There even Pavle Djurisic was captured, but according to some he managed to save himself, how I do not know, and accordingly he is now in Bosnia.

Ilija and Milicko were in the same group with Milinko, his cousin. The sons of the late Milonja: Spiro, Leko and Danilo, as well as Radomir with the youngest son from Opasanica, also had been with us. About their fate, I do not know, but there is no hope that any have been saved, because none of them crossed the border to Austria.

Of fugitives from Maribor and Ljubjana I learned that the massacres had been done en masse. In Maribor about 3,500 were slaughtered, and in Kamnik about 900; one group had been slaughtered in Radovlica, another at Zidanimost, another at Sloven-Gradec and others in other places.

Our retreat from Montenegro took place on December 5, 1944. Oh how many hardships, strains and sufferings during this long and painful travel, accompanied by hunger and cold across the Bosnian Mountains and everywhere in hard fighting, and stricken down by typhus—it is hard to describe all this even a little bit. As a result, there was an almost total loss of our men.

From Milija's letter I learned that he was not informed (at that time) about the falling of the late George (Lasic). He had been killed on May 5, 1944, during the bombardment of Podgorica. At this same time Bogic Gogic and the son of Radisav Milosevic were also killed. These two were with him in the same trench. I was not at that time in Podgorica, as I was on an official mission. If I had been there I would have died with them. Maybe it would have been better for me, because I would not endure the sufferings which I experienced and that I am suffering today. At that time many were killed en masse. Day in and day out we started to fall so that now there is perhaps one per cent of us living today.

Milija is interested about what happened after he left Crna Gora. Oh, dear Milija, I would have to narrate to you long about our hardships. All that we experienced together in 1941 and in 1942 was only a song. Many of our graves are scattered from the Adriatic Sea to Neretva and the Drina Rivers and Serbia, through Bosnia, Croatia and Slovenia.

The most trying times were from October to November 1943, when the Lim Valley and Lijeva Rijeka were occupied by Communists; we had occupied these places many times, and we were finally compelled to leave Montenegro.

In Vasojevici none of our men are left. All army officers and intellectuals have perished, and about the soldiers we don't have to say anything. (A list of several pages of scores of dead acquaintances follows.)

Here of us Chetniks from Montenegro we can number hardly 30 men. With me here is Simo Mijuskovic from Niksic.

Yours,
Branko

At the end of April, 1946, they loaded us in freight cars and took us to Sendgwarden, northwest from Wilhelmshaven. Here we were able to go freely in the nearby countryside. As there was some crowdedness in the rooms, this was greatly welcome to all of us "neither war prisoners, nor free men." In Sendgwarden before long we received new index cards: segregated P.W.X.D.P. index cards; my number had been G 22,719,315. That meant that we were now "displaced persons".

In October, Colonel Dunjic called a conference of teachers to tell us that General Damjanovic had asked to get more teachers for our children in Eboli, in Italy, where there were a great number of settled Chetniks. After a delay to obtain papers, three of us (Radenko Gordic, Nektarije Marinkovic and myself) left for Eboli on December 16, 1946. After a train trip through France and Italy, we arrived at the camp at Eboli. At the end of December, 1946, we three began our work in the high school; I taught the Serbian language in the lower classes of high school and French in the upper classes. Gordic taught the history of Serbian literature in the upper classes, and Marinkovic, geography.

There were about 12,000 former Chetnik fighters at Eboli, plus several thousand women and children. Except for pure air and good climatic conditions, these people lacked everything. They were living mostly in barracks with the shape of long barrels of steel, and a few under tents. Even when the weather was very mild, you could not escape the impression that these persons were living in sloth and dirt and misery. I was sorry to see the small children, very miserably clad and dirty, playing before their barracks or running around the camp. In the classroom there was no liveliness or expression of joy on their faces.

General Dragoljub Mihailovic, leader of the pro-Government resistance forces, as he appeared after his capture by the Communists. A short time after this he was executed by the Communists—supposedly for "treason."

CHAPTER TWELVE: THE RETREAT IN YUGOSLAVIA

In Eboli, one of my students in the final year of high school, a youth nicknamed "Mrgud", had already seen an incredible amount of warfare and suffering. This is a condensation of the account "Mrgud" Bojanic wrote of his experiences:

The concentration of Chetnik forces from Crna Gora took place in October-November 1944, on the sectors of the Bjelopavlicki and Ljesanske brigades, that is, in the districts of Podgorica and Danilovgrad. There were other units from Boka Kotorska, on the sector of Risanj, Bar and a battalion around Cetinje. The sector in Boka was held by the Vucedolska and Grbljanska brigades and gendarmerie. The men in Boka sector were about 1,800. The commander of Vucedolska brigade was Army Captain Ivan Janicic, and of the Grbljanska brigade, Captain Djuro Ivetic. The commander around Cetinje was Vukasin Bojovic.

On November 12, 1944, a telegram was recieved from Supreme Command saying that the English had landed in Dubrovnik, with two motorized divisions. One was advancing in the direction of Kalinovik, with the other going to Niksic. Our advanced units had gotten in touch with them, and the meeting was very cordial. There were no Reds there.

This news was communicated to all our fighting forces; there was great rejoicing in our ranks, because it was thought that the worst had passed.

The assaults by the partisans were continuing and were more and more pressing. Their main forces had been on the sector Bogatici-Garac-Ostrog-Kupinovo. On November 18, a carrier from Niksic declared that the English were already in Niksic, with the partisans. The next day, about 7 in the morning, there had begun great machine gun fire from Ostrog and Bogetic. It had been clear that there had also been English artillery.

Under these circumstances, Vojvoda Djurisic on November 25 sent messengers to the English, led by Niko Nikcevic, who spoke English fluently. We awaited their return for six days, after which one of the messengers came back and told us the following: "We talked with the English commander in Niksic. He met us and told us 'We are fighting units of the English army, and have no orders to mix with other questions among you and the partisans, much less to make peace or to receive and protect you!"

On November 28, 1944, a new message was received from main headquarters which ordered Vojvoda Djurisic to move our forces in the direction to Sandzak to unite our fighting forces. The coastal units had joined us five days earlier. The evacuation started on December 1; the first units to move were of the Kolasinska Brigade; the last left December 8. From Podgorica to Lijeva Rijeka we endured awful weather—rain, snowstorms and strong winds. On this part of our trip the only serious fighting took place on Veternik Mountain, which was entrenched by two Partisans brigades. After two days of hard fighting, the Partisans had been driven off. We captured only two English cannons and 20 cases of ammunition. On December 11, 1944, Djurisic ordered the Storming Brigade to go in the direction of Planinica and Verusa, because we had received information that in Verusa there were about a thousand Partisans who intended to cut our advance at Raskovo Guvno.

The commander of the Storming Brigade gave the disposition and on December 12, at 8:00 a.m., started battle. The attack had been prepared in great secrecy, and caught the Partisans almost unaware. Most of them had been surprised sleeping in houses and huts. The sentinels, except for two, were overwhelmed and beaten before they were able to give warning by shooting their rifles. When we surprised them and mingled with them, they thought we were Partisans. In the night melee the Partisans had 430 dead and some wounded, but from our side there had been only four dead and twelve wounded. Their defense had been very weak, because they had been really surprised and unaware of our assault; by this awful slaughter, the whole right Partisans' wing had been completely destroyed.

The snow fell to a depth of about 6 or 7 centimeters [2-3 inches] but there was an open sky and the airplanes could find us. There were machine gunnings, bombings, and putting fire to the houses. The air above the roads from Podgorica to Kolasin were filled with airplanes. On December 14, about 8:00 p.m., we started for Kolasin, and arrived in Lipovo near Kolasin about 9 the next morning. From Lipovo to Rudo we moved in a forced march. The first units reached the villages around Rudo on December 29, and the last on January 2, 1945. All the villages around Rudo were filled by our armed forces. From Lipovo to Rudo there was no fighting, except small skirmishes at Mojkovac.

On January 1st to 6th, we were preparing to celebrate [Orthodox] Christmas, and meanwhile the fighting forces reorganized. The army was formed into three divisions (the First, Fifth and Eighth) and each had two regiments of 2,500 fighters. The Storming Brigade was a special unit assigned to the Fifth Division. This brigade consisted at that time of 20 army officers, 80 under-officers, and 750 fighting men. From 1941 up until now (that is January, 1945) this bridage had lost 3,800 fighting men and its men were constantly replaced. The commander of the First Division was Army Major Ivan Ruzic; the commander of the Fifth Division was Army Major Leko Lalic, and the commander of the Eighty Division was Lieutenant Colonel Vaso Vukcevic.

Christmas was spent in Rudo and nearby villages, and on January 9, we began to move in the direction of Visegrad. The last units left Rudo. The weather was awful, the ammunition carriers had blocked the advance, as their horses had frequently fallen down with their burdens. The old men wrapped their heads with shawls, and under their covering one heard their steady grumbling, asking each other: "Where are they going?" I heard one of them say; "Oh, God, why does this shameful thing happen to me, instead of my staying home to perish there; now nobody will find even my socks." Hearing him talk this way, I said: "Do not talk so, old man, and do not be faint-hearted; you ought to give some encouragement to these young men."

"And who are you?", he asked.

"I am Mrgud, commander of the Third Battalion of the Storming Brigade", I continued.

"And what a beautiful name, and may God Bless you with good!" continued the old man. He asked: "And could you tell me Mrgud, where are we going to, in the name of Almighty God!" I was startled by such a question and I was preparing to answer when he cut me off: "Listen to me; tell me the truth and do not lie to me, because nobody I asked would tell us the turth."

"To tell the truth, I also do not know how long we will go, or how far, but at any rate to Ozren Mountain in Bosnia."

"Where is this mountain?" inquired the old man.

"It is rather far; we have to travel four or five days."

"What are you talking about? In the name of God, nobody will find our steps anymore!" concluded the old man.

We crossed the bridge at Visegrad. Before us, on the other bank of the Drina River, there was a great mountain called Semec, covered with snow up to a meter deep. On January 16, 1945, all of our army was on Semec. This was our first encounter with high snows and very rigorous cold. The army, with the civilians and wounded, was settled under pine trees in dense woods. There was a lack of fires everyplace, except by the units deep in the rear. It was snowing continuously; vision was hampered. Compasses were hardly being used; it had been better to let the old woman lead us.

There was enough flour and bread, but little meat. The hardest task was supplying feed for the cattle. The fighting units were generally well supplied, except that we did not have enough ammunition, taking into account what was awaiting us farther on; ammunition is a life and death question for fighting forces.

Among all our forces, the most sympathy was for the youth regiment, which had been organized of 1,012 boys of 15 to 17 years, divided into three batallions. Each of these battalions had three companies; each company had 5 machine guns, and the rest only rifles. Vojvoda had ordered that these boys should be saved from fighting, but they asked to get to the first ranks in fighting. The morale among them was excellent, but they hated the cold and snow. They used to say to themselves: "The cold is harder for us than for the Partisans." Through the fighting, snow and other hardships, they would sing, as though their souls had been touched with victory.

On January 19, in the morning, we left Semec Mountain and before dark, arrived in the Lower and Upper Brankovic villages. These villages, formerly had about 400 houses, but they had been completely burned in 1941 and 1942 by Ustasi. One could find some stalls which had not been burned, and these were used for sick, the wounded, exausted, and refugees. The army settled on the snow nearby under the open sky. Snow continued to fall. In these villages, under these circumstances, we stayed until January 26. At the center of our forces were the refugees, wounded, and the National Committee retreating in the direction of Sokolovic. This column crossed the highway running from Pale to Vlasenica, and continued toward Mendojevic in the direction of Olovo and Kladanj. The First Division was at the head of the column, and the Eighth ahd Fifth Divisions on both sides of this column. In the direction of Semec-Olovo the hardest fighting was being engaged in by the Fifth Division, with the Storming Brigade, while the First and Eighth Divisions did not have serious fighting.

The Partisan's 36th division, which had occupied Devetak and

Dzimlije, was destroyed by our First Division, which continued toward Kladanj, where there previously had been hard fighting. In this new fighting at Kladanj on January 27 and 28, we suffered 124 dead and 104 wounded.

We had a very difficult job taking care of the sick and the wounded, whose number mounted daily. Transporting these wounded was awful. Horses were the only means for their transportation, and it happened often that a horse with a wounded person would fall down in some abyss. Although as an officer of the Storming Brigade I was fighting every day, I considered myself lucky not to have been in the "ambulance" section, which transported the wounded and buried the dead.

At the end of January, we got information that five or six men were infected with typhus, which spread great fear among us. I knew previously that typhus fever was an awful disease, but I could not imagine that it would so mercilessly destroy life. Looking at a typhus-blistered face, one would not be able to recognize his own brother.

From Olovo to Ozren we traversed the Krivaj Valley, starting January 29 and arriving at Vozuce February 2, 1945. In this valley, the snow was like an iceberg; the road was very straight, so that the column could barely advance one by one. In transporting the wounded there were scenes before which one would shut his eyes, because of the sorrow; the wounded were suffering so much, many of them asked in the name of God to be killed on the spot.

There had been about 100 young girls who carried the wounded on their backs, and they had been glad and bold that they could give this help in distress. Each one looked at the wounded as though he had been her brother, and they strove to ease the pain and distress.

We were bothered by another terribly enemy—lice, from which no one was able to defend himself. This was the producer of our large graves through the spread of typhus. We washed everything every second day in boiling water, but all was in vain. Among the people there was a settled conviction that the lice were coming from underground.

In Ozren, we were joined by Chetniks numbering about 3,800 men. On February 4, the battle against the Partisans started near Tuzla. The plan for attack was made by Vojvoda Djurisic. On the right wing, in the direction of Simin Han, was our First Division; nearby was the Fifth Division, and to the left of them was the Eighth Division, the Racic group, and the Ozren Chetniks. At this battle, fought along the entire front, we had 652 dead. The number of Partisan casualities cound not be calculated easily. The Partisans whom we made prisoner told us that Tuzla had been defended by 9,000 men.

The wounded and the refugees were settled in the following villages: Pejanovici, Orahovica, and Svinjanisica. On February 11, the order was issued to cross to Trebava. In doing so, a Partisan division attacked our column in the center, where the wounded and cvilian refugees were. The Eighth Division and the Headquarters Battalion immediately went to the fighting, and they beat the Partisans down. In this two-hour battle, the Partisans left 600 dead, and about 300 as prisoners. The commander of Lipovo Battalion, Lieutenant Branko Bulatovic, was killed.

Near Trebava we settled at the following villages: Serbian and Moslem Brapska, Korzuci, Trebava Village, Duge Njive and the front lines, toward Modric and Posavina. Here reigned an awful typhus epidemic, so that we Chetniks coming from Montenegro were decreased by one half.

On February 12, a regiment of the Eighth Division finished crossing the Bosnia River, entered Rudanka, and fought hard against the Partisans, but was forced back with 27 dead and 40 wounded. On this same day the Fifth Division was fighting at Duge Njive and Modric, and 72 Partisans were made prisoners, most of them were Moslems.

Our main headquarters was placcd in the village of Koprivna. The wounded were settled in Vucjak in the village of Bozinici, protected by the First Division. In this sector were about 2,000 Vucjak Chetniks under the command of Branko Kovacevic, who betrayed us. He gave the Communists our signs of recognition, and with two of his battalions he personally took part in this disaster. All the Partisans wore Chetnik insignias. In this whirlwind fighting, we had 482 dead. Many of the victims had been sick with typhus, which had already almost wiped out the ambulance group. This hideous attack was on March 8, at about 11:00 p.m.

We stayed in Vucjak until March 21. Then we passed between Derventa and Zeravci and entered Bela Brda, where we stayed from March 22 to 27, and then went through Matajnica in the direction of Lijevce Polje.

On March 29, the First Division, "Leteca Bosna" and the Chetniks from Herzegovina fought hard at Matajnica with a Lika Partisan division, which they completely destroyed. We crossed the Vrbas to Lijevce Polje on March 30 and April 1, 1945. The fighting forces settled in the villages to get some rest and some supplies for the move towards Slovenia. On April 4, suddenly, two divisions of [Croatian] Ustasi attacked our ranks at the spot where the highways from Bozinci and Topola crossed.

Unfortunately, the above account written by my student "Mrgud" Bojanic was not completed any further, at least in the brief time before the camp at Eboli was dispersed. However, the general information of this massive Chetnik retreat from Crna Gora was confirmed by the accounts of others in the camp who also had taken part in the massive exodus. One of these accounts is by a student and former soldier by the name of Nedovic, who was born in Berane, and who was with the units on the Adriatic Coast near Podgorica which Mrgud mentioned joined the main party late in November of 1944. Nedovic was with the "Youth Regiment." I shall condense Nedovic's account greatly for the chronological period duplicating Mrgud's account already given (November, 1944 to April 4, 1945), and then let Nedovic continue the account of the Chetnik retreat from where Mrgud's stopped. Here is Nedovic's account from the start of the retreat:

The gathering of the army and the people started at Zlatica in Doljane. The leaving of Podgorica and the nearby area took place on December 3, 1944. There gathered about 15,000 persons—about 10,000 fighters and the rest civilians. Here we received orders to move. The message was as follows: "All fighting forces direct to Gorazde, where you will meet the first tank units of our allies." Here at Zlatica we had been forced to spend the night in caves along the Moraca River. Allied airplanes were continually dropping bombs on the nearby hills in Donji Kuci and Piperi above Mrke. Although there was no snow, it was very cold and rainy. The men, women and children gathered around fires in the caves, in which there was much humidity, and from above, because of the great rain, water dripped almost all night, so that there was very little dry space. All night we listened to the wails of women and children and consoling by the men.

Here we stayed about three days under the hardest conditions. What is important to stress is that the people—even women and children, in spite of their sufferings and distress—were not willing to stay back, but with great eagerness were willing to continue to go to the unknown. It was believed that the retreat would last only to Vasojevici, and that we would have to stay in the forest for only a couple of months, until our allies would come from Salonika to free Yugoslavia.

On December 5, 1944, we started our move toward Bratonozici and Vasojevici. We moved along the old road, through Mazanica, on the left bank of the Moraca River. On the highway, we watched a continuous stream of German motorized units, and on the hills we saw units of the German army, protecting the convoy. Our troops moved in formations of the old brigades; in each there were also old men, women and children of the respective units, despite Djurisic's order that civilians should go separate in the middle of our units, under the command of Spiro Stojanovic.

Late in the evening we stopped at Bioce, on the left bank of the Moraca River, and thus again we were in caves, as the few houses had been burned in 1941 by the Italian punishing expedition after the July uprising in Crna Gora and Mountains. Here we stayed for two or three days, to regroup and to make our way across to the right bank of Moraca, because there the wooden bridge had also been burned in 1941.

From there we crossed to the right bank of the Moraca, and all of our column headed toward Pelev Brijeg and Vjeternik. Now we were going by the highway in the direction of Jelin Dub, Klopot, and Pelev Brijeg. Some men had horses, but mothers were carrying their children on their backs. Supplies were very bad; each one carried with him some corn and flour, and at night they made meals in kettles for their families. But there had been many who had nothing of their own to eat. Some meat was distributed to them, because we had taken some cattle with us. Even at Zlatica the cattle were distributed and each brigade cared for its part of the distributed herd.

[Nedovic goes on to describe in detail the continuing journey to Pelev Brijeg, then to Duske in Lijeva Rijeka county, then toward Planinica, back again to Duske after a day in an aborted move on Partisans near Brskut, then to Matesevo over a mountanous route, and then through the ruins of Kolasin. From there they continued and . . .]

We spent the night at Bablja Greda, in the Low Lipovo under the open sky. The night was awful. We made fires on the snow. The women and children were also out under the open sky. We had already been hungry. The sights were awful: shivering persons wrapped in an overcoat or a blanket around the fire; the crying of children and wailing of women ceaselessly from all sides. The exhaustion and the unknown added to the fear.

The next night was spent in the lower Trebaljevo. Here we were mostly settled in houses and barns. For the first time since Duske in

Lijeva Rijeka we could get some supplies—mostly potatoes, cabbage, and some cheese. The village had been settled, but in the houses were only women. The sheep and cattle had been taken away somewhere. Here was provisionally settled a small German detachment to protect the partisan families. Here we stayed two or three days.

From Trebaljevo the column moved during the night by a narrow path, along the Tara River. One whole family—man, woman and two children—found an awful death that night in the waves of the river, as their horse and they fell off a precipice into the Tara. Because of the darkness and the fast current of the river, no one was able to give any help.

We spent the night in Bjelojevice below Bjelasica; the next morning we arrived at Mojkovac. Our columns were gathering at Ulosevina, east of Mojkovac. At Ulosevina we stayed for some days, and spent the night around the campfires under the open skies, soldiers as well as women and children. From here we went forward by the old road through Bojine Njive to the Lepenac River. Fighting with the partisans took place at Jabuka.

We were compelled to cross the bridge at Slijepac heading toward Bijelo Polje. The crossing of this bridge during the night was difficult, even though Djurisic was there in person to ease our crossing of it, as the Germans were not willing to let us cross the bridge because they were hurrying to retreat. Thus we crossed to Bijelo Polje the next afternoon in speed marching, because we feared the Allied airplanes here.

In Bijelo Polje we were able to buy some foods, especially fruits; it was rare to be able to buy bread and meat, and this only with Italian lire. Bijelo Polje was filled with Communist inscriptions on the houses. We learned that several hundred persons had been killed by Allied bombing a few days before, including a large number of partisans attending a meeting in the Hotel Radovic, which was leveled by the bombs.

The following night we spent in Nedakusi, downstream from Bijelo Polje. With my brother, sister, and father I went to a Moslem house at the entrance of the village Nedakusi, left of the highway, where we were very well received. The Moslems were very kind toward all who spent the night in this village, either by their good will or by fear, I do not know, as I was unacquainted with the situation in this area.

After spending Christmas (Julian calendar) 1944 in Rudo, my unit, the Youth Regiment, started to move toward Visegrad along the railroad tracks toward Medjedja, and then soon to the right to cross the mountains between Rudo and Visegrad. We crossed Vikra Mountain at night in snow, ice and almost unbearably cold.

In Visegrad we didn't spend the night; but immediately crossed the bridge at the Drina River, and spent the night under the open sky at Semec Mountain, on the left (northwest) bank of the river. In front of Tmor Mountain, we went right and advanced over the low slopes of Romanija Mountain, with Devetak Mountain to our right. The snow was very high, and movement was very difficult. Our Eighth Division was moving on the slopes of Romanija Mountain as our left protecting wing. The right protecting units were moving across Devetak Mountain toward Han-Pijesak. There were our strongest forces, because we were awaiting the onslaught of the partisans from Srebrenica and Vlasenica.

We stayed seven days in the former Upper and Lower Brankovice in January, 1945. We got food by slaughtering cattle which we had been driving from Rudo. The settlement had been hit very hard: the villagers had been Serbian, but had been completely annihilated by Ustasi. It was now deserted, and only two or three barns remained. The majority spent seven days around campfires under the open sky. The snow was very high.

In Olovo, for the first time, we saw Ustasi. Because we were strong and in very large units, they did not dare attack us. The small town of Olovo we crossed in column one by one. Here for the first time we were able to buy bread with Croatian money, and the Moslems would sell these supplies.

From Vosuce we continued to Pejanovice, where we stayed the night in Serbian houses. We got some supplies, though not in great quantity. Our right wing was settled in the village in Orahovica, where our Chetniks units of the Eighth Division were attacked by partisans. We got orders to go toward Pasini Konaci, but the Eighth Division stayed to continue the fighting. We were ordered to attack Tuzla.

At Tuzla our forces had attacked (on February 4) from Zenica and other of our units from Turija and Purjacici; the Youth Regiment had been displayed in the upper and lower Brijesnica. The civilians, women and children had been also with us, though they did not take part in the fighting around Tuzla. Because the partisans had been reinforced by tank units coming from Zvornik, we were compelled to leave Tuzla without occupying it. We came back again to Pasini

Konaci. After we continued our journey through the Krivaja Valley and then the Bosna River, in the direction of Maglaj. Even before Maglaj we spent the night in a Serbian village, whose name I have forgotten, and in which among the villagers had been typhus epidemic. Here we encountered our Eighth Division's headquarters and one regiment. We were told about the typhus epidemic and were ordered to settle only in barns. The right column under Djurisic was coming from Tuzla, through the Spreca River Valley in the direction of Doboj.

From this epidemic village we moved toward Maglaj, where we arrived at night. We did not stay in the town, but continued in fighting display, because we feared that Ustasi might attack us; they had occupied this town previously. Getting out of Maglaj, we turned to the right to some Moslem villages, and here we spent the night settled in the houses. Food was given us by Moslem villagers. Ustasi from Maglaj came here to have some talks, without staying long, and without plundering; they told us that some Chetniks units had come previously and plundered.

From these villages we came to the highway linking Maglaj with Doboj, and took it in the direction of Doboj. At about 10 kilometers from Maglaj, we turned to the right, heading toward the Ozren section. We spent the night on the lower slopes of the mountain, in a Serbian village. We were very well received and supplied, because this had been a Serbian Chetnik village. The Ozren Chetniks were holding from Purjacici to Tuzla, because the partisans were fighting us, coming from Majevica. The next day we went to another Serbian village where we were better able to get supplies. In this village in Ozren we spent four days, coming in contact with the First Division of Leko Lalic, which was fighting the partisans from Tuzla to Doboj.

From here we went through the Spreca Valley along the railroad tracks Doboj-Tuzla and we went down to Doboj, crossing the bridge at the mouth of Spreca in the Bosna River. We left Doboj on our left and went along the right bank of the Bosna toward Srpska and Turska Grapska. We met other Chetniks who did not take part in the fighting at Tuzla who told us now that they had had no orders from the main headquarters to do so. From Srpska Grapska way down to Modric, even to Obduvac, we met the fighting corps of Racic, Kalabic and Keserovic. In Koprivna Village, in this area, had been the headquarters of General Draza Mihailovic. Because we were unable to settle there, we went forward about 30 kilometers to the village of Vranjak, where we stayed in houses that night. Here we encountered a great number of sick from typhus, and others who were convalescing. They looked like spectors—living cadavers wrapped only in sooty blankets; they were even barefooted.

Among our Chetniks nobody had been sick with typhus until now. We stayed in the area of Trebava about 17 days, and our men also got sick with typhus in great number; within some days the number of sick reached to nearly 4,000. Every day 10 to 15 died. Here my brother Vojislav was stricken by the epidemic. We had no medicines to fight the epidemic.

Cica (the nickname for Gen. Draza Mihailovic) invited Pavle Djurisic and the entire committee from Crna Gora, together with all regimental commanders to a meeting. There were rumors that Pavle protested that he had given the order to retreat to Bosna, because from Crna Gora we would have been able to retreat toward Greece; then there were rumors that Pavle and the entire national committee had decided to go to Slovenia, even without Cica's orders. In addition, there was talk that Draza counseled that the civilians should go back and that only the fighting men should stay. Djurisic was against this proposition and he declared that he was not able to do that, as their fate was one.

The opinion of the fighting men and the civilians was that we should at any cost proceed toward Slovenia, because the partisans had already occupied Modric, and Doboj was also endangered. Our left fighting wing which had been on the left bank of the Bosna, was defeated at Rudnik, although the partisans also suffered very great losses.

It was decided to cross the Bosna River in the area of Vucjak Mountain. There was no bridge, and the mass of people of Koprivna were forced to cross the river by rafts and crude boats. Draza and many Chetniks stayed in the area of Trebava, but the main headquarters and the sick crossed, as well as Ruzic's Fifth Division, our Youth Regiment, and the civilians.

Our regiments with Djurisic fought bloodily against the partisans on the front line Gracanica-Srnce-Tubrava, and the Chetniks units from Serbia fought on the front between Gradacac and Modric. Both received some help from Trebava's First and Second Chetnik Brigades.

In the area of Vucjak, where we crossed the river, there were

Vucjak Chetniks who were inclined, as far as we were told, to the partisans. After 4 to 5 days here, we were attacked by partisan forces. On this occasion we suffered our greatest losses since leaving Podgorica. About 800 men were either killed, wounded, or were made prisoner. The partisans in the night even reached the "ambulance" section of sick and wounded and simply cut the throats of 60 sick men.

Civilians infected with the epidemic and children were ordered to recross the Bosna River at Koprivna, where the rafts were. This was done immediately, but in reality this was a hopeless effort, because the situation was already very bad and worsening. Returning to the other bank, we stayed there two or three days looking for some means to get out of this very dangerous situation. The partisans were tightening the circle around us.

We were ordered again to cross the Bosna River to get to Vucjak. This was done because the Vranjak was taken by partisans. Among us was a real panic, and the people were eager to cross the river to get to the left bank. Officially it had been ordered that the first to be evacuated must be the sick and the civilians—women and children.

On behalf of Pavle, and even for the main headquarters as far as they told us anything definite, there had been sent messengers to Zagreb to get permission to go to Croatia and continue to Slovenia. The delegation was composed of some high-ranking army officers of the main headquarters: Branko Drljevic, Krivokapic, Dusan Pavlovic, and others. Settled in the houses in this area, we awaited the results from Zagreb.

The village in the area of Vucjak, where we were abiding at the time, had been plundered by the disloyal Vucjak Chetniks. We settled in the villages of Bozinci, Glogovci, Orahovica and Trnjani. The typhus epidemic was at its peak. The scenes were awful. A few of the sick were in the elementary schools in the villages of Trnjani and Glogovac, but the majority of them were lying in the cold under the open sky, gathered around fires. Men died en masse, so that it was very hard to bury them.

We were told the delegation had successfully done its duty in Zagreb. From here, with a special delegation, General Miodrag Damjanovic was sent to Slovenia. The order was given to prepare for moving forward; the most difficult was to evacuate the sick. Six hundred ox carts were allotted for this purpose. We also awaited the arrival of

Chetniks from Herzegovina.

Two days before our moving forward, General Mihailovic visited our fighting units. This was the best proof that there had been no misunderstanding on our going to Slovenia, and that he alone had been advising us. I personally saw him for the first time in my life arriving on horseback accompanied by six army officers also on horseback. He came to our sick unit, took off his military cap and gave the last farewell in front of some fresh graves. He stopped in front of one of our regiments and made a short speech in which he especially advised the units to be careful when crossing through Croatia and to behave kindly in Slovenia. We learned later that Cica had visited other units of ours and also made speeches.

Then all of us were ordered in the beginning of March, 1945 to proceed forward. We crossed the highway Derventa-Bosanska Samac and arrived at Zeravac Village, along the railroad from Derventa to Bosanski Brod. There we spent three days under the open skies because the Ustasi were not willing to let us enter the village; however, they gave us some supplies. We proceeded farther to the Serbian villages which had been left unburned in the vicinity of Bosanski-Brod, and there we were able to get some supplies, most without payment. Here again we were ordered to separate the sick from our units, because of the typhus epidemic. These sick were gathered at the nearby railroad station and were evacuated to Zagreb and Brod, and some elsewhere. We were told that those sick who went to Brod suffered bombardments, so their fate was uncertain. Those taken to Djakovo, or somewhere near the city, we were informed had been given great care and consideration, so that they had recovered very quickly.

Afterward we crossed a small stream and continued toward Bijela Brda in the vicinity of Derventa. At Bijela Brda we were received excellently and supplied very well. Here my brother recovered from typhus, and my father was stricken. To the left and right of us there were all our fighting units, as well as of Djurisic. The left wing occupied the line of Matajnica-Prnjavor, from where great partisan forces attacked us; the right wing was in the area of Derventa.

Now we were ordered by main headquarters to go back to the area of Vucjak. We covered 56 kilometers in speedy marching. We moved along the right bank of the Sava River, along the old road, and headed toward the Vrbas River, in the direction of Srb Village.

As there was no bridge on the Vrbas at Srb, we were compelled to cross the stream by rafts and crude boats to get to the Lijevce Polje area. There we settled in the Serbian village Gaj. We stayed about a week in Lijevce Polje, because our units needed rest after these exhausting days. In my opinion, if the march had been done immediately, we could have escaped the partisan pincers, had we not lost twenty precious days at Trebava and Vucjak.

As soon as our presence in Lijevce Polje was known, the Ustasi attacked us, among them the notorious "Devil Division" under the command of the notorious criminal Boban; this division came directly from Zagreb. All Ustasi forces were concentrated along the highway from Banja Luka to Bosanska Gradiska, which highway was lined with bunkers.

After we had left Vucjak and crossed to the Ustasi terrain nearer to Zagreb, our units divided. Dragisa Vasic, Zarije Ostojic, Lalatovic, and the entire Mlavski and Kosovski Corps with two brigades, as well as all Bacevic units, the Pljevlja Brigade, which had been with Pavle Djurisic's forces, the Priboj Chetniks, and two Sarajevo brigades left the main headquarters. It was believed that about three thousand Chetniks were left with Cica, and that he again retreated to Ozren with the Ozren Chetniks. All these units now joined Pavle Djurisic's forces under his command. With him also were Bishop Joanikije and the entire National Committee from Crna Gora, Boka and Stari Ras, which had been enlarged to comprise Herzegovina and the parts of Bosna. With us had been also the "flying Bosna"—about six hundred Chetniks.

On the other side of the Vrbas, Prnjavor was in partisan hands; beyond the Sava River were Ustasi, so that we were in a triangle whose two sides were held by Ustasi, and the third by Partisans.

At this time we received a message from the national forces in Slovenia that the forces of Vojvoda Jevdjevic and the two corps of "Dobrovoljci" were on the Kupa River and that they were waiting for us near the Croatian Karlovac; these forces had been sent from Ljubljana to aid Pavle's and our other forces. Their help had been requested by Pavle Djurisic when we were in Vucjak.

After a week of rest, the order was given to break the Ustasi lines from Banja Luka to Bosanska Gradiska. It was advised that all carts with the sick—there had been about five or six hundred sick—should be left where they had been, and the less sick should be loaded on horseback. The most sick were left in Serbian homes and the chiefs of the village should take care of them. (My father died in the village Gaj on April 3, 1945.)

Our attacks were made, as far as I remember, on April 8. The attack was at midnight on the line of Razboj-Laktasi-Ilidza. Our positions were as follows: on the highway were gathered rows of six fighters in order that the column should be forceful; the vanguard was ordered to overcome two or three bunkers on the highway, and to keep them at any cost, even of their lives, so that the other forces would be able to break the pincer. It was settled and said openly among the soldiers that they were going to certain death, and as long as someone was left alive, he should go forward. Among our ranks there was some firm belief for success in breaking the Ustasi ranks.

Exactly at twelve at night, the storming began. Above our heads there started the hellish fire from the Ustasi machine guns and explosions from mortar fire and grenades. But happily they did not foresee the direction of our move, and there were no losses on our side.

The break was not successful, because the vanguard started to talk with the Ustasi to let us continue forward. All the vanguard, in the strength of two regiments, here surrendered to the mercy of Ustasi. The commander of this vanguard was the commander of the Grahovo Chetniks, Ivan Janicic, who previously had been commander of the Sixth Regiment (I think). Half of the Second Regiment also surrendered.

Even before the first assault against the Ustasi began, there had been circling above our heads a Croatian airplane that threw some leaflets, signed by Sekula Drljevic, in which he asked us to surrender to "the Croatian army", which would receive us and supply us as their own brothers. This greatly demoralized our forces because of the incredible suffering already endured.

The next day, at ten in the morning, a great Ustasi and Home Guards force attacked our units. Among us there was a panic because of the tanks on the Ustasi sides, from which there was the hellish firing machine guns, and cannons were fighting from afar—probably from Bosanska Gradiska. At the same time partisan mortars were throwing on us a hellish fire from the other side of the Vrbas. Almost by bare hands we warded off the assaults. The units of Branko Ostojic and Pavle Djurisic destroyed three Ustasi tanks with bombs. In this battle 37 fighters from Pavle and Ostojic's ranks were killed.

In the evening of the same day, there was given the order to break the circle around us. At that time Djurisic with his assaulting battalion was placed as vanguard and they started the fighting at ten p.m. in the same line and in the same direction, as well as with the same intention as the first assault.

This night about 600 Chetniks from Herzegovina led by the Priest Perisic and Army Captain Milorad Popovic broke the encirclement. They headed toward Kozara Mountain, but three partisan brigades opposed and almost annihilated them, so from these six hundred men only six survived. (One part of these Chetniks under Priest Perisic had escaped the partisans, but in returning the Ustasi encountered them and finished the slaughter.)

We were compelled to retreat. The next day there was a lull. The third attempt to break the encirclement was prepared, but not started, because it seemed hopeless. Then there was much talk of how to go about surrendering. Meanwhile, there was a conference among the commanders and the National Committee. The opinion was almost unamimous that Pavle Djurisic should surrender us to the Ustasi authorities, but he did not consent to this. He asked only to keep a small number of fighting units and the separation was made in this order: the group of Chetniks under Vuk Kalajit, a force of about 2,500 to 3,000 fighters, turned back toward the great mountains over the Vrbas; they would try to go to Sandzak and Crna Gora. To them were given all arms, about 500 automatic weapons, as well as ammunition and supplies; the second, a group numbering about 1,000 men, surrendered to partisans by crossing the river Vrbas. We learned that all of them were killed. A group of about 1,000 men went with Djurisic, Ostojic, and Vasic and other commanders, and headed toward Banja Luka to join the Chetniks under Vranesevic in this area. The remainder of our forces, about twelve thousand men, surrendered to the Ustasi and Croatian Home Guard.

This surrender had been settled in Bosanska Gradiska, in nearby buildings and courtyards of the ex-penitentiary, which previously was the Ustasi's concentration camp during the Ustasi terror, in which thousands and thousands of Serbians had been slaughtered by Ustasi and thrown into the Sava River. There were still traces of blood and an awful stench. We remained there for five days under conditions which should not be described, and would hardly be imaginable to men of sound mind.

In the penitentiary, Sekula Drljevic, coming from Zagreb, gave us a short speech, pleading that here should be formed purely

"Crna Gora" brigades, stressing that the Croats are our brothers and would take care of us. On his advice were formed the First, Second, and Third Brigades of our forces—one of "Nikac of Rovina", the second of "Bajo Pivljanin", and the third, as far as I remember, of "Marko Miljanov".

On the fifth day we started to Zagreb on foot, in the direction of Bosanska Gradiska-Okucani. At Okucani we stayed two to three days, keeping front lines toward Ptunj and Pakrac against the partisans. Then we took the direction of Novska and Popovaca. From Popovaca we went to Dugo Selo, near Zagreb, where we were loaded on trains and went through Zagreb, crossing the Sava River southeast of Zagreb, to Velika Gorica in the area of Turopolje. There we had remained about 15 days. We settled in houses and were very well treated and abundantly supplied with food. Another part of our forces went to Jastrebarsko Village, west of Zagreb, where they were also very well treated. We learned that Djurisic's group had come back from Sanski Most, and some days after us surrendered in Bosanska Gradiska to the Croatian authorities. We learned that they also had been in Zagreb some days before Easter Day. There was talk that Savo Vuletic had guaranteed Djurisic that nothing bad would happen to him.

My group from Velika Gorica went to Zagreb on the second day of the Easter celebration, because Sisak was already in the hands of partisans and they were fighting from Turopolje east of Zagreb. On the edge of Zagreb there was fighting against the partisans. This was on May 7, 1945. We crossed toward Samobor in a speedy march. On the cross road between Zagreb and Samobor-Jastrebarsko we learned from the Croatian soldiers that Karlovac was in partisan hands, and that our Chetniks from Jastrebarsko had gone toward Celje, and generally toward Slovenia. Not listening to the "new commanders", we continued toward Somobor and then to Slovenia.

When we arrived in Samobor we were met by Bosko Agram from Niksic, who was considered now as the main commander in place of Djurisic. With pistol in hand he ordered us to go back. He detained us by force for 24 hours, which cost us very much later. From Samobor to Celje the highway was so congested that we were compelled to go on our own wherever we could. It was learned that about 150,000 Ustasi left Croatia in the same direction, not knowing to where. Our purpose was to reach Slovenia, where we expected to find our regrouped national forces. This was in vain. We were very surprised that Ljubljana was already in partisan hands. All of us headed forward, not knowing where.

Finally we arrived in Celje, where the German surrender found us—that is, the taking of the German military forces in this area. In Celje we found a great number of our men. Here I did not remain long, but with my brother and sister continued to Dravograd, and then through Udine-Trevise, Fodia-Rimini-Ancona-Bari-Toronto until we reached Eboli, in Italy.

In Italy I had found very few of our men. Later, from the fellows who managed to escape, I learned about the disastrous fate of those who had escaped to Klagenfurt and were handed by the Allied military forces to Tito's partisans. They had been slaughtered in thousands at Jasenice, Kamnik, Kocevje, and other places in Slovenia.

That is the end of the account by Nedovic. Pavle Djurisic and other officers who surrendered with him were burned alive by Ustasi at Velika Gradiska.

A wooden cottage typical of Bosnia and parts of Serbia.

CHAPTER THIRTEEN: TRYING TO AVOID
BEING SENT TO THE REDS

About the end of May and in the first days of June, 1947, our transfer began from Eboli in Italy to Germany. Our train from Salerno moved toward Naples and Rome, then to Bologna, Mantova, Bari, and Salzburg in Austria. In Salzburg our train stopped very long, so that we had opportunity to get out. In a group I encountered many friends, among them old professor Milos Zecevic. He seemed weak, and I wondered why he waited for us so long in the night to come to the station. "I learned that our men were coming from Italy", he said, "and I wanted to see some of my friends and greet them. This is the only joy left to us these days."

Leaving Salzburg about midnight, our train continued to Germany, until we arrived at a great camp. The train stopped on the rails between many barracks. Immediately we were surrounded by English soldiers, who gathered us in a space, watching attentively that nobody escaped. After we were regrouped, guarded from all sides, they took us to some barracks to the west. In front of the gate there were other English soldiers, who again counted us, opened the gate and let us in.

Surrounded by barbed wire, to which we had been accustomed since 1941, we again found our men from Eboli. Even these new barracks were similar to those in Eboli, having the shape of elongated barrels of steel. Now we knew the name of this camp—the notorious Munster Camp in Eastern Westphalia.

About the end of July and the beginning of August, 1947, there began the notorious Maclean Commission, whose duty it was to investigate each individual in the Münster Camp, in order to separate those guilty of "war crimes". The men went in groups to the investigations, accompanied by English soldiers. Then came my turn. The English soldiers took us to a corridor and with gestures pointed where one should enter the office. Inside there was seated a middle-aged man in civilian clothes, rather skinny, with a thin mustache turned upwards and a little bit askew, clinging to the cheeks, similar to that of Kaiser Wilhelm II. This "investigator" spoke Serbian perfectly, but one could conclude that he was an Englishman by the brevity of his questions. After the generalities, he asked me where I had been during the war. I started to tell him all from March 27, 1941, the demonstration in Krusevac, joining our front line on the border, coming to my war unit on April 1, 1941, fighting against Fascists in Vrmusa in northern Albania, coming back, the defeating of our armies, becoming a war prisoner, taken by the Gestapo and deported to Germany. I showed him my war prisoner number on a metal plate, which I keep as a souvenir. When the "investigator" saw it, he told me: "You could have bought this."

"It is true that I could have bought this, but I did not; that would have been dishonest and I have never done anything dishonest in my life," I answered him almost in fury. I added: "In 1943 under this number, I was registered by the German camp authorities and declared to the Red Cross in Geneva. This I could officially verify." The "investigator" looked down his nose, thanked me and told me that I could go.

When I returned to the camp, I told my fellows what had happened. Many concluded, by my description of the investigator, that this had been Fitzroy Maclean. We knew that this British officer had been with the Communist partisans in the last years of the war, and that he personally had greatly helped the Communists come to power. Nevertheless, I did not expect what I experienced shortly afterward.

About the end of August, 1947, the investigations ended. Waiting for the results of the commission, many fellows tried to escape, either by cutting barbed wires, as we had done in different war prisoner camps, or in other ways. In the soldiers' camp there were many such attempts. From this, the officer's camp, we personally watched the escaping of Savo Radovic, from Cetinje. He escaped very skillfully. It looked as if he had very quickly finished his investigation, went out of the barracks where the investigation had been done, and unnoticed, started to walk peacefully in the opposite direction. Some of us watched him as he disappeared into a depression behind the offices. The next day we learned he was not among us anymore: he escaped.

On September 2, the news spread that on this day would be the separation of "criminals" to turn them over to Josip Broz Tito. I was mustered in the second group in the right wing. In front there was a large group of English soldiers facing us. The first from our ranks was loudly called forth: "Army Major Zivojin Mladenovic." We stretched our heads to the left, but the man did not appear quickly. Nevertheless, he finally appeared from some rear rank, very possibly in the third group.

As Mladenovic was moving toward the English soldiers, he bent his head, shaking and raising his hands in dispair. I was acquainted with him from Eboli; he had belonged to the Dinara Chetnik Division. He seemed more comic than tragic; I was almost about to laugh, when it was called: "Professor Milija Lasic." I left my line in wooden sandals and headed forward. I noticed my cousin, Dragutin Lasic, and told him to quickly hand me my shoes so that I would not go barefoot to Belgrade. Behind me came Milos Pavicevic, before the war a staff army major and in Eboli commander of the Zeta Regiment. Others were called, but I did not pay any attention; the most urgent thing for me was to get my shoes, and I was steadily looking for Dragutin. The group of those who were called was growing. When there were about sixty of us, the English soldiers quickly shoved us to the gate on the other side of the barbed wire, because they were fearing some disorder; other English soldiers guarded us on the other side. The others were called by groups, and they then separated them and joined them with us, so that we were moving little by little closer to the fence of barbed wire.

Many of our fellows were looking at us with eyes filled with tears. There I noticed Golub Butric, a teacher and army major in reserve, from Berane; he was almost crying. I told him: "Why are you sniveling there, stupid man! Find Dragutin immediately and tell him to bring me my shoes very quickly; he knows where they are." Within seconds, both of them brought my shoes and threw them over the barbed wire. I told Dragutin to take my belongings and to watch my trunk very carefully, as it contained my manuscript. I put my shoes on, and tightly laced them.

When the last of us "war criminals" had been taken out of the camp, the English guards were increased. We learned there were 142 men to be handed over to the Communists in Belgrade. The English guards were arranged on both sides of us, and behind; it looked as though the guards outnumbered us. We headed to the north side of camp, and stopped in front of a small camp, on which there was written "Y". The special guards opened the gate, carefully counting us many times and let us in. It was about two in the afternoon. It was very hot but the sky was serene.

There was a general sense of frustration among us. Many thought that even tonight we would be transported to Yugoslavia. I did not believe this: I preferred to believe that even this separation of "war criminals" would turn out to be some new English comedy. Anyhow, the men started to settle in the barracks. There were 33 Chetniks, mostly high officers. There were also many State Guards and "Zbor-asi" or Nazi followers. I settled in a room with Army Major Vlado Djukic and Army General Svetomir Djukic.

That night the General and the Army Major discussed our fate. I was very tired, and went to bed, turning my head toward the wall and going immediately to sleep. In the morning when I awoke, about 7:00 a.m., I saw that the General and the Major were still awake in their beds, and I shouted to them: "Are you still here? I thought you were about to go to Belgrade, and had left me here all alone! That would not have been kind!"

General Djukic stretched himself, sat on the bed, and said: "You Vlado, did not sleep all night through, while this, God bless him, Lasic, did not even turn in his bed!"

The Major answered him: "With that light shining all night in the windows, it has been hard to sleep. But how did you know, General?"

The General replied: "You know Vlado, I did not shut my eyes all night through, but I have been silent not to wake anyone."

The men were living almost in constant fear. The bringing in of the priest Prostan, Dusan Dzakovic and some other fellows from family camps brought still more frustration to the souls of individual men. We learned that General Damjanovic, whom the English had confined in a single house out of the camp, had been handed to the Communists with us and was to be transferred to Belgrade. The counting of us twice a day continued.

The fear of being delivered to the Communists did not diminish, especially among the "Zborasi". Ratko Parezanin was the first among them; he got sick to his stomach and went to the infirmary. Some Chetniks with Lieutenant Colonel Radovanovic and Marko Cucuz found a better escape. These 10 profitted from the slumbering of the English watchmen, way up in the tower (inherited from the late Hitler), and one by one they slipped underneath the barbed wire, just beneath the watchman, and disappeared into darkness and hard rain. Many others were studying plans to escape. In addition they let free "19 Petrovics", among them the notorious Marisav Petrovic, involved in the great tragedy in Kragujevac, where more than eight thousand students and teachers were massacred by the German occupational force in 1941.

Soon we were visited by the local English commander in this area. He gave us great hope that we would not be handed over to the Communist government in Belgrade. He declared to us that in this case he would never be an officer in the English forces; in addition, he told us that he would have the opportunity to open for us the gates to the camp, and let us scatter.

So the "Y" camp became less frustrated. We organized two English courses. I was the teacher for the beginners, and for the advanced courses was an English Army Major, who was the head of the guards in the camp. I gave lessons every morning for two hours to the beginners. In the advanced course I was also a student. There we had the opportunity to ask questions of the English Major, which sometimes had no connection with "grammar". We asked him why the English were victims of Communist propaganda, and why they betrayed their most faithful allies from two world wars. The Major was silent. . . . Others asked him why Ireland stayed neutral during the Second World War. The Major started to laugh and told us that millions of Irishmen took part in the struggle against the Axis powers. Probably he was thinking of the Irish-Americans!

As the days were running away, our friends came to visit us. These visits could have been more frequent, except that the English emptied the camp at Munster. For a long while we did not know where this mass of people had been transported.

The most important visit, however, had been the coming of a special envoy, Mr. Bevan, from the English minister of foreign affairs. He had been appointed with the personal right to free any one of us. This envoy arrived at the "Y" camp in the first days of December, 1947, and immediately started to make individual investigations every day in the morning and afternoon. We learned that for many years he had been English Consul in Zagreb, and that he spoke Serbo-Croatian fluently, which was very welcome to us.

One day, my name was on the list of investigation for the afternoon. The second on the list, after me, was an Army Major, Cedomir Milic, from the State Guard, whom I had not previously known. Major Milic approached me and asked me to go somewhat apart from the others. When we were separated enough, he addressed me with the following words: "Mr. Lasic, I have a document and I do not know if I should show it to this Englishman. I would like you to give me advice on this point."

"Very well Major, I would like to see the document, and then I will give you my opinion," I told him. Major Milic displayed a sheet of paper in the form of a postcard. There was written with a type-writer the following: "I ordered captain of the first class Cedomir

Milic to immediately *join the ranks of the state guards*." After that there had been made a underline and it continued: "I order all of our regular Yugoslav army units in the country, that they should give help to Cedomir Milic, first class captain, and to help him in any case of emergency." It was signed: "Colonel Dragoljub Mihailovic."

When I read this, keeping the paper in my hand, I told him: "Major, you should show this to this Englishman, keeping it in your hand, and let the Consul read it. Then you should ask him if he understood this well. When he tells you that he has understood all, in front of him you should fold this paper and keep it as a precious document in your wallet." Milic and I did not talk anymore of his role as an agent of Mihailovic in the German-controlled State Guards.

Soon my turn came. I entered the office and sat on the chair shown me. The Consul asked me immediately: "In what relationship have you been with the late George Lasic?" I told him that he had been my younger brother. Then the Consul continued: "In what relationship was your brother George and Pavle Djurisic?" Immediately, without any reflection, I told him: "Their mutual relationship was very good. You know, sir, we had been in the struggle against the occupiers of our country and against the Communists as well. This meant we had the same purposes and goals. This purpose was mutual for the late George and Pavle." After that, the Consul got up, stretched his hand and finished: "Thank you very much, Mr. Lasic."

After this "investigation" I went out and stayed nearby to wait for Milic. I did not wait long. As soon as he got out, we went somewhat aside and he told me: "I did exactly what we had discussed before: I showed the Consul Draza Mihailovic's order from 1941, which he read from my hand and told me he thoroughly understood and personally recognized the signature of Mihailovic. Then we exchanged greetings and I was allowed to leave.

For the results of this new investigation, we did not wait long. On December 12, 1947, a list was placed on the bulletin board. On this list I found my name, as well as the name of Major Milic. There were 38 men on this occasion who were investigated and freed.

The evacuation of us who were freed was done very quickly. I entered my previous room and found Major Djukic. He looked frustrated. He told me that this was the final decision—all those who had been left in "Y" camp would be handed over to the Communists. He complained that he had no tools to cut the barbed wire. I convinced him that I would provide this within a week. When we parted, we hugged each other with tears filling our eyes. He tried to help me to carry my belongings to the gate, but I would not allow him to do that. By the way I met the General, who was also very much frustrated. We greeted each other with the wishes that all our fellows would soon be free. I had no time to greet other fellows and take leave of them, except those who were near the gate. Finally the gate opened wide, and we 38 left "Y" camp, with the heavy impression that more than 70 of our Serbian brothers could soon be delivered to the hangman's noose in Belgrade.

On leaving the camp, we got official papers that we had been freed without guilt. In addition they gave us tickets to travel to the localities assigned. I had been assigned to the camp of Bohalt and took the train to the camp. On the train I was worried about being able to come back to Vlado Djukic with tools for cutting the barbed wire. In Bohalt some of us arrived in the morning. There I found that our fellows greeted us with joy. Here I found many of our acquaintances, among them two professors from Zendgwarden—Radenko Gordic and Nektarije Marinkovic—and Army major Mijuskovic.

I did not lose any time. I immediately got in touch with army Major in Reserve Golub Butric and confided my purpose to find scissors to cut the barbed wire. Together we went to the city of Bohalt, brought a large scissors for this purpose, and wrapped it in papers tied with cloth. When we came back to our camp, we started to gather some cigarettes that I should bring to the "Y" camp. The other two fellows began to get some supplies for the fellows there. Both of us, Butric and I, were doing this to mask my return to the camp to visit Vlado Djukic. Within three days all was ready for this purpose. We found a long box, made from carton, which was handy to pack the scissors in. Two other fellows and I went to the railroad station nearby, and on December 18, we again were near "Y" camp. On the way from the railroad station heading to the camp, I took the scissors from the box and put them in the pocket of my trousers, underneath my military overcoat. The scissors almost reached to my shoulder, and I feared the sentinels would notice when we went in the gate. We three stood in front of the gate and gave signs that we wished to be allowed in. The English sergeant went to the army major; the army major appeared at the window of his office, and greeted us with waving hands. The sergeant went forward to open the gate. There had been great change in getting visits in the "Y" camp for all concerned these last days: visitors should wait in a room by the guard. The English sergeant explained this to us, and addressed me personally: "You specifically can go wherever you want!"

I disappeared between the barbed wire and my previous barracks and I speeded my pace. When I came in front of the room, I knocked at the door and entered without waiting for a reply. Fortunately I found Army Major Djukic alone. Even before our greeting I pulled the scissors from my pocket under the military overcoat, unwrapped them, and hid them under Vlado's bed. Then we embraced and I told him: "Major, I fulfilled my promise! I wish you very much luck and success in cutting the barbed wire . . ." We went out together to greet some of the other fellows. We found even General Djukic. We hugged each other in greeting. They had been delighted that I did not forget them. I apologized that this visit was only to bring some cigarettes and tobacco to Vlado. The time of visit was ended, and many fellows accompanied me to the gate. On the way many fellows told me that this was our last meeting: "We will be surely delivered to the slaughterers in Belgrade." With little conviction, I repeated my opinion which I had when we came together to the "Y" camp. The gate opened and we three from the Bohalt camp found ourselves on the other side of barbed wire. We immediately headed toward the railroad station. From my heart a heavy burden had fallen—maybe I had done a good deed and had succeeded in easing the escape from out of "Y" camp for a group of fighters for freedom and martyrs of my people.

I spent the next three and a half years first in a displaced persons camp and then working in the supply section for the military government in the French Zone of occupied Germany. But I still sought a new permanent country of residence.

CHAPTER FOURTEEN: HEADING FOR AMERICA

In Germany I filled out forms to emmigrate to either France or the United States of America. It looked as if the French had assigned me to emmigrate to the U.S.A., and very soon I was summoned by the American consulate in Baden-Baden. I got a leave of absence and went there.

Exactly at 10:00 a.m., I entered the office of the American Consul. As soon as I entered and was offered a chair, the Consul asked in which language he should talk, and he began: "You know, Mr. Lasic, in your document there is nothing to prevent your emmigrating to the United States of America; the only thing not clear for us is that you were treated as a private, while your position in civil life would correspond to the rank of an officer in the army." To this question I smiled and answered: "Sir. . . in the First World War I was a volunteer and this, by the law of my country, was recognized after the war as having been my stint in the army. Accordingly, I was enrolled in the Yugoslavian Army as a private and took part in war from the first days of mobilization on March 28, 1941, to the end of the war as a private." After this the Consul handed me a list of many organizations which had been active during the war in Yugoslavia. There had been the Ustasi, "Zbor", and many organizations under initial letters or in full. This angered me and, rather violently, I rejected this list, so that the Consul was compelled to catch it. The Consul only smiled, while I added: "Sir, I am not acquainted with any of these organizations, I had heard some existed, but for the most on the list I do not even know what these initials mean. I can tell you only that I belonged to the Army under the command of Draza Mihailovic, who fought on the side of our allies for four full years. But all these other organizations were real rabble serving the occupiers of Yugoslavia. Even the Communists, as you called them "partisans", have been the traitors of our country, because, indirectly, they helped Fascists and Nazis to disrupt our fighting forces. With this rabble I never had any connection." The American Consul looked straight into my eyes and, visibly satisfied, stood up and very cordially shook my hand, and accompanied me to the door, saying: "Your case will be decided very soon and before long you will go to a medical examination in Rastatt."

In July I went again to Rastatt to get the medical examinations and other formalities for emmigration to the United States. I took leave of my French friends and thanked them that my countrymen and I had been treated so well. In Rastatt, however, it did not go smoothly. First, one German physician rejected me on the examination. I would have to wait for the examination of the American doctor, who fortunately sent me for a detailed examination to a nearby sanitorium. There I was more fortunate. The German head of the sanitorium, a specialist in tuberculosis, ordered an X-ray for my lungs. With the new X-ray examination, I went back to Rastatt. I did not know the result of this new examination because the head of the sanitorium did not tell me, but the American physician told me that the results had been all right. The German expert had said: "There has not in the least been any findings of tuberculosis, earlier or today, in the man in question." This fact gave me reason to suspect the fairness of the previous German doctor, of whom had been said that he used to be bribed, and I was convinced of the fairness of the German doctor in the sanitorium.

After the physical examination, it had been left with the American Consul in Rastatt. When it came my turn, according to the list of names, I went in. This was a tall, gaunt, young man. His secretary, Miss Maric, spoke fluently in Serbian and English. Finishing the generalities, the Consul started to question me about the situation in Yugoslavia in the beginning of the war. Not waiting for the translation on the part of Miss Maric, with my own words I answered him in English about our continuation of the fighting against the occupiers of our country, and the fight of Draza Mihailovic, telling him that we fought for a full four years during the war on the part of our Allies—French, Englishmen and Americans, and for the same ideals and goals. When the Consul asked me what I thought about Tito, I asked Miss Maric to translate my words, word for word as follows: "You are helping Tito now and the whole Communistic rubble in Yugoslavia, while I, from my own experience, know that the Communists are plain traitors of our country, and that they helped during the occupation mostly our common foes during the last war. Josip Broz-Tito, together with the entire rabble now in power in Belgrade, does not fight for the interest of Yugoslavia, and in the end he will betray also the United States of America."

While Miss Maric was translating my words, the Consul did not look at me straight in the eye anymore, but started to look down and began to write something on a sheet of paper that was in front of him. This last examination had been done, and now it was necessary only to look on the list to read my name. Unfortunately, there were some persons who were rejected. One man was rejected on the doctors' examination, while his wife and his small son had passed the examination.

From Rastatt the evacuation of displaced persons was gradually begun. First we started to pack heavy belongings (those of us who had any), to be transported to the transit camp near Bremerhaven. The hand luggage we would take with us. At the end of August 1951, I was assigned to travel with a group for the transit camp. With me were a small number of Serbians, mostly married to German women, or with wives of other nationalities. In the transit camp I found many Serbians and some Slovenes. Evacuation had been very slow—each group would wait for the coming of some American ship, according to the list.

There was also a special order of life in the transit camp; bachelors were living separately, while the married had special buildings to live in. I was assigned to a large building in which were mostly living Poles; I was only living with Polish people, and I started to "Mov po Polski", as far as I was able to talk. It is important to stress that if one Slav gets into contact with any Slavonic group of people, immediately he is able to communicate. I also found many Serbians scattered in other rooms. The grouping by ethnic groups took place between these buildings, in walking or in the common mess hall. In this way we waited for our ship.

Even in this camp, I began to give a course in English for our Serbians. I gave lessons in the morning and in the afternoon in a classroom at the end of the camp. Every day there were 18 to 30 students. I taught them the most basic things which I prepared in advance and verified myself. It was interesting, and heartbreaking, to see the men suffering to pronounce and learn the most basic words and expressions. In the next lesson, I would repeat and ask them to express this or what they had learned. But even this repetition was not easy, because the men could not learn it. Here I felt how we language professors had been lucky when we gave lessons to the young men who very quickly understood and retained.

After the lesson in the morning or in the afternoon, I had to cross all the camp. Somewhat to my right when I was heading to the building where I stayed, I saw the men issuing from a large building where movies were shown. I never got to this building, but one day in front of this movie, I asked some men what they had seen inside.

One of them was eager to explain to me: "Sir, you know the German lady, in the German language, very kindly explained to us how we should move in the streets in America, where to cross to the other side of the street and many other useful explanations. One thing is of great importance for all of us who are intending to go to the United States, and this is that the Americans at the entrance to their country should put a beam of rays on every individual, and they could without rummaging us see even the smallest needle and not only the things of greater value. You should go there yourself to see these wonders!"

Gradually the evacuation of this mass of homeless people out of this camp took place. Many of my friends, Serbians, and some Slovenes, had been evacuated to Bremerhaven some days before me. Finally came my turn. My preparation was easy, except that I was unable to find one of my younger countrymen, Dr. Miljkovic, to whom I had loaned a book. I looked in vain for him everywhere. Meanwhile, he had come in my room and left the book under my pillow. Not suspecting anything, I put the book in my suitcase and I went to try to sleep. In the morning on September 28, 1951, we started to be moved according to plan. Our travel to Bremerhaven did not last very long. When we got out of the train, we prepared to undergo the customs checking, the last on the German territory. At my turn, I opened my hand luggage wide and handed it to the customs officers. The customs officer immediately opened the book I had gotten last night and hurriedly put in my bag. To my great surprise, and to the surprise of the customs officer, inside were 2,500 Nedic's dinars, some French francs and one ruble! I told the customs officer that I was unaware who had put this money in my book. This customs officer started to look at these bills and said: "All this is now of no value!" In his presence I tore up the money and put it into a wastepaper basket, and I continued to show him the other things.

We headed for the ship. I tried to read what her name was— "General Turgis". On this ship were loaded about 2,000 displaced persons. We were settled in large rooms in bunk beds. I was assigned to the room near the bottom of the ship. The organization on the ship was perfect from every point of view, as was the food. The children were given special foods and separate rooms. We adults got three meals a day and this by groups, because the dining rooms were not able to receive all at once. In addition, there was a plan for the work on the ship, every person having some job. I was assigned as an aide in the infirmary.

The ship "General Turgis" advanced through the ocean. In the first hours, while we were crossing the English Channel, we were still able to look at the English coast. The following days we could watch only the huge waves around us, so that the ship which in Bremerhaven looked very large now looked like a small bark striving against the waves. Although I did not get seasick, many did.

When the weather was beautiful and when the wind was not blowing, which was very seldom, I strolled on the deck with my countrymen. One day, a fellow of mine—a tall giant—confided to me that he had with him five dollars. When he had been in Germany a relative of his had sent him twenty dollars, of which he had spent fifteen, and five dollars was left. He was undecided what to do with the five dollars. I consoled him that he could use them as soon as we landed on the American shores. But he was frightened by the "unknown rays" about which the German frauline had been talking when they had been in transit camp. I told him that this German lady wished to frighten our men not to take valuable things from Germany, and that we could have American money on us as far as the German customs officer had not taken from each of us in Bremerhaven. My countryman, however, continued to be worried about his five dollars and often started to talk about it. One day, when we were standing at the rail on the deck, I told him: "Listen to me, man, fold this five dollars tightly and throw it into the ocean; there is enough space and depth to get rid of it. Otherwise if you start anymore to bother me about what to do with your money, I will ask all of my countrymen to help me and we shall throw you overboard, even though you are a big tall man, and throw you into the ocean together with your money to be free of you and your five dollars." Never again did we talk of this five dollars.

Our ship was nearing her destination. We learned that we would land in New Orleans, not in New York, and this meant that we would travel longer than we thought. One day, I think on November 9, our ship started to cross by some islands of which one was rather long; we concluded this was Cuba. The weather was very beatiful and all of us were delighted standing on the decks. Finally we entered the Mississippi River, whose waters were choppy and filled with large fish, which were more numerous than in the ocean.

The "General Turgis" reached New Orleans rather early on

October 10, 1951. However, we spent the night on the ship, because of the checking of our papers. During the night, after the name calling, we entered the office where they gave us our papers. All this was already prepared; nevertheless the clerk started to check over all papers again, and gave us information on how to keep them and handed them out to us.

The next day, about 10:00 a.m., we started to descend from the ship and landed on the soil of this great country, with the great hopes that were with us. With our first steps we were greeted by a fine gentleman, who told us that he was a "Yugoslav Consul" here, which looked to me somewhat suspicious, taking into account our experience in Germany. This gentleman understood us very well, and pulled out his visitor's card on which was printed on the left side at the top a Yugoslav coat of arms; in the middle was "Basile J. Rusovic, Royal Yugoslav Consul". No doubt, this was a man who had stayed loyal to our country. We thanked Mr. Rusovic very gladly, and learned that he was challenging, even by his title, all those responsible for putting Yugoslavia under the yoke of the Communists.

The true "Yugoslav Consul" led us Serbians to the customs house, and left us there to make other necessary steps connected with us. The customs house really was a large hall. To the right of us there had been set tables loaded with cakes, pies, and big cups for coffee and big pots of boiled coffee. Some ladies of the Red Cross offered us cake and coffee.

When we were served and refeshed, we went to the other part of this hall. There we were met kindly by some uniformed officials; we saw that these were the American customs officers. They indicated that they were to see our belongings. We tried to open our hand luggage and small trunks, but they started to mumble something, and then turned over our belongings, writing on them "O.K.". With my "knowledge" of English, I saw that this meant: "all is all right", and this I explained to my countrymen. We told the customs officer we had some other belongings. They led us to a large pile of trunks, from which we took our belongings piled there during the night. As soon as we found our trunks, the customs officer would turn it to the other side and put on the famous "O.K.". None of the customs officers allowed us to open our belongings. When we later regrouped with our belongings, I told my countrymen that we could have packed an elephant or a jackass and they also would have been welcomed to the United States and stamped "O.K.". To that of my countryman with his five dollars, I said: "It would have served you right if we had thrown you in the ocean, because you had been frightened by this German fräulein, who filled your head with 'beams of rays' before you came to America!"

About this checking of our luggage, we started to make jokes. I explained to them that in the Serbian language elephant means stupid—you are stupid as an elephant; the word jackass in our language means not intelligent—not intelligent as a jackass. Other meanings are for the Americans. The word elephant means strong—as for example strong as an elephant; while the word jackass means enduring—as for example enduring as a jackass; so, if we were elephants or jackasses, we would be welcome to the United States. This came from the fact that the Americans were divided into two political parties, Republicans and Democrats. Symbollically, the first is represented by an elephant and the other by a jackass. According to this, in every case, we were welcome to this great country!

Our "Royal Yugoslav Consul" again gathered us Serbians around him. He gave us tickets for the Greyhound bus from New Orleans to Chicago, or to some other locality. In addition, we got some dollar bills for the fares from here to the place of our destination. Those who would go to Chicago got $27.00 each. From the customs office we went in groups to a large restaurant where we were to wait for our bus to take us to Chicago. Refreshed, supplied with tickets to pay for the bus, and with dollars, we loaded onto the bus rather early in the afternoon.

We were travelling to different localities, but we were not able to orient ourselves. In fact this was not necessary, because the driver knew where he was taking us. We were thus more interested in getting something to drink in the bus stations, where we stopped. We would ask the driver how long we would stay. In one of these cafeterias we asked for a piece of pie and a coffee. The waiter immediately served us, giving us containers of cream for the coffee. This time there was a problem among us how to open the pitcher! Luckily in the cafeteria there were other guests and I watched one of them pouring the cream into this coffee; I watched him as he opened the cover, pulling it towards him to open the spout. As though I had known that already, I pulled the lever toward me. Very quickly among us, this problem had been solved!

Watching on the next bus stops, I was gradually getting into the customs of the people without any difficulties. One felt that there was no cold attitude to which we had been accustomed in Germany. The people here are eager to help you, to teach you even by gestures if one could not explain by words. Our traveling was long lasting and the fatigue and the not sleeping was bothersome. However, all of us were more glad than ever before; already one could feel that we were living under normal conditions of life. During October 13, we learned that we were not far from Chicago. The driver of the bus had been changed many times, and we continued forward. Somewhat about midnight, the bus began circling a large body of water. We supposed that this was Lake Michigan. Finally, we crossed some large streets and very soon stopped in front of a tall building—the Raleigh Hotel. Immediately we got rooms to sleep, two fellows in one room, not to pay too much. Our rooms we paid in advance. A special clerk from Serbian National Defense was at hand to explain to us what was necessary to know; he offered us loans if anybody needed it.

So on October 14, 1951, our long journey had ended. New life had been opened to us, which surely would be better than the sufferings which we had left behind, forever.

ENEMIES ON ALL SIDES

APPENDICES

EDITOR'S NOTE: With the exception of certain maps and illustrations, the remainder of this volume, in six appendices and a map supplement, is extracted from *Jugoslavia*, "B.R. 493A (Restricted) Geographical Handbook Series for Official Use only," which was published in October of 1944 by the British Naval Intelligence Division. These appendices therefore reflect the views of that time of British Intelligence, and are not to be taken as necessarily being the views of the author of this book.

ETHNIC MAP   BASED ON LANGUAGE USE
IN THE 1930s

EUROPE PRIOR TO WORLD WAR ONE

EUROPE PRIOR TO WORLD WAR TWO

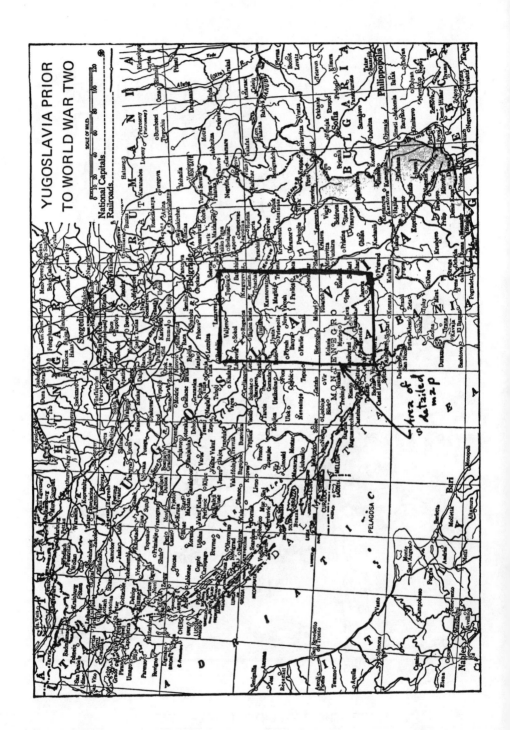

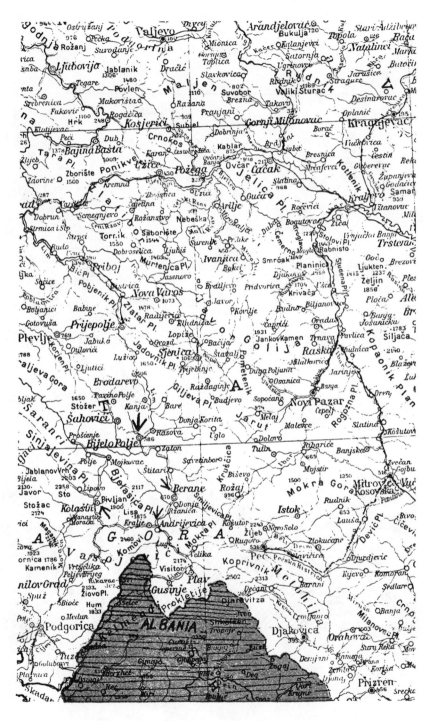

DETAILED MAP OF AREA OF MONTENEGRO AND SERBIA

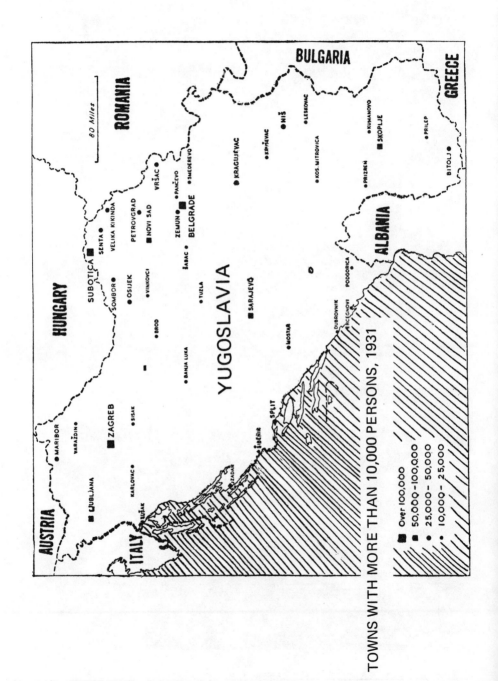

TOWNS WITH MORE THAN 10,000 PERSONS, 1931

Over 100,000
50,000-100,000
25,000- 50,000
10,000- 25,000

APPENDIX ONE: Origin of the Southern Slavs (Yugoslavs)

Comparatively little is known of the peoples occupying the territory now included within Jugoslavia before the coming of the Slavs. It is clear, however, that already in these regions there was a considerable population of varied origins whose history extends back at least a thousand years before the main Slav infiltrations took place.

That the area was peopled even at the time of the early Iron Age (Hallstatt period), long before the dawn of history, is attested in many localities by archaeological remains, but the first historical references to the descendants of these ancient peoples are those made by the ancient Greeks, who, about the fifth century B.C., referred collectively to the various tribes inhabiting the western and central Balkan peninsula as the Illyrians and Thracians. As far as Jugoslav territory is concerned, the Illyrians occupied the area west of the Vardar and north of Epirus (i.e. mainly the lands that physically have been described as the Dinaric region). The Thracians occupied the area to the east of this, including the territory that in later history was to become Serbia.

The characteristics and mode of life of these peoples are obscure, but it is thought that of the two, the Illyrians were the later comers who drove the Thracians eastward into the central Balkan regions.

Along the seaboard, the movement of Greek colonization brought settlers in the seventh and sixth centuries B.C.; while, in the north, the migrations of the so-called 'Celtic' peoples at the beginning of the fourth century greatly affected the whole area between the Danube and the Adriatic. It was not until well on into the third century that Roman influence began to be important in the area. Pirates from the Illyrian coasts interfered with the commerce of the Adriatic, and the result was two Roman expeditions in 229 and 219 B.C. By this time, the Illyrian tribes had formed a kingdom with its capital at Skodra (Scutari, Skadar) in Albania; and during the next two centuries, especially after 168, there were intermittent Roman expeditions demanding tribute. In A.D. 9, the whole area was finally annexed and incorporated by Tiberius as part of the Roman empire under the name of 'Illyricum'. The term, however, was used in widely different senses, and places as far apart as Vienna and Athens formed part of an 'Illyricum' at different times.

By some authorities the modern Albanians are thought to represent the only relic of the ancient Illyrian population that has survived to the present day.

Over a period from about 770–550 B.C. the coastlands and islands of the eastern Adriatic were influenced by the spread of Greek trading colonies. These were most frequent in the central coastal districts where there were important colonies at Vis (Issa), Korčula (Korkyra nigra), Hvar (Pharos), Trogir (Tragurion) and Split (Salona). The Greek colonization was, however, never very strongly felt and it had little influence on the life of the peoples inland.

At about the same time, at the beginning of the fourth century B.C., there was a marked infiltration in the north and north-west, in Illyria, of the so-called 'Celtic' peoples from central Europe. Though these peoples have left a record of their influences in the place names of Dalmatia and elsewhere, they represent a strain in the population that was quickly assimilated by the Illyrians.

The influence of the growing Roman empire to the west began to be felt in the third century B.C. ··· From then onwards, the Romans made a number of expeditions into the area, but they did not finally annex it until A.D. 9. Of the varied lands that constitute present-day Jugoslavia, only that coinciding with the northern and central parts of the Bačka remained unsubdued, outside the Roman frontier. Culturally, the Roman influence was of the greatest importance. Commerce and industry flourished, and the indigenous population was largely Romanized, while Roman roads were built widely across the country from the coasts inland. The Illyrian peoples of the western Balkans, especially, became an important source of man-power for the Roman legions, while more than one emperor came from humble Illyrian stock. The massive remains of the great palace of Diocletian which still front the sea at Split harbour are a reminder of this fact. Widespread and considerable though these cultural influences were, the composition of the indigenous population can hardly have been affected, for the Roman officials and merchants settled mainly in the towns and in the mining centres, and they cannot have been numerous relative to the rest of the population.

The fifth century A.D. brought great changes, for the invasions associated with the break-up of the Roman empire greatly affected Illyria. Visigoths, Huns, Ostrogoths and Avars, together with many lesser groups, passed through the area or raided into it. They disturbed the existing population and may themselves have contributed 'pockets' of people and some ethnic strains, but they certainly did not settle in any large numbers. At the end of the fifth century A.D. the western Balkan peoples seem substantially to have been what they were in the fourth century B.C., except that culturally they had fallen under the civilizing influence of Rome.

THE COMING OF THE SLAVS

All this was changed in the latter part of the sixth and the first half of the seventh centuries. To the north, the Slav peoples were expanding in all directions from their homeland around the Pripet marshes. They seem to have been driven southwards by the Avars centred in the plain of Hungary, and this widespread movement had a great effect upon the population of the Balkans. By A.D. 650, the newcomers were in full occupation of the western Balkans, and they spread southwards, even to the Peloponnese. It is impossible to estimate what was the proportion of the Slav newcomers to the indigenous population, but, at any rate, the newcomers proved dominant, and assimilated the other peoples to their own language. So widespread were the Slav settlements that much of the Balkan lands, including mainland Greece, became known by the eighth century as Sclavinia.

There were three exceptions to the assimilation. In the cities of the coastlands, the Latin civilization was maintained, and here the pre-Slav elements continued in strength, and Illyria became a 'Slavonic land with a Latin fringe', although succeeding centuries were greatly to increase the purely Slav element within the fringe itself. A second exception to assimilation was formed by the scattered and transhumant remnants of the Roman provincials who preserved a separate identity here and there in the interior. They were known as 'Mavrovlachs' or 'Morlachs'; there was a 'Major Vlachia' in the region where the frontiers of Bosnia, Dalmatia and Croatia meet, and a 'Minor Vlachia' as far north as Požega between the Sava and the Drava, while northern Dalmatia and Croatia were known as 'Morlacchia' in the eighteenth century · · · One of the regions of Serbia is still known as 'Stari Vlah', i.e. Old Wallachia. Although they managed to maintain their separate character for a long time, all these remnants were destined to become completely Slavonicized. Finally, in the south, there were some tribes who had escaped Romanization and now, too, they escaped Slavonicization, and so became the Albanians of later times.

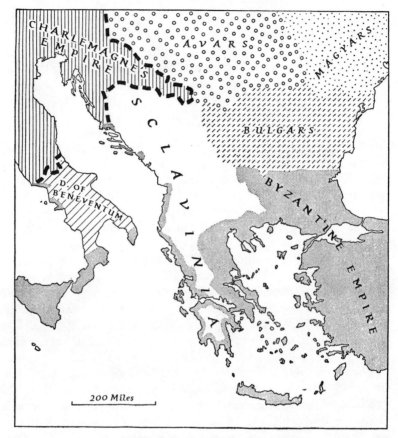

The Balkan peninsula about A.D. 800

Based on R. L. Poole, *Historical Atlas of Modern Europe*, plate 4 (Oxford, 1902). This map shows dominant political groupings rather than ethnic distributions; thus Slavs were also to be found in the areas marked as 'Avars' and 'Bulgars'. The outermost limits of Charlemagne's empire are indicated; the facts do not warrant a definite line, and authorities differ in their estimate of where it should run. The Franks here left a trace of their former rule in the name of the 'Fruška Gora' mountains, south of the Danube in Srem. So widespread were the settlements of the Slavs, that, by the eighth century, the southern Balkan lands and mainland Greece were known as 'Sclavinia'. The limits of the Byzantine empire were, of course, indeterminate and constantly changing.

The Slavs who inherited the western and central Balkans comprised three groups—the Slovenes, Croats and Serbs (or *Slovenci, Hrvati* and *Srbi*). These names are of ancient derivation. Originally, practically all Slav tribes seem to have been known by the general name *Sloveni*, possibly from *Sclaveni*, from which the word 'Slav' is in fact derived. One tribe retained this general name in a slightly modified form to the present day, i.e. in *Slovenec* (singular), *Slovenci* (plural), or the 'Slovenes', as we call them.

It is thought by some authorities that the name of the other two groups—i.e. the Serbs and Croats—represent their original local tribal names, for both words are known to be of ancient origin. Thus the word 'Sirbi' (Srbi) is mentioned by classical writers of the first and second centuries with reference to a Slav people in Russia, while, according to other authorities the word for Croats (Hrvati) is derived from an ancient Slav word for 'Carpathians'. Sixth-century writers called the Croats, 'Chrovati', 'Horvati', and 'Hrvati'. Whatever may have been the origin of these older words, the expression Jugoslav (i.e. 'Southern Slav') is comparatively modern. It dates only from the eighteenth century when it first appeared in scientific literature and gradually spread from this into common usage.

The early distinctions between the three Slav groups are obscure, but, in any case, they were to be accentuated by cultural factors. In the early Middle Ages, the Slovenes and Croats fell under western and Roman Catholic influences and adopted the Latin alphabet, while the Serbs fell under the influence of the Greek Orthodox Church and adopted the Cyrillic alphabet.   · · ·   This distinction was to continue throughout all later history.

The Turkish Period

The Turkish period from the fifteenth century onward contributed very few ingredients to the mass of the Jugoslav people. Turkish officials and soldiers formed only a very small element in relation to the total population of the area, and, as the Turkish frontier retreated, these emigrated back to Ottoman territory. Fig.   shows the western borders of the Turkish *čiflik* which marks the extreme limit of Turkish settlement on the land. Any appreciable Turkish settlement was limited to Macedonia—to the valley of the Vardar and the country to the east. The descendants of these settlers, or many of them, still remain here, for Jugoslav Macedonia, unlike Greek Macedonia, was not emptied of its Turkish element by exchanges of population after the war of 1914–18.

But although the Turkish period contributed no very great element to the population, it had a profound effect upon the Jugoslavs. The Turkish advance into the Balkan lands, during the latter part of the fourteenth century, resulted in numerous Slav migrations that continued, in one form or another, for five centuries or so—until after the liberation of the Christian states. The migrations were due to the fact that the establishment of the alien Moslem civilization created general conditions—economic and political—distasteful to most of the Christian population. There were specific causes too.

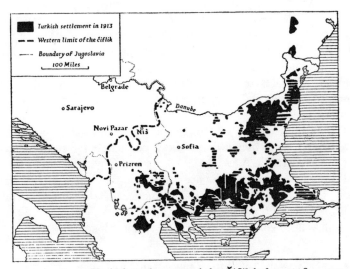

Turkish settlement and the *Čiflik* before 1918

Based on two folding maps in J. Cvijić, *La Péninsule balkanique: Géographie humaine* (Paris, 1918).
For the effects of the exchanges of population in the Greek lands after 1923, see N.I.D. Handbook on *Greece*, vol. 1, Fig. 108.

. . . Recruitment for the janissaries led many parents to seek refuge with their children in other lands·

An important factor in the subsequent history of the Slavs was the arrival of the Magyars in the plain of Hungary about the year 900. This Finno-Ugrian people inserted, so to speak, a wedge between the South Slavs on the one hand, and the Czechs, Poles, Slovaks and the Russians on the other.

But although isolated and although dominant in the Balkan peninsula, the history of the South Slavs was itself far from being uniform. For some 1,300 years after their arrival they were divided into groups with separate destinies, and it is convenient to consider each of these groups separately. They were distributed as follows:

1. The Slovene lands
2. Croatia-Slavonia
3. Dalmatia
4. Bosnia and Hercegovina
5. Montenegro
6. The Vojvodina
7. Serbia
8. Macedonia

The general category of 'South Slavs' also includes the Bulgarians, who are not considered here. They are basically Slav with Ural-Altaic peoples superimposed.

Taken together, the history of these separate units presents a double character—'Balkan' and 'Central European'. On the one hand, there is the 'Eastern Question', and the influence first of the Byzantine and then of the Ottoman empire. On the other hand, there is the problem of the Austro-Hungarian empire and its constituent populations. The merging of these two themes into one, with the development of the Austro-German policy of *Drang nach Osten*, was the immediate prelude to the war of 1914, and to the political realization of the unity of the South Slavs.

PHYSICAL DIFFERENCES

In this country so many successive 'layers' of peoples have been superimposed throughout prehistoric and historical times, that there is wide variety in the physical characteristics of the people. The prevailing type encountered amongst the Southern Slavs generally, may be summarized as broad-headed, broad-faced, tall, and mainly brunet, with the head small for the stature.

The most striking feature in the distribution of physical types in Jugoslavia—in so far as these can be differentiated—is the dominance of an unusually tall and broad-headed people over a wide belt of country coinciding with the western mountain systems of Bosnia, Dalmatia, Montenegro and western Croatia. The average stature throughout this region is tall (i.e. more than 5 ft. 8 in.) and with this stature the head is often very broad. The hair is generally dark, the face very long, with the nose arched or aquiline. Of these peoples, the Montenegrins tend to be the tallest; indeed, they are among the tallest peoples of Europe.

The Serbians, to the east, also vary considerably in their characteristics, but the great majority have dark-brown and black hair and

* J. Cvijić, *La Péninsule balkanique: Géographie humaine*, p. 128 (Paris, 1918).

are tall in stature. They do, however, include a small number of tall and surprisingly fair-haired, long-headed peoples, and because of this, the percentage of people with fair or light coloured hair is higher in Serbia than in any other part of the Balkan peninsula (5%–10% in Serbia as compared with less than 5% in other parts of the peninsula).

In the north of Jugoslavia, these characteristics become somewhat obscured in the Drava, Sava and Danube country, where admixture has been particularly great. The Slovenes show a stronger tendency to medium-brown-to-blonde hair, while light and light-mixed eyes total nearly 70%. Within Slovenia, however, there are many local differences.

LANGUAGE

The Indo-European Background

Linguistic unity has been one of the few constant factors in the troubled history of the Southern Slavs, and the consciousness of this unity has more than once been used as a political lever. Although there are several enclaves of Turkish, Albanian, Italian, German and Magyar speakers within it · · · the region of South Slav speech to-day extends in a continuous belt from the Black Sea to the Alps. This speech belongs to the Slavonic group of the Indo-European family of languages, and, judging from the signs of close relationship that still exist between them, it is likely that the Slavonic group at one time formed a single unit with the Baltic group of languages (Old Prussian, Lithuanian and Lettish or Latvian).

There are three main divisions within the Slavonic group:

(i) The Southern division, consisting of Serbo-Croat, Slovene and Bulgarian.
(ii) The Eastern division, consisting of Russian, White Russian and Ruthenian (also called Ukrainian and Little Russian).
(iii) The Western division, consisting of Polish, Kashubian, Slovincian, Sorb (or Wendish), Czech and Slovak.

Unlike most of the Indo-European language groups, the several languages of the Slavonic group did not enter upon their separate development until the eighth century—a comparatively late period. For a long time, the original Slavonic language remained a 'bundle' of dialects, and the fact that its essential unity was unbroken until after the age of Charlemagne is shown by the way in which *Karl*, a form of the emperor's name, was borrowed into Slavonic in the sense of 'king', as attested in Russian *korol'*, Serbo-Croat *kralj* and Polish *król*. Not only was the actual division of the Slavonic dialects into separate and distinct languages a recent happening of the ninth century, but linguistic evolution from the parent Indo-European had also been slow. As a result, the whole Slavonic group of languages shows more homogeneity and less differentiation than do such groups as the Romance and the Germanic languages. With the Baltic group, Slavonic comes next only to Sanskrit, Greek and Lithuanian in its importance for the study of the original Indo-European language.

Serbo-Croat and Slovene are the two major languages in Jugoslavia to-day, and they are spoken by about 84% of the total population. Their separation was the inevitable result of geographical factors, political events and diverse cultural influences, but they are kindred languages and the close ties of affinity between them remain strong.

SERBO-CROAT

The term Serbo-Croat is a convenient label invented by grammarians to describe a language now written in two alphabets—Cyrillic and Latin. . . . Despite its double name, the language forms a complete unity and is called by Jugoslav scholars the Serb or Croat language (*Srpski ili hrvatski jezik*). According to the census of 1921, there were 8,911,509 Serbo-Croat speakers in the kingdom and to-day they form about 76% of the total population.

In view of the part played both by historical and geographical factors within the area of Serbo-Croat speech, it is not surprising that a diversity of dialects has arisen · · · but it is not easy to draw exact lines of demarcation between them. The three major dialects are 'Kajkavian', 'Čakavian' and 'Štokavian'; these names are derived from the three words *kaj*, *ča* and *što*, which in their respective territories function as the interrogative pronoun 'what'. In the east and south-east, there is a number of less easily defined dialects which mark a transition between Serbo-Croat on the one hand, and Bulgarian and Macedonian on the other.

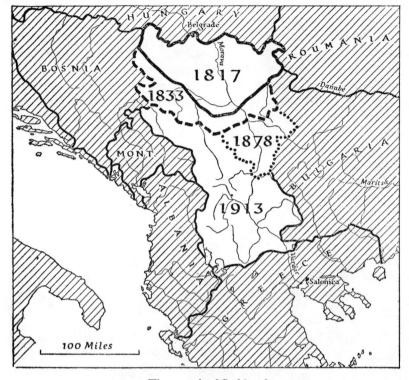

The growth of Serbia, 1817–1913

THE JUGOSLAVS IN 1914

Though the 'Illyrian Provinces' had so quickly passed away with the defeat of Napoleon, the possibility of some union among the various Southern Slav groups was never lost sight of during the nineteenth century. South Slav consciousness was fostered by the linguistic and literary work of Vuk Karadžić (1787–1864) among the Serbs, and by that of Ljudevit Gaj (1809–72) and Bishop Strossmayer (1815–1905) among the Croats. Moreover, the disciples of Jernej Kopitar (1780–1844) among the Slovenes were making closer contacts with the Croats and with the Jugoslav movement in general. But this growing feeling of common nationality had many difficulties to contend with, and the ultimate union of all the Southern Slavs was far from being a foregone conclusion. They were scattered among so many different political and administrative units which made concerted action difficult. The various

Estimate of Jugoslav Population in 1914

The figures are only very approximate estimates. They are based on the Austrian and Hungarian censuses of 1910, supplemented by information in *Peace Handbooks: vol.* IV, *The Balkan States*, part ii, no. 20. 'Serbia,' p. 9 (H.M.S.O., London, 1920).

A. Attached to Austria

Dalmatia	Serbo-Croats, 611,000
Carniola	Slovenes, 491,000
Styria	Slovenes, 410,000
Carinthia	Slovenes, 82,000
Küstenland	{ Slovenes, 267,000 { Serbo-Croats, 171,000

Made up as:

Trieste	{ Slovenes, 57,000 { Serbo-Croats, 2,000
Görz and Gradisca	Slovenes, 155,000
Istria	{ Slovenes, 55,000 { Serbo-Croats, 168,000

B. Attached to Hungary

Croatia-Slavonia	{ Serbs, 645,000 { Croats, 1,638,000
Vojvodina	{ Serbs, 382,000 { Croats, 7,000 { Bunjevci and Šokci, 63,000
Fiume	{ Slovenes, 2,000 { Serbo-Croats, 13,000
Rest of Hungary	{ Serbs, 79,000 { Croats, 186,000 { Slovenes, 70,000

C. Attached to Austria-Hungary

Bosnia and Hercegovina	{ Serbs, 825,000 { Croats, 400,000 { Moslem Serbo-Croats, 610,000

D. Serbia

Serbs	3,000,000
Macedo-Slavs	550,000

E. Montenegro

Serbs	250,000
GRAND TOTAL	10,789,000

units, too, had different historical backgrounds, and, not least, there was the antagonism between the Roman Catholic and the Orthodox sections of the population. But, with the twentieth century, the Jugoslav ideal advanced by leaps and bounds. A variety of circumstances drew the Southern Slavs together, and affected both those within and those outside the Austro-Hungarian Monarchy.

Within the Monarchy, the unconstitutional régime in Croatia, and the attempts to suppress the Croat language and nationality were rapidly destroying any pro-Hungarian feeling among the Croat population. Some of the older generation, it is true, were still doubtful about an alliance with the Orthodox Serbs, but the leaders of the younger generation were avowedly in favour of breaking away

Jugoslavia in relation to Austria-Hungary

Based on C. Grant Robertson and J. G. Bartholomew, *An Historical Atlas of Modern Europe*, plates 21 and 40 (2nd ed., Oxford, 1924).
C. Carniola; K. Küstenland; S. Salzburg.

from Hungary. Croat feeling was reflected in Dalmatia, and the Resolutions of Fiume and of Zara (Zadar) in 1905 were signs that Roman Catholic-Orthodox antagonism was breaking down, or, at any rate, was being submerged in other issues. Even so, it must be remembered that both resolutions professed allegiance to Hungary provided that an autonomous Croatia-Dalmatia could be secured. The Catholic Slovenes and the Orthodox Serb peoples of south

Hungary were not such important groups, but here, too, the Austro-Hungarian régime was producing dissatisfaction and unrest that increased as the twentieth century went forward. Finally, in Bosnia the whole situation was unstable, and all sections of the population supported the demand for a greater measure of autonomy.

Among the Southern Slavs outside the Monarchy, the most important feature of the twentieth century was the change of régime in Serbia when the Karageorgević dynasty came once more to the throne (1903). The contrast between Serbian democracy and the alien rule of Austria and Hungary became all the more glaring. An increasing number of Southern Slavs now felt that any hope of liberation lay with Serbia, and the triumph of the Serbian armies in the Balkan Wars of 1912–13 aroused great excitement throughout the South Slav world. The favourable Concordat made by Serbia with the Vatican in June 1914 helped, moreover, to allay Roman Catholic suspicions of Orthodox intolerance. The other independent state was Montenegro, and this, despite the dynastic rivalry of Nicholas and Peter, was, early in 1914, about to enter into the closest fiscal and diplomatic union with Serbia. Jugoslav ideas were in the air, and Serbia was accused of pan-Serb aspirations in the Balkans.

But the factors affecting the fate of the Southern Slavs inside the Austro-Hungarian Monarchy could not be separated from those affecting the Slavs without. There was an inevitable interaction between the domestic policy of Austria-Hungary towards the South Slavs within the Monarchy, and the foreign policy of Austria-Hungary towards the Southern Slavs outside. Serbia was not only the 'Guardian of the Gate' blocking expansion to the south-east, but she was also a 'Piedmont' that might do for the South Slavs what Savoy had done for Italy. Thus it was that the German-Austrian dream of economic penetration towards Turkey and beyond, became interlocked with the racial problem of the Dual Monarchy. The 'Eastern Question' or the 'Macedonian Problem' or the 'Germanic Threat' in Europe could not be separated from the 'South Slav Question' or the 'Croat Problem' in Austria-Hungary. With the outbreak of war in 1914, all the problems were put into a melting pot.

APPENDIX TWO: Historical Outline of Yugoslavia, 1914-1941

The War of 1914–18: Main features of the War of 1914–18; The Treaty of London, 26 April 1915; The Serbian Government and the Jugoslav Committee; The break-up of Austria-Hungary; Negotiations at Paris and Geneva, 1918

The New State of 1918: The component parts; The Italian frontier; The Austrian frontier; The Hungarian frontier; The Roumanian frontier; The Bulgarian frontier; The Albanian frontier; A survey of the new state

The Democratic Experiment, 1919–29: Centralism versus Federalism; Party rivalries; Economic progress, 1919–29; The *Skupština* murders

The Royal Dictatorship, 1929–34: Government by decree, 1929–31; The Croat problem, 1929–31; The Constitution of 1931; Unrepresentative Government, 1931–2; The Growth of Opposition, 1932–3; The Economic Crisis, 1931–3; Foreign Affairs, 1932–4

The Regency, 1934–41: The legacy of King Alexander; The elections of May 1935; Problems of Federalism; The Concordat, 1937; Foreign Relations, 1934–8; The elections of December 1938; The *Sporazum,* August 1939; Prince Paul and the Axis, 1940

The Final Crisis, 1941: German intimidation; Prince Paul's motives; The *Coup d'Etat*; The Invasion

THE WAR OF 1914–18

Main features of the war of 1914–18

The story of the Jugoslav contribution to the war of 1914–18 is too complicated to tell in detail, but certain trends of opinion and certain outstanding incidents in the war must be mentioned, however briefly, as essential clues to a right understanding of the Jugoslav problem to-day. The first and most decisive factor was the heroic Serbian army, which thrice drove the Austrians back across the frontier in 1914, and, after succumbing to superior Austrian, German and Bulgarian forces, made a great retreat over the Albanian snows. After an interval of recuperation at Corfu, it played an important part in holding the Salonica front and, supplemented by volunteer Jugoslav Legions, shared in the final Allied victory over Bulgaria. Without this heavy sacrifice of life (and Serbia and Montenegro probably lost not less than one out of five million souls), all political efforts would have been in vain.

The second tendency was entirely opportunist; the Serbo-Croat

Coalition in Zagreb continued to attend the joint parliament in Budapest and to profess loyalty to the Hungarian crown, and indeed attended the coronation of Charles IV, who succeeded his uncle, Francis Joseph, in 1916. It thus was able to husband Croatian resources and to maintain its autonomous institutions unimpaired till the end of the war, but it steadily declined to make any public disavowal of its colleagues abroad and maintained secret contacts with them, in the same way as did the Czech 'Maffia' with the Czech National Committee of Masaryk and Beneš.

Thirdly, there was parallel action among the Croats and Slovenes in Austria, and when the Austrian parliament was again allowed to meet in May 1917, their leaders in it, Monsignors Krek and Korošec, put forward an open claim for the union of the Jugoslav lands of the Monarchy in a single free state under the Hapsburg sceptre, of course suppressing any reference to the completion of that union by the addition of Serbia and Montenegro.

Finally, the Jugoslav Committee, consisting of over twenty fairly representative exiles from all the different provinces of the Monarchy (the most notable being Franjo Supilo, Ante Trumbić, the sculptor Meštrović and the advocate Hinković), made London its headquarters and put forward manifestoes claiming unity and independence and repudiating the Hapsburgs.

The Treaty of London, 26 April 1915

A serious complication was introduced by the Treaty of London of 26 April 1915, by which the Entente (Britain, France and Russia), in return for Italy's entry on their side, assigned to her wide territories in Gorizia, Carniola, Istria and Dalmatia, inhabited by an overwhelmingly Slovene and Croat population of not less than 700,000 · · · A special clause reserved Fiume as the port of Croatia. The provisions of the Treaty, though a strictly guarded secret, were discovered by the Croat leader Supilo in conversation with the Russian Foreign Minister Sazonov in St Petersburg: and it became known that both Russia and the Serbian Premier Pašić—a man of narrowly Serb nationalist outlook—were inclined to leave the Catholic Croats and Slovenes to their fate, if the territory where the Serb and Orthodox population predominated could be secured for Serbia and, with it, ample access to the Adriatic. This caused a temporary revulsion of feeling in favour of Austria-Hungary; and the Jugoslavs in the Austrian army fought manfully against Italy, knowing that they were defending Slav soil against Italian aggression.

The supreme command on the Isonzo was given to Marshal Boroević, an Orthodox Serb belonging to one of the *Graničar* (Frontiersman) families long in Hapsburg service.

King Alexander I

The Serbian Government and the Jugoslav Committee

By the winter of 1915 the conquest of Serbia, by Austrian, German and Bulgarian forces, once more closed the ranks of the Jugoslavs, whose sole hope lay in unity; but for the next eighteen months a deadlock ensued. The Russian Revolution and the entry of America weakened the position of the reactionary and pan-Serb Pašić, and his party split into Old Radicals and Young Radicals, the latter demanding democratic institutions no less than national unity and equality. On 20 July 1917, the Declaration of Corfu was signed between Pašić as Serbian Premier, and Trumbić as President of the Jugoslav Committee in exile, and this may be called the birth certificate of the future Jugoslavia. It declared in favour of the union of all Serbs, Croats and Slovenes as a single nation, under the Karageorgević dynasty: the new state was to be 'a constitutional democratic and parliamentary monarchy', with equality for the two alphabets, the three national names and flags and the three religions, with manhood suffrage in parliament and in the municipalities. The details were left to a future Constituent Assembly, and, in particular, the Declaration of Corfu left open the question whether the state should be centralized or federal.

During the following winter, after the disaster of Caporetto, Italian statesmen were in a more chastened frame of mind, and long negotiations, at first of an entirely informal and non-committal kind, were conducted in London between representative Italians (first General Mola, then Signor Torre) and the Jugoslav Committee under Trumbić. On the basis of an agreement between them, subsequently known as the 'Pact of Rome,' a 'Congress of the Oppressed Nationalities of Austria-Hungary' was held on 8 April 1918 at the Roman Capitol. Active propaganda was now started on the Austrian front, and this had a direct effect in blunting the point of the Austrian offensive on the Piave. The success of the Congress influenced President Wilson, who, during the summer, revised that one of the Fourteen Points which recommended 'autonomy' for the subject races, and now insisted upon Jugoslav and Czechoslovak unity as essential parts of his programme.

Unhappily, the increasing readiness of the Allied governments to recognize the Jugoslav idea was counterbalanced by the jealous, narrowly pan-Serb attitude of the Serbian Premier Pašić, in the teeth of strong opposition from the Young Radicals. At the same time that Mr Balfour accorded British recognition to the Czechoslovak National Council, he was willing to extend similar recognition to the Jugoslavs, if once the two groups (Serbian Government and Jugoslav Committee) could show their unanimity. But Pašić, on the contrary, dismissed his Ministers in Washington and London for espousing a Jugoslav programme, and when the war ended, agreement had still not been reached—with the result that the Italian government went back upon the Pact of Rome and demanded of the embarrassed Allies the fulfilment of the Treaty of London.

The Break-up of Austria-Hungary

Emboldened by the American endorsement of the Pact of Rome, Mgr Korošec had organized a Jugoslav National Council, openly aiming at national unity.

The confusion of this initial period was increased by the fact that the Prince Regent was with his troops advancing northwards from the Salonica front to Belgrade after the surrender of Bulgaria on 29 September, while the Serbian government was in Paris and Corfu and had a strict monopoly of telegraphic communications. The delegates of the National Council in Zagreb—its President, Mgr Korošec, and Dr Čingrija, Mayor of Dubrovnik—reached Paris only to find a virtual rupture between Pašić and the Old Radicals on the one hand and the Jugoslav Committee, supported by the Young Radical Opposition (which had a paper majority in the *Skupština*) on the other hand. The leaders of the latter were actually threatening to start a Republican campaign, in the erroneous belief that the Crown Prince was a mere tool in the hands of Pašić.

Under strong French pressure a conference was held at Geneva between the three groups, and, on 9 November 1918, a Declaration was signed, constituting the new Jugoslavia 'from to-day as an indivisible state-unit,' the cabinet being composed of representatives of the two rival Serbian parties (Old and Young Radicals), of the Jugoslav Committee and of the Zagreb National Council. The governments of Belgrade and Zagreb were to retain their respective functions until a Constituent Assembly could meet and draft a new constitution for the whole country. But the Geneva decisions remained operative only on paper; the Prince Regent, when at last the true facts reached him, appointed Protić (who was with him in Belgrade) as Premier, Trumbić as Foreign Minister, and Pašić as principal delegate at the Peace Conference. Centralizing tendencies rapidly asserted themselves, in view of the dangers threatening from all sides; for the Entente governments, under pressure from Italy, withheld their recognition from the newly united state.

Thus did the various sections of the Jugoslav people rush into union, without any very clear idea of the lines on which it was to be worked out, and without any generally recognized bargain or contract. This affected the whole future development of the new state and still affects it to-day.

213

THE NEW STATE OF 1918

The component parts

The new Jugoslav state which came into existence between the Declaration of Zagreb on 29 October 1918 and the proclamation of 'the kingdom of the Serbs, Croats and Slovenes' on 4 December, was constituted out of the following elements:

1. The independent kingdom of Serbia.
2. The independent kingdom of Montenegro.
3. Croatia-Slavonia, hitherto possessing some measure of 'Home Rule' under Hungary.
4. Dalmatia, an Austrian province.
5. Carniola, part of Styria, a small corner of Carinthia and two small fragments of Istria—all these were former Austrian provinces.
6. Baranja, Bačka, and the western portion of the Banat, together with the districts of Prekomurje and Medjumurje—all formerly integral parts of Hungary.
7. Bosnia and Hercegovina, formerly administered jointly by Austria and Hungary.

The territorial formation of Jugoslavia

P. Prekomurje, and M. Medjumurje. Both these areas, like the Vojvodina, formed integral parts of the old kingdom of Hungary.

A survey of the new state

A census, taken on 31 January 1921, provides a picture of the new state at the beginning of its history.* It included twelve million people, and of these some 83 per cent spoke Serbo-Croat or Slovene. The main linguistic components were as follows:

Serbo-Croats	8,911,509
Slovenes	1,019,997
Germans	505,790
Magyars	467,658
Albanians	439,657
Roumanians	231,068
Turks	150,322
Czechs and Slovaks	115,532
Ruthenes	25,615
Russians	20,568
Poles	14,764
Italians	12,553
Others	69,878
Tota	11,984,911

The preliminary census report was accompanied by a number of maps showing the distribution of these elements.

Equally important were the religious differences, especially the difference between the Roman Catholic Croats and the Serb Orthodox. · · ·   The strength of the different religious confessions was as follows:

Orthodox	5,593,057
Roman Catholic	4,708,657
Greek Catholic (Uniate)	40,338
Moslem	1,345,271
Protestant	229,517
Jewish	64,746
Other religions	1,944
Without religion and unknown	1,381
Total	11,984,911

Economically, the population of the new state was largely rural in character, 80 per cent of the population being supported by

* *Résultats définitifs du Recensement de la Population du 31 Janvier 1921* (Sarajevo, 1932).

215

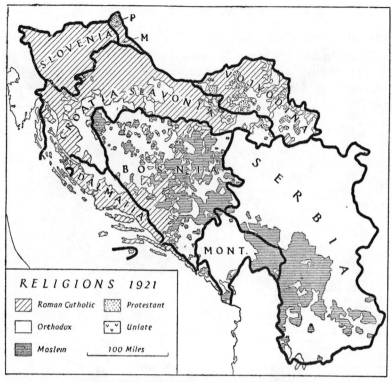

Historic divisions and religious faiths

Based on a folding map in *Résultats préliminaires du Recensement de la Population dans le Royaume des Serbes, Croates et Slovènes du 31 Janvier 1921, publié par la direction de la Statistique d'Etat, Belgrade* (Sarajevo, 1924).
The boundaries of the historic divisions are shown as they were in 1914; the international frontier is that of the new state that came into being after 1918.

P. Prekomurje and M. Medjumurje—both these areas, like the Vojvodina, formed parts of the old kingdom of Hungary.

Orthodox was roughly equivalent to Serbs; the Moslems of Bosnia were Serbs, while those of Montenegro and Serbia itself were largely Albanians. The Roman Catholics included Croats and Slovenes.

agriculture. There were only three towns with populations above 100,000—Belgrade, Zagreb and Subotica. Much of the area had been depopulated by the warfare that had disturbed the area almost continuously since 1912. A period of peace for economic recuperation was badly needed. The new state also stood in need of a period of rest to work out its political destiny and to devise some satisfactory means of holding together the diverse peoples now suddenly brought together within a common frontier.

The Albanian frontier

Albanians had been steadily pushing forward into the area around Peć since 1691 · · · and in the years after 1878 the further settlement of Albanians in the districts of Kosovo, Metohija and

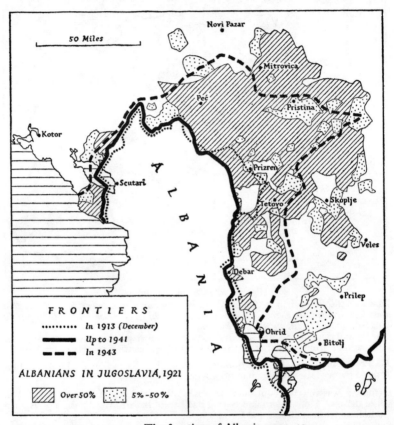

The frontiers of Albania, 1913–43

Based on (i) E. P. Stickney, *Southern Albania or Northern Epirus in European International Affairs*, 1912–33, pp. 96, 108 and 109 (Stanford, Cal., 1926); (ii) H. W. V. Temperley (ed.), *A History of the Peace Conference of Paris*, vol. IV, p. 338 (London, 1921); and (iii) Jugoslav Census, 1921.

Novi Pazar was encouraged by the Turkish government. The Jugoslav census of January 1921 stated that there were nearly half a million Albanian-speakers within Jugoslavia. · · · At the time of the census, the frontier was still undetermined, and various alternatives were eagerly canvassed. Ultimately, the line originally sanctioned by the Council of Ambassadors in 1913 was laid down.

GOVERNMENT, ADMINISTRATION AND LAW

Introduction: The New State of 1918: The *Vidovdan* Constitution of 1921: The Constitution of 1931: Political Parties.

The realization of South Slav political unity in 1918 gave a new significance to many of the antagonisms and contrasts of culture, creed and regional consciousness that had existed for centuries among the constituent groups of the new state. Not the least important of these differences was the inequality of experience in government responsibility, and this inequality provided a major difficulty when the time came to face the constitutional problem of the new kingdom.

Serbia

Serbia had long been accustomed to various forms of self-government. Throughout the nineteenth century there had been a strange sequence of constitutions and of fundamental laws, either decreed by the sultans or promulgated by the Serbian princes under the pressure of popular demands. A national assembly (*Skupština*), together with a 'council of state', had been instituted in the time of Kara George. Although the *Skupština*, in its early days, was little more than a gathering of armed warriors who expressed their opinions 'by a thunder of cheers or of hisses', by the middle of the century it had become a regularly constituted, but irregularly convoked, assembly. The first Serbian constitution of any importance was that imposed by the Turks in 1838. Miloš was confirmed as hereditary prince of Serbia, but the executive power of the council of state was strengthened in order to restrain the prince's despotism, and an oligarchic régime was thus inaugurated. This constitution was replaced in 1861, during the reign of Michael, by one which brought more power into the hands of the prince and regularized the position of the *Skupština* through limiting the control of the state council. Soon after Michael's death in 1868, the regency began to reform the constitution in a manner that would almost certainly have gained the murdered prince's approval. The reformed constitution of 1869 had all the outward signs of a liberal and democratic instrument designed to expedite the working of normal parliamentary government. In practice, however, its provisions tended to restrict the powers of the *Skupština* and to strengthen the autocratic methods of the executive. The rise of a 'Radical' movement in the 'seventies led to agitation for further constitutional reforms in the 'eighties, and in 1889, shortly before his abdication, King Milan, in a last bid to save his position, appointed a commission, representing all parties, to draft another consitution. This document, which was approved by a more or less intimidated assembly, was considerably more liberal in character than its predecessors, and its major innovations included a statement of the parliamentary responsibility of ministers, a wide extension of the franchise and a promise of freedom for the press. In 1894, five years after his accession, Alexander dissolved the *Skupština*, abolished the constitution of 1889 and restored that of 1869. The Radicals were naturally strongly opposed to this arbitrary suspension of a liberal constitution. The political blunder of his marriage forced the king, in 1901, to find some means of regaining popularity. A new constitution was devised, more democratic, it is true, than that of 1869, but certainly less liberal than that of 1889, and for the first time in Serbian history, a second chamber was created. Once again, in March 1903, Alexander temporarily suspended the constitution, but when he attempted to restore it a few weeks later, it was too late. In June, Peter Karageorgević accepted the crown offered to him by the *Skupština*; one of his first acts was to recover and strengthen the constitution of 1889 —the franchise was extended, proportional representation was introduced and changes were made in the membership of the national assembly, which was now to meet annually. It was under this revised constitution of 1889 that Serbia was governed until the creation of the united kingdom in 1918.

Montenegro

Montenegro had known a primitive form of self-government since the end of the seventeenth century and an elective senate had been created in 1831. Prince Nicholas promulgated a 'constitution' in 1868, and the laws of the country were later codified, but in effect the prince retained all executive power in himself. In 1905, Nicholas granted another constitution; it provided for an assembly of two classes of members—a majority chosen by universal manhood suffrage and an *ex-officio* minority nominated by the king; ministries were made responsible both to the crown and to the legislature; liberty of expression and of religion was also guaranteed. These concessions to modern democratic principles made the constitution an impressive document, and, indeed, it was fully intended that it should make a favourable impression on foreign states. Nevertheless, Nicholas's jealous hold on his own authority, together with the absence of a quickened political consciousness among the Montenegrin populace, prevented any effective application of the constitution and restrained any development in the legislative power of the national assembly. Skill in the art of parliamentary government could not therefore be among Montenegro's contributions to the constitutional needs of the triune kingdom.

Croatia-Slavonia

Between 1868 and 1918, Croatia-Slavonia was governed under the terms of the *Nagoda* which placed it under Hungarian supremacy.
· · ·   The Croat assembly (*Sabor*), it is true, had its origins in the *Sabor* of the independent medieval kingdom, but its function, as defined in the *Nagoda*, was to advise and assist the Hungarian-appointed governor (*Ban*). Because of the limited nature of the suffrage in the province (there were only 49,000 voters in a total population of 2,600,000), the assembly could not in any way be regarded as truly representative. Despite the more apparent advantages of autonomous status for fifty years, with the use of the Serbo-Croat language permitted in all public services, the principles and methods of real self-government were largely unpractised among the inhabitants of Croatia.

Slovenia and Dalmatia

In Slovenia and Dalmatia, on the other hand, conditions had been more favourable. The various regions which went to form these provinces had each possessed its own Diet since 1861 · · ·
and the ground was thus prepared for the training of skilful parliamentarians. Moreover, under a somewhat restricted system of suffrage, each of the regions shared in elections to the central parliament at Vienna (indirectly between 1867 and 1893), and universal manhood suffrage was introduced in 1906.

Bosnia-Hercegovina

No constitution was granted to the provinces of Bosnia-Hercegovina when they were transferred to Austria-Hungary in 1878, and even when a constitution was promulgated in 1910, on their formal annexation and incorporation by the Dual Monarchy $\cdots$ it was not conceived in a democratic form. A Diet elected by restricted voting was established, but its powers were only those of consultation; it could not initiate bills and the approval both of the governor and of the Austro-Hungarian Finance Minister had to be obtained before any projects of law voted by the *Sabor* could become effective. General administration was centralized under imperial heads of departments; local government, too, was centralized in the same way under officials who relied upon the authority and assistance of the governor.

Other regions

In the Macedonian areas of South Serbia, retained by Turkey until the Balkan War of 1912, Turkish administration still lingered on and no attempt had been made to educate the people. Political experience was also slight among the Serbs of the Vojvodina. With a limited suffrage, they returned deputies to the Hungarian parliament, but local government was everywhere dominated by officials from Budapest.

THE NEW STATE OF 1918

The diversity of the Southern Slav political heritage became evident when the kingdom of the Serbs, Croats and Slovenes was proclaimed on 4 December 1918. Full agreement had not been reached between the representatives of these three peoples on the constitutional pattern of the state. Indeed, the name of the new kingdom itself was an indication of the reluctance of the leaders of the different groups to be brought into a closer and larger unity.

The Declaration of Corfu, on 20 July 1917, which had been issued by the Serbian premier and the president of the Jugoslav Committee $\cdots$ proclaimed the future union of the Serbs, Croats and Slovenes as a constitutional, democratic and parliamentary monarchy under the Karageorgević dynasty. The two alphabets, Latin and Cyrillic, and the three main religious bodies were to receive equal privileges. A constituent assembly was to be elected by direct, equal and secret ballot, and to be charged with the task of drafting a constitution for the new kingdom. Beyond these provisions, the Corfu manifesto only declared that local autonomy should be granted in accordance with natural, social and economic conditions. The

THE NEW STATE OF 1918

question whether the state should be centralized or federal was thus left to the constituent assembly.

The interpretation of the last clause in the Corfu declaration produced considerable differences of opinion among the 296 members of the provisional assembly. This assembly, which met at Belgrade in March 1919, consisted of the surviving members of the former Serbian *Skupština* and elected representatives from the various provincial assemblies outside Serbia. Eventually, in September 1920, a law was passed for the election of a constituent assembly. Elections were held in November and, among other things, they were notable for their freedom. The constituent assembly had 419 members, divided among fifteen parties. Five of these parties (Radicals, Democrats, Communists, Social Democrats and Agrarians), which broadly represented centralist views, gained 290 seats, while the three large parties, whose hopes were largely based on federalism (Croat Peasant, Slovene Populars and Moslems), obtained 101 seats; the remaining seats were distributed among minor parties (see p. 340). A committee, composed of forty-two members drawn proportionately from each group, was appointed to consider the draft constitution presented by the government. The assembly decided that the government's plan should be discussed first, then the committee's recommendations, and finally individual drafts and amendments submitted by any group consisting of at least twenty deputies. Each plan was discussed in turn; there was a Croat draft stressing the advantages of federalism, and a Slovene plan 'representing federalism in politics and state socialism in economics'; there were other plans (e.g. the Protić scheme) intended to effect a compromise between centralization and federalism. In May, a preliminary vote was taken on the government draft, which was centralist in tone, and it was provisionally adopted by 227 to 93 votes. A lengthy and bitter debate followed, clause by clause, and then, on 28 June 1921, the final vote was taken: 223 deputies voted for the draft, while 35 were against it. The two government parties—Democrat and Radical—obtained the support of the Moslem Organization through an assurance that agrarian reform in Bosnia would be accompanied by general compensation to the Moslem landlords and that the new administrative divisions would not cross the boundaries of Bosnia. At the final vote, 163 deputies, including the members of the Croat Peasant Party, were absent; both Croats and Slovenes contended that a centralist constitution had been imposed upon them despite their protests.

GOVERNMENT, ADMINISTRATION AND LAW

THE *VIDOVDAN* CONSTITUTION OF 1921

The first constitution of the new kingdom was adopted on *Vidovdan* (the feast of St Vitus) which was also the anniversary of the Serbian defeat at Kosovo in 1389. · · · Its general provisions declared that the official title of the state was 'the kingdom of the Serbs, Croats and Slovenes', and that the state was a constitutional, parliamentary and hereditary monarchy. The title was adopted after the Democrats and Radicals had rejected the name of Jugoslavia, which had been advocated by the other parties. The official language of the state was to be 'Serbo-Croat-Slovene'—a philological figment designed to bring the linguistic clause into line with the triple nature of the state's official title. The fundamental rights and duties of citizenship were enunciated in accordance with the doctrines of Western liberalism: all citizens were to be equal before the law, the liberty of the individual was guaranteed and there was freedom of religion, of the press, of association and of education.

Oblasti—administrative divisions, 1921–9
Based on official Jugoslav sources.

THE CONSTITUTION OF 1931

On 6 January 1929, King Alexander declared that the *Vidovdan* constitution was abolished, and assumed the responsibility of absolute power. Various decrees, all aimed at the complete unification of the state, were issued from time to time · · · and finally, on 3 September 1931, the king promulgated a new constitution which, with minor alterations and subject to the establishing of Croatian autonomy in 1939 · · · was still in force in 1941. The preamble to the decree of promulgation made it clear that this definitive constitution was to provide a wider basis to national unity and policy. The name of the kingdom was changed to Jugoslavia, and the state was declared to be a constitutional monarchy under the Karageorgević dynasty. The fundamental rights and duties of citizenship were again enunciated in an impressive manner, and the liberties guaranteed in the *Vidovdan* constitution were re-asserted. The interpretation of these liberties, however, was made doubtful by the statement that they were granted 'within the limits of the law', and the law remained as under the dictatorship. Furthermore, all associations for political purposes, or indeed for physical training, formed on a religious, regional or particularist basis, were expressly forbidden. It was argued that this new constitution, although it contained a substantial residuum of the constitutional principles laid down in that of 1921 and, for that matter, in the Serbian constitution of 1903, provided a first step towards the re-introduction of parliamentary democracy, while it also ensured the continuance of royal power. Its promulgation was not received without misgiving; its Serbian critics complained that it was a mere disguise for autocracy, while Croats, Slovenes and Moslems protested that it did nothing more than prolong centralist government from Belgrade.

CENTRAL GOVERNMENT

The Monarchy

Under the constitution of 1931, the king is granted not only the general powers defined in 1921 · · · but also the unconditional right to determine the succession to the throne in the absence of male heirs and to appoint regents in the event of the heir succeeding during his minority. Legislative power is again exercised jointly by the crown and the national assembly, and all of the king's acts must be countersigned by the responsible minister.

GOVERNMENT, ADMINISTRATION AND LAW

THE FIRST DECADE, 1918–1929

The Constituent Assembly of 1920 consisted of no less than fifteen political parties, with 419 representatives.

(1) *Radical Party*

The Radical party, formally created in 1881 by Nicolas Pašić, had virtually ruled Serbia between 1903 and 1914. Originally an agrarian socialist party, by 1919 it had become a more or less conservative group representing the Serbian *bourgeoisie* and wealthier peasants, but it also received some support from *prečani* Serbs of the former Austrian and Hungarian lands. When the new state was formed, the Radicals advocated a centralist or unitarist system, although a small group within the party urged that the change from the old régimes should be cautious and gradual.

(2) *Democrat Party*

In 1919, dissident Radicals joined with members of the former Serbian opposition parties and with Serbs from Croatia and the Vojvodina (led by Pribičević), as well as with scattered Liberal elements from Croatia and Slovenia, to form the Democrat party. The Democrats showed more enthusiasm than the Radicals for the Jugoslav ideal even if it meant a vigorous centralism, but, under the influence of more liberal elements, they also showed a greater willingness to conciliate the Croats.

(3) *Serb Agrarian Party*

Created in 1920 to express the dissatisfaction of the peasants with government in the interests of townspeople, the Agrarian party drew its strength mainly from Bosnia and Serbia, and opposed centralism.

(4) *Croat Peasant Party (Hrvatska Seljačka Stranka or HSS)*

The Croat Peasant party had been founded at the beginning of the century by Stephen Radić and its aim was to establish a peasant republic. Under the limited franchise prevailing in Croatia-Slavonia, the party did not gain much parliamentary success before 1918, although its social and cultural influence was great. With the collapse of the Austro-Hungarian Monarchy and the extension of the franchise, the Croat Peasant party become an important political organization: between 1918 and 1924 it demanded the establishment of an independent Croat republic; after 1924 it stood for Croatian autonomy.

The following table shows the strength of the parties in the Constituent Assembly of 1920:

Democrat	92	Social Democrat	10
Radical	91	*Džemijet*	5
Communist	58	Croat Union	4
Croat Peasant (*HSS*)	50	Party of Croat Rights	3
Serb Agrarian and other small		Republican	3
Peasant parties	39	Others	13
Slovene Popular	27		
Moslem Organization	24		419

The conflicting opinions of these political groups soon became evident in their reactions to the draft constitution of 1921.

The Croat Peasant party (*HSS*) refused to sit in parliament, both on Croat national and on republican grounds. The Communists, who were strongest in the industrial areas of Slovenia and especially in Ljubljana, withdrew from the assembly; so, too, did the Social Democrats, the Republicans, the Slovene Populars and the smaller Croat parties. Thus when the two government parties— Radicals and Democrats—obtained the support of the Moslem Organization · · · the 'Centralists' found themselves in an even stronger position than their numbers in parliament seemed to imply, and there was left only a handful of uninfluential Peasant parties to form an opposition.

Although the government had only a small majority, it did not hesitate to act ruthlessly against members of the opposition and Radić, among others, was thrown into prison. After the *Skupština* murders in 1928 the whole of the Croat Peasant-Independent Democrat bloc withdrew from Belgrade; the Croat Peasants went to Zagreb, where they set up an extra-legal anti-parliament.

UNDER THE DICTATORSHIP AND THE REGENCY

In January 1929, King Alexander had assumed absolute power and appointed an ostensibly non-party cabinet with General Živković, commander of the Royal Guard, as prime minister. The king governed through ministers responsible only to him, and the *Skupština* was abolished.

Parliament was restored under the constitution of 1931, but the ban on all political association on a religious or regionalist basis and the conditions imposed by the electoral law of 1931 · · ·
made it not only difficult for many of the former parties to contest elections, but also led to the imprisonment of their leaders.

The Economic Crisis, 1931–3

Economic conditions in Jugoslavia began to deteriorate in 1931. During the first six months of that year, exports and imports fell by 25 per cent. The trade balance for the same period showed a deficit of over 265 million dinars. A loan arranged in May at Paris of 1,025 million francs at 7 per cent was used to stabilize the dinar. But matters became rapidly worse. The National Bank's foreign credits became exhausted and a series of temporary expedients was adopted. In August came the cessation of German reparation payments, which meant a loss of 700 million dinars a year, entailing the necessity of severe cuts in administrative salaries and pensions and an increase of taxation. The collapse in the prices of agricultural products now hit the country severely, and in June the government in desperation undertook to buy up the whole wheat harvest at about 60 per cent above the world price, an arrangement that greatly added to the country's financial embarrassments.

The full force of the economic catastrophe came in 1932, at a time when political unrest was at its stormiest stage. The first serious blow had been a run on the banks in September 1931, which followed the British government's repudiation of the Gold Standard. Just when the banks most needed credit, the National Bank found it necessary to deny them such facilities, and the banks were only given moratoria on condition that they came under government control. Then the government's grain monopoly, intended to protect the peasants against the collapse of cereal prices, worked disastrously. The government agents were unable to store all the quantities of wheat received, much of which was consequently ruined. On the other hand, many of the peasants were paid in bonds, which were not available for the payment of taxes. The whole scheme was dropped early in 1932, at a loss of over 400 million dinars to the tax-payers. Other disasters took place. The winter was exceptionally severe and was followed by extensive floods. Some 30,000 persons were homeless. The scarcity of fodder resulted in the slaughtering of a quarter of the country's cattle, which made the export of stock impossible. Something had to be done for the peasants, bewildered by the collapse of their whole economy, exasperated against the urban *gospoda* (gentry) who ruled and exploited them, and unable to repay the debts which, especially in the Serbian districts, they had contracted in the carefree years of prosperity.

In March, the government announced a moratorium of six months for peasant debts. This expedient was also followed by unhappy consequences. The peasants found themselves unable to obtain any credit at the time of year when they most needed it and were accustomed to having it. Their creditors had less prospect than ever of recovering their debts. The peasants were unable to buy anything. Retailers were unable to pay wholesalers, who, in turn, could not pay manufacturers and importers. The number of bankruptcies and compulsory settlements in 1932 was more than three times as great as that in 1930. There was even an outcry for a general moratorium on all debts. Nevertheless in October the government continued the suspension of peasant debts indefinitely, and it lasted till 23 November 1933.

Meanwhile export trade had been falling heavily; the National Bank's supply of foreign exchange ran short; exchange control was introduced with increasing severity, till in March it was made illegal for money to leave the country. Foreign trade was in consequence almost paralysed. To meet the desperate situation the government began to negotiate for clearing agreements with most of the European countries. In June the Commercial Secretary to the British Legation reported, 'it seems likely that when any form of trade revival appears there will be a great re-orientation, due not only to changes in international relationships but to the fact that old business connexions have been severed and old sources of credit cut off during this period of currency control.' His prediction was indeed fulfilled.

Foreign Affairs, 1933-4

Amid these disasters the country experienced a relaxation of interest in public affairs, the problem of the next meal being uppermost in most men's minds, though bitterness against the government was prevalent in all districts. At the same time Jugoslavia's international position was deteriorating. The victory of the 'Left' in the French elections of May 1932 meant that France would withdraw from her position of paymaster to Jugoslavia. As *La Volonté* interpreted the situation, 'France has voted against the policy of the European *status quo* which inevitably entails conflict. She has realized that the policy of alliances with a view to encircling Germany is no longer practicable, and that the burden of armaments, incompatible with a minimum of prosperity, does not even assure security'. The Jugoslav government soon felt the truth of these words, for in July, Jugoslavia failed to obtain the fresh loan of which the régime was in pressing need and only secured a moratorium of one year for the payments due on previous loans. On the worst of terms with her neighbours, Italy, Hungary and Bulgaria, and with her French patron alienated and preoccupied, Jugoslavia was in a position that justified anxiety.

In this period of political violence and economic depression at home, the importance of foreign affairs became more urgent. Here the king inaugurated policies which rapidly produced satisfactory results. In September 1933, King Boris of Bulgaria was passing through Jugoslavia on his way home. At King Alexander's suggestion, the two monarchs met informally in Belgrade station and the foundation was laid for a mutual friendship, which in 1934 led to a Jugoslav-Bulgarian *rapprochement*, a more conciliatory régime in Serbian Macedonia, the suppression of the Macedonian Revolutionary Organization in Bulgaria, and finally, in 1937, to the pact of eternal friendship between the two states. Immediately after that interview, the king made a tour of Roumania, Bulgaria, Turkey and Greece, which was a prelude to the inauguration, on 9 February 1934, of the Balkan Entente, in which it was not his fault that Bulgaria was not included. The king was doing his best to find security by linking the Little Entente (Jugoslavia, Roumania and Czechoslovakia) and the Balkan States. Danger was apprehended from Italy and from a revived union, whether Hapsburg or Italian, of Austria and Hungary.

The challenge of Germany to the established order was veiled by the friendly attitude of the Nazi Government towards Jugoslavia, as shown by General Göring's visits to Belgrade and by the German-Jugoslav treaty of commerce in May 1934, which facilitated the diversion of German tourists from Austria to the holiday resorts of the Jugoslav coast. Nevertheless the visit of M. Barthou to the Little Entente Conference and to Belgrade in June gave the government an opportunity of making the most emphatic declarations that they would resist the slightest revision of the *status quo*. Strained relations with Hungary developed into an open dispute before the Council of the League of Nations in June 1934, when the Hungarian representative complained of the difficulties caused by the severity of the Jugoslav frontier control, and the Jugoslav reply, with a wealth of corroborative evidence, accused Hungary of training terrorists and assisting them in their attacks on the Jugoslav government.

Early in October 1934 King Alexander left by sea for an official visit to Paris; after landing at Marseilles, on 9 October, he was assassinated while driving through the streets; M. Barthou was at the same time mortally wounded. It is no secret that the king intended to carry a stage further the discussions and plans for Balkan consolidation in view of the disturbing developments in Central Europe. But it is less known that he had latterly reached the conclusion that the dictatorship was a failure, and was firmly resolved on his return to revert to constitutional government. The outburst of grief and rage throughout Jugoslavia was a sure sign that his people, an overwhelming majority of whom disapproved of the dictatorship and desired a return to democracy, none the less recognized that in the eyes of the enemy he was a symbol of unity and independence and had been removed for that reason. Popular legend at once constructed the tale that with his last breath he gasped, 'Protect Jugoslavia for me'.

THE REGENCY, 1934–41

The legacy of King Alexander

King Alexander had been respected, indeed liked, throughout Jugoslavia, even by those who most deplored his policy of the forcible fusion of incompatible elements. The universal expressions of grief at his death were the tributes of his peoples to a brave and sincere monarch. Convinced that federalism would mean disruption, he had believed that only the use of force could serve the unity of the state. At his death Alexander left the country torn by dissension and distrust, with more party differences even than under the parliamentary system, the ills of which he had set out to cure.

It was to a country overshadowed by economic distress as well as by political bitterness that the young King Peter II was brought from his preparatory school in Surrey. King Alexander had left a will appointing a triple Regency consisting of his cousin Prince Paul, Dr Stanković (a distinguished Serbian specialist and Professor of Medicine at Belgrade University), and Dr Perović (a Serb official, for a time Ban of the Coastal *banovina*). As substitutes for these three he had nominated General Tomić, commandant of the Belgrade garrison, M. Banjanin (a well-known Serb journalist in Zagreb, an active member of the Jugoslav Committee during the war of 1914–18, who rallied to the dictatorship and became a Senator), and Dr Zec, a little-known Serb official. Five of the six names were greeted by the general public with feelings of unreserved amazement, for politically they were unknown. Even of Prince Paul this was in the main true, though he was the only possible member of the Royal family for such a post.

It was upon Prince Paul that the mantle of authority had been conferred; and hopes were aroused that he would inaugurate a return to constitutional government. Early in November he received a memorandum from 250 leading Croatian ecclesiastics, ex-ministers, bankers, writers and artists, urging a general amnesty, especially for Dr Maček, free elections and the appointment to high office of men respected for their characters and abilities. This appeal was strikingly supported by a similar memorandum from fifty of the most eminent Serbian intellectuals. But Prince Paul walked warily, knowing that he was distrusted by many Serbians as a 'foreigner' educated in Russia and at Oxford. He interviewed leaders of parties likely to accept the existing constitution, especially the Radicals, who had already applied for registration as a party. But he retained the Uzunović cabinet appointed by King Alexander in January 1934. Meanwhile the Foreign Minister, M. Jevtić, was engaged at Geneva on the difficult task of branding Hungary with complicity in the murder of the late king, without recourse to war, without loss of national dignity and without stimulating the anger which was felt in the country and the government. The Memorandum which the Jugoslav government presented to the League and then published to the world at large was a formidable indictment of Hungary, the more so as it was now known that for many months past Belgrade had made representations to Budapest regarding the terrorist activities conducted from Janka Puszta, and that among the persons of whom it had complained by name were some of those now implicated in the Marseilles crime. Yet nothing had been done to fulfil the undertakings of Budapest to suppress terrorism on Hungarian soil.

The discussions of the League of Nations, however, ended in only a qualified condemnation of Hungary. Nevertheless M. Jevtić was made prime minister, with a cabinet containing no prominent politicians except General Živković and one of the younger Radicals, M. Stojadinović, a financial expert.

The Elections of May 1935

The new government made the conciliatory gesture of releasing Dr Maček and Dr D. Jovanović from Mitrovica prison in which they had cemented a firm friendship, and the censorship was relaxed, but the premier announced that the existing constitution, which was designed to prohibit opposition parties, would be upheld. In

February 1935 the *Skupština* was dissolved and elections announced for 5 May. It was the first electoral contest to be held for eight years, and it was anything but free. . . . The opposition was prevented from holding meetings or publishing appeals, the press being only permitted to print official announcements and speeches. Several of the opposition leaders were temporarily interned. The voters were subjected to the most open intimidation and violence, and state employees received instructions such as those issued by the Ban of the Coastal *banovina* (*Primorska*) to his subordinates on 20 March: 'This (the official) list must have a majority, and every official who does not vote for it will be held responsible and punished without mercy'.

The first published results of the elections—Government 1,738,000, Opposition 983,000—were so vigorously challenged that they were revised to show Government 1,746,982, Opposition 1,076,346. When allowance was made for all the voters whose livelihood depended on their support of the Government, as well as for the abstention of the Radicals (the 'grand old Serbian party') and the Slovenes, and for the official tampering with the figures which was assumed as a matter of course, the elections amounted to a moral victory for the opposition. The electoral method, however, attributed 301 seats to the Government and only 67 to its opponents.

These scandalous elections were quickly followed by dramatic consequences. The deputies of the opposition bloc boycotted the *Skupština* · · · and met in a counter-parliament at Zagreb. The aged Catholic Archbishop of Zagreb requested an audience of Prince Paul, and laid before him a statement of the grosser outrages committed during the elections in his diocese, and the text found its way into the Vienna *Reichspost*. The three Croat Ministers resigned and were quickly followed by General Živković and M. Stojadinović. The Prince Regent then took the bold step of inviting the Croat leader to visit him. Dr Maček drove in a royal car from Belgrade station to the palace, cheered by the Belgrade crowd. After his interview with Prince Paul, he spent the evening with the Serbian Democratic and Agrarian leaders and reached agreement about their common aims. He accepted the Dynasty, the common Army and Foreign Office, but insisted on both a democratic basis for the state and its federation, and suggested the formation of a neutral ministry to govern till the autumn during the negotiations for the revision of the constitution.

The result of these promising events was that on 23 June the Regents invited Dr Milan Stojadinović to form a cabinet. The new government was accepted as one of appeasement and reconstruction, and it included Dr Spaho, the Moslem leader, and the Slovene leader, Mgr Korošec. On the other hand, except for the War Minister, General Živković, who was believed to favour conciliation of the Croats, there was a clean sweep of the figures connected with the dictatorship. The rest of the cabinet consisted of new men, either Radicals or Croatian non-political experts. Most of Dr Jevtić's three hundred deputies submissively transferred their support overnight to the new premier.

Problems of Federalism

Dr Stojadinović proceeded cautiously. He relaxed the censorship and spoke approvingly of the American two-party system, a change from the totalitarian attitude of his predecessors. But he was in no hurry to reach a settlement with Zagreb. His immediate aims seem to have been to give the régime that organized popular support which it had hitherto lacked, and to prevent the consolidation of an united *prečani* front. In August 1935, he announced the formation of a new government party, the JRZ (Jugoslav Radical Union) composed of Radicals, Slovenes and Moslems. He thus proposed to unite the strongest Serbian party with two special interests from the new provinces. The party's policy was described as including democratic government and a wide measure of autonomy. The promises seemed fair, and were welcomed by the Opposition in Belgrade and Zagreb with the proviso that the government would be judged by its deeds rather than by its words. In July a Concordat with the Holy See, which the late king had ardently desired, had been signed and it was hoped that relations with the Catholic Church would now be untroubled. Much satisfaction was caused on 1 December by a generous amnesty for political offences, which affected some 10,000 persons.

The government, however, gave no sign of an early return to true parliamentarism. Whether on that account (as was stated) or on account of personal jealousy at the promotion of a young colleague to the highest office, the committee of the Radical party announced on 31 March 1936 that they had decided to join the opposition. The Serbian foundation was thus removed from Dr Stojadinović's JRZ, which was left consisting only of the Slovenes, the Moslems and the premier's official adherents. It was not clear whether the government was gradually liquidating the dictatorship by comparatively mild administration of the law, or merely camouflaging, with phrases and gestures, the re-entrenchment of the Army and a sprinkling of ex-Radicals in absolute power.

All shades of opinion were agreed that a solution of the Croat question must be found, and that quickly, before an explosion could take place in Europe, when the Croats might rebel and Jugoslavia be dismembered. Prince Paul had a long and cordial conversation with Dr Maček in December 1936, and they appear to have agreed on the necessity of federalism, though differing on methods of procedure.

The outlines of a possible federal solution were beginning to take shape. The Dynasty, the common Army and Foreign Office were already accepted by Dr Maček. He was now prepared to leave to the central government at least state finance, commerce, posts and telegraphs, and customs. The number and extent of the proposed federalized units were thornier problems. There were eight possible units which could claim autonomy on historic, linguistic or racial grounds—Serbia, Montenegro, Macedonia, Croatia-Slavonia, Dalmatia, Bosnia-Hercegovina, Vojvodina and Slovenia. About Slovenia, there was no dispute. The existing *banovina* of the Drava contained hardly any Jugoslavs except the Slovenes, and their title to autonomy was accepted by all who would discuss federalism at all. But the Serbians were vigorous in declaring that Macedonia and Montenegro must be included in the Serbian unit. To which the reply of the *prečani* was that in that case the former Hapsburg provinces, except Slovenia must be theirs. That Dalmatia should be joined to Croatia-Slavonia was agreed, the only doubtful area being the extreme east of Slavonia, Srem, which was rather to be reckoned as a part of the Vojvodina.

This left the two difficult problems of Bosnia-Hercegovina and the Vojvodina. In the former, the Croat minority would prefer attribution to Croatia, the much larger Serb element would vote for union with Serbia, and the Moslems would desire autonomy. The Croats, if faced with the alternative of Serbia or autonomy, would choose the latter and so give the Moslems a majority. While the Moslems, if refused autonomy, would prefer Croatia to Serbia. Any scheme of partition by which only the solidly Serb eastern border of Bosnia-Hercegovina would be merged in Serbia was resented by the Serbians, who pointed out that the number of Serbs then left in Croatia would be vastly greater than that of the Croats in Serbia. This difficulty applied with equal force to the Vojvodina, which the Serbians claimed on the grounds that the Serbs were the largest single element in the population, that in the past the Vojvodina had been the cultural centre of Serbism and that it was geographically and economically tied to Belgrade.

The Concordat, 1937

The summer of 1937 had been marked by a curious outburst of popular feeling in Belgrade and Serbia. In July a bill, embodying the terms of the Concordat, negotiated by the Jevtić government in 1935 and largely the work of King Alexander himself, was laid before the *Skupština.* ・・・ The bill was carried, amid an uproar inside and outside the *Skupština*, on 23 July by 167 votes to 127. The Synod of the Orthodox Church duly excommunicated all the Orthodox Ministers (except General Marić, since that might have alienated the Army) and the deputies who had voted for the bill. The JRZ ejected those of its members who had not voted for the bill. Eventually in October Dr Stojadinović capitulated and announced that the bill would not be sent on to the Senate (where he was not sure of a majority). The excommunications were lifted in February 1938, and the assembly for the election of the new patriarch, in which Orthodox Ministers had a legal right to vote, was summoned for the 24 February. Thus the project of a Concordat was indefinitely shelved and the Roman Catholic Church remained the only considerable religious body whose relations with the state were unregulated.

The whole episode was a remarkable illustration of the character of Serb Orthodoxy. The cry of 'No Popery' was perhaps the one expedient by means of which Serbian chauvinists could arouse serious opposition to the government in Serbia. The Orthodox Church in Jugoslavia is revered by the Serb peasants as the beloved and historic expression of their nationality. The Serbian bourgeoisie, accustomed to ignore their own nominal religion, were irritated to find their government coming to terms with their bugbear, the Catholic Church, which insisted on spiritual independence and ecclesiastical discipline and whose head was not amenable to secular control. Dr Maček and the Croats ignored the whole affair, whether from a desire not to see Serbo-Croat relations embittered by a religious issue, or from a suspicion that the Concordat was a bribe to detach the Catholic hierarchy from support of Croatian claims.

Dr Stojadinović's successful retention of power, caused even the Radical leaders eventually to make common cause with the Croats.

On 8 October 1937, Dr Maček for the HSS and M. Adam Pribičević for the SDS joined with the three Serbian leaders, M. Aca Stanojević (Radical), M. Davidović (Democrat) and M. J. M. Jovanović (Agrarian), in signing a manifesto of policy, which was sent to Dr Stojadinović. Its value lay not so much in the programme outlined, which was extremely vague, but rather in the spirit of Serbo-Croat co-operation which it fostered and which received tumultuous expression from the Belgrade crowd, when Dr Maček visited the capital in August 1938, accompanied by his Serb colleagues from Croatia and the Vojvodina, and spoke from a balcony to enthusiastic thousands.

Democratic arguments and defiance, however, continued to rebound off the broad shoulders of Dr Stojadinović. He rejected all demands for the revision of the constitution on the grounds that the European position was too delicate for such an experiment, that the Croats could not yet be trusted not to use autonomy as a step to secession, and even that no constitutional change could be made till the king came of age.

Foreign Relations, 1934-8

The most striking feature of Jugoslav trade in the period after the disastrous year of 1932 had been the rapid development of commercial relations with Germany. The German economic penetration had begun, after 1919, with the deliveries of machinery and technical equipment on account of reparations. German firms followed up these deliveries by supplying the demand for renewals and adapting their goods to suit Jugoslav requirements. German manufacturers thus became well established in the Jugoslav market. After the commercial treaty of 1934 Jugoslav raw materials began to be exported to Germany in rapidly increasing quantities, a process accelerated by the cessation of Jugoslav trade with Italy in 1935-6. In March 1936, Germany granted new preferential rates and quotas, to the value of 450 million dinars, in respect of Jugoslav exports of cattle, pigs and wheat; while the Jugoslav government placed considerable contracts for rolling stock, machinery and bridging material in Germany. In June 1936, Dr Schacht visited Belgrade to propose a great increase in trade by barter, and as Germany offered to take Jugoslav raw materials at prices well above world parity, it was not surprising that she obtained them. At last the unfortunate Jugoslav peasant was finding a sure market for his produce, although a large part of the price failed to reach the actual producer.

The bonds of goodwill between Germany and Jugoslavia thus became proportionately stronger and the resistance of the Jugoslav government to a possible German annexation of Austria correspondingly weaker. In the autumn came a further sign of Jugoslavia's changing international position. In his speech at Milan in November, Mussolini referred to 'the extraordinary improvement of atmosphere' between Italy and Jugoslavia and stated that there 'now exist the necessary moral, political and economic bases' for friendship. The Jugoslav premier alluded several times in speeches, early in 1937, to the continued improvement of relations with Italy, and finally Count Ciano visited Belgrade and signed a treaty of friendship on 25 March 1937. Moreover, in the meanwhile, on 24 January, a pact of 'eternal and indissoluble' friendship between Jugoslavia and Bulgaria had been signed. In itself this was all to the good. It was a further step on the path of Jugoslav-Bulgarian amity and was enthusiastically received in the country. But there were those who felt alarm at the successive departures from the policy of reliance on France and the Little Entente (Jugoslavia, Roumania and Czechoslovakia); and in April 1937, the leaders of the Serbian parties united to protest in that sense. Dr Stojadinović was able to reply that the links with Jugoslavia's old friends were as strong as ever, but that he had succeeded in converting old enemies also into friends. In other words, and in view of the heightened tension in Europe, the premier was ensuring his country's safety by conciliating all parties who might affect her position.

Behind these arguments were the growing strength of the anti-democratic powers of the Axis and the good relations of the premier with them, as well as the prosperity brought by German trade. In due course, therefore, the German conquest of Austria was taken calmly by official circles and the Belgrade press; and this attitude was defended by Dr Stojadinović in the Senate on 16 March 1938, on the grounds of German official declarations that the new German-Jugoslav frontier was henceforth inviolable and of his information that the Czechoslovak government were satisfied with the similar German declarations concerning their frontiers.

The elections of December 1938

The agitated summer of 1938 wore on; the government appearing increasingly pro-Axis, the people equally devoted to the Democracies. To strengthen his position, and to break up the apparently united Serbo-Croat opposition, Dr Stojadinović could either have admitted some of the Serbian leaders to a share of power or come to a compromise with Dr Maček. Acting no doubt on the justified belief that the popular forces behind Dr Maček were far more effective than those of the Serbian parties, he approached the Croat leader, but without success, since his proposals fell far short of the federalism which Dr Maček demanded. But the surrender of the Western Powers at Munich in September 1938, and the revelation of Dr Stojadinović's realism in not having trusted to them seemed to offer him an excellent opportunity for an electoral victory. The usual official pressure on electors and, no doubt, some official tampering with voting-papers, combined with insistence on the bankruptcy of democracy in Europe and his promise that, if returned to power, he would negotiate with Dr Maček, seemed to assure success at the polls. The elections were held on 11 December (see p. 344). The approximate results of the elections may be compared with those of 1935 as follows:

	1935		1938
Government (Jevtić)	1,746,982	Government (Stojadinović)	1,643,783
Opposition	1,076,346	Opposition	1,364,524

The complex electoral law gave the Government 306 seats and the opposition 67; but the facts remained that the opposition had considerably increased its votes and come within a reasonable distance of defeating the official lists.

As Dr Stojadinović seemed determined to continue his régime of the 'strong hand', five Ministers—M. Cvetković (a Serbian), two Moslems and two Slovenes—seized the opportunity to resign when a fellow-Minister, on 3 February 1939, made a Serbian chauvinist speech with derogatory references to the *prečani*. Thereupon Dr Stojadinović presented the resignation of his Cabinet, which was promptly accepted. Thus the supposedly indispensable strong man disappeared from the scene. It subsequently transpired that immediately after the elections in December Prince Paul had conducted confidential negotiations with Dr Maček and had been assured that the Croats utterly distrusted Dr Stojadinović. The Prince now installed M. Cvetković in power with a mandate to achieve a settlement with the Croats.

The new government, like its predecessor, was drawn from the official JRZ and contained no outstanding political figures except the premier and the Moslem leader, Dr Spaho. This time determination to reach a settlement of the Croat question was sincere.

Hitler's seizure of Prague in March 1939—which evoked such consternation and rage as to show beyond all doubt the sentiments of the whole nation towards both Germans and Czechs—was like the writing on the wall, warning Prince Paul and his rather colourless team of politicians to agree with the Croats while there was yet time. The Frankist party, which had been almost negligible for many years (see p. 339), began to raise its head, and there were already hints that its extremist wing, under Pavelić, was being held in reserve by the Axis powers as a means of pressure upon Belgrade. Few, if any, then foresaw the rôle reserved for Pavelić in 1941.

The Sporazum, August 1939

For over six months, highly confidential negotiations were conducted between Prince Paul and Dr Maček, and it was not till late in August that all difficulties were overcome. Dr Maček had originally demanded that all the lands of the former Monarchy should form a single autonomous unit, that the constitution of 1931 should be abolished forthwith, and that a coalition government should then steer a new constitution through a Constituent Assembly. He eventually agreed to the creation of three *banovine* in the first instance —a Serbian, a Croatian and a Slovene respectively—subject to two modifications, that the southernmost tip of Dalmatia around Kotor, and the easternmost district of Slavonia, known as Srem (Syrmia), should be assigned to Serbia, and that portions of Bosnia and Western Hercegovina added to Croatia. These three provinces would be run on federal lines, and Maček, who would have preferred to add two more federal units—the Vojvodina and Bosnia-Hercegovina— insisted on leaving open the possibility of some particular district later voting itself into, or out of, one or other federal unit. All of these proposals, however, came to nothing.

By this time it was abundantly clear that Prince Paul, who all along had tried to keep the two questions, national and constitutional, strictly apart, and to solve the former without yielding on the latter, was now bent upon separating the Croats from their allies of the Serbian Opposition. The Regent undoubtedly feared that Hitler and Mussolini might make trouble if Jugoslavia adopted a frankly democratic settlement of her internal problems, though the endless demonstrations in favour of the Czechs were unmistakable signs of what the country was feeling, and how utterly out of sympathy it was with the hedging policy of the Regent.

The so-called *Sporazum* of 26 August 1939 was in the end

concluded in such a way as to give no little offence to the Serbian Opposition and to postpone the constitutional issue, as Prince Paul had wished. Dr Maček was reproached in many quarters for not having insisted on the inclusion of his allies of the three parties in any joint action. In actual fact he only yielded to the direct appeal of the First Regent, recognizing that a European war was imminent and that to leave the Croat question still unregulated would have been to play into the hands of the Frankist extremists.

The *Sporazum* provided for the creation of a new *banovina* which was to be known as 'Croatia'. It comprised a population of 4,400,000 out of a total of 14,000,000: of these 164,000 were Moslems and 866,000 Serbs, the Croats forming 74 per cent of those inside the new boundaries. The office of Ban was restored to its historic importance, and the *Sabor* or Diet of Zagreb was revived for specific purposes—foreign affairs, defence, commerce, transport and public security being reserved for the central government. The legislative power was to be shared by *Sabor* and crown, and the Ban was to be appointed and dismissed by the latter. At the same time the existing artificial *Skupština* was dissolved, and the government was authorized to prepare a new electoral law, and laws on the press, and rights of association and assembly.

The new government formed on this basis was a coalition, under M. Cvetković as Premier, with Dr Maček as Vice-Premier and M. Cincar-Marković as Foreign Minister.   Maček, and his nominee for the Banship, Dr Šubašić, who enjoyed the Prince's confidence, lost no time in setting the new autonomy in motion, with its centre at Zagreb. There was a political amnesty, and the Zagreb press became so out-spoken, not to say indiscreet, as to become the envy of the still much-censored press of Belgrade. The dominant note of the new régime in Croatia was that 'the peasant wants to be, and will be, the chief factor in his fatherland'. But there was much unrest below the surface, and a crop of outrages in Zagreb itself prompted Dr Maček to issue a manifesto denouncing these anarchic tendencies as unchristian and as endangering the national future. This was an unmistakable hit at the Frankist extremists, who now looked to Hitler for the achievement of a mock-independent status for Croatia. The *Sporazum* undoubtedly produced some measure of agreement, but the opportunity for a real political settlement had been missed.

Prince Paul and the Axis, 1940

In February 1940 the four Foreign Ministers of the Balkan Entente (Jugoslavia, Greece, Turkey and Roumania) conferred in Belgrade and issued grandiloquent pronouncements calculated to cover up the painful fact that the Balkan Entente had come to an abrupt end. M. Cincar-Marković quite gratuitously argued that the Balkans were not threatened from any side, and paid compliments varying in warmth to Italy, Bulgaria and Hungary—to the first especially for 'her wise attitude of non-belligerency'. Though this Balkan window-dressing deceived no one, there can be no doubt that Jugoslav-Bulgarian relations showed a steady upward tendency. Another sign of the times was the restoration of trade relations between Belgrade and Moscow, after an interruption of 20 years (Jugoslavia having been the most intransigent of all European states towards Soviet Russia), and the marked satisfaction publicly displayed by the Bulgarian Foreign Minister at this step on the part of the neighbouring state. The intense alarm at the long series of Germany's aggressive acts and the sense of insecurity generated by the loss of the Škoda armament works as a source of military supply and by the inability of the Western Powers to make good even one per cent of the deficiency, help to explain the current of Russophil opinion which now spread through Serbia and Croatia, and led to the dispatch of first a trade, then a military, delegation to Moscow. The restoration of diplomatic relations followed logically. On the other hand, M. Stojadinović was interned by the government in the remote mountain village of Rudnik.

The fall of France in June 1940 and the September *Blitzkrieg* against Britain caused almost universal dismay in Jugoslavia; and though the way in which Britain rallied round Mr Churchill caused corresponding jubilation in all sections of the Jugoslav nation, it was realized that Britain would not in the near future be in a position to send practical help to her friends in the Balkans, and there were therefore a few opportunists in high quarters who favoured a 'realist acceptance of hard facts'—a euphemism for coming to terms with the Axis. While the first German troops began to arrive in Roumania, ostensibly as 'instructors', and while Berlin scarcely deigned to conceal its plans, Belgrade made a great show of neutrality, but talked very categorically of resistance to aggression from whatever quarter, and of the impossibility of permitting the transit of foreign troops across Jugoslav soil. Italy's treacherous attack upon Greece still further incensed Jugoslav opinion against the Axis, and the

Jugoslav General Staff, encouraged by the success of Greek resistance, was inclined to join hands for the defence of Salonica against Italy. Berlin privately encouraged Belgrade to take possession of Salonica while the Greeks were occupied elsewhere, but the trap was altogether too obvious.

On 6 November, General Milan Nedić was replaced as War Minister by General Pešić, a distinguished officer of the previous war, who had latterly made several doubtful incursions into politics and diplomacy, but who seemed best qualified for a Pétainist role. This occurred only a few days after Italian planes had twice dropped bombs on Bitolj (Monastir)—as a sort of reprisal, it was alleged, for the Jugoslav refusal to allow Italy to outflank the Greek right wing by crossing Jugoslav territory. This gave rise to two entirely contradictory versions of Nedić's departure—on the one hand that he was dismissed as anti-German, and on the other that he had submitted a memorandum urging agreement with the Axis and had resented its rejection. The latter is now known to have been nearer the facts. Already those in authority in Jugoslavia were reduced to a policy of anxious negation, clinging to neutrality and playing for time, but utterly at a loss where to rearm or to find allies.

At this early stage of the Balkan tragedy the Turks were specially alarmed and annoyed at King Boris's visit to Berchtesgaden, and warned Sofia that they would not remain inactive in the event of a Bulgarian attack on Greece. They saw the Balkan Entente dissolving before their very eyes, and proposed to Belgrade an immediate Turco-Jugoslav military convention. This was not merely refused by Prince Paul, but carefully concealed from all Jugoslav statesmen, save the pliable Cvetković and Cincar-Marković. Another feature of Prince Paul's balancing policy in these final months of crisis was his cordial response to overtures from Budapest, almost certainly made under prompting from Berlin and Rome. The 'pact of lasting peace and eternal friendship' signed by Hungary at Belgrade on 12 December was received without enthusiasm by a public which had in no way forgotten the fate of Czechoslovakia.

THE FINAL CRISIS, 1941

German intimidation

It was early in 1941 that Jugoslavia showed the first open leanings towards the Axis. On 15 February M. Cvetković and M. Cincar-Marković were summoned to meet Ribbentrop at Salzburg, and to the

Führer's mountain eyrie at Berchtesgaden. At this meeting Cincar-Marković appears to have assured Hitler that Jugoslavia had done all in her power to prevent Greece from accepting British help, and was now ready to give him a guarantee that she would not become an instrument of British policy against the Reich. Hitler thereupon suggested as a fitting achievement of Jugoslav policy the adhesion of the three still neutral Balkan Powers—Jugoslavia, Bulgaria and Turkey—to the Tripartite Pact between Germany, Italy and Japan; otherwise he made no specific demands and was full of soft phrases, stressing his eagerness to see Jugoslavia take her rightful place among the powers of South Eastern Europe.

Prince Paul was now in the toils. At the very moment when Cincar-Marković was absent on a brief return visit to Budapest for the purpose of ratifying the new Hungaro-Jugoslav Pact, Bulgaria took the final plunge; and on 1 March her premier, M. Filov, flew to Vienna to sign Bulgaria's adherence—a step which was at once followed by the entry of German troops into Bulgaria. Prince Paul, too, visited Berchtesgaden in dire secrecy on 3 March. On his return he argued that it was specially difficult for him to make concessions to Germany, owing to his close contacts with Greece and Britain, yet he felt impelled to save the country from war at all costs. In the end it was decided to resume negotiations with Germany. At this stage Prince Paul still hugged the illusion that in return for signing the Tripartite Pact, he would be dispensed from giving the Axis military help or even from opening his territory to German troops in transit. On 13 March the cabinet resumed its discussions, and by this time it was doubtful whether even adherence to the Tripartite Pact would avert warlike complications. As there were already grounds for fearing that Germany was looking round for puppets capable of replacing those actually in power, it was considered wiser to remove M. Stojadinović out of harm's way; on 19 March, in agreement with the British and Greek governments, he was sent from his place of internment to Athens and thence to the island of Mauritius, That Prince Paul consented to the banishment of Stojadinović is generally ascribed to fear lest the latter would overthrow the weak Cvetković and assume control of the situation.

When the cabinet met again on 20 March, Prince Paul was already resigned to what he regarded as the inevitable, and held that the patriarch and the chiefs of the opposition should be informed of the position. In the diplomatic corps it was already feared that Paul's intense unpopularity might provoke an upheaval and that his overthrow, if it took place, might involve the Serbo-Croat *Sporazum*, upon which national unity precariously rested. The first public sign of trouble came on 21 March with the resignation of four Ministers. During the crucial discussion the War Minister, General Pešić, absented himself. Maček's attitude was extremely reserved, but he did not vote against compliance with the German proposals, though by doing so he would probably have tipped the scales against Prince Paul.

The final proposals which Cvetković and Cincar-Marković were instructed by the Prince Regent and cabinet to take with them to Vienna, were that Jugoslovia should adhere to the Tripartite Pact, but with a special protocol suspending certain clauses; in return for this, she would be given a guarantee of her existing frontiers and not compelled to join in the impending military action of the Axis. It is, however, scarcely credible that any of the Ministers can have seriously supposed that they would be let off with an agreement which gave Germany nothing save a paper pledge, and those who resigned were therefore convinced that secret clauses were held in reserve. In any case, the Premier and Foreign Minister left Belgrade on 24 March for Vienna, despite the parting warning that under no circumstances would Britain 'condone' such action. They signed the Pact next day and returned to Belgrade on 26 March to be confronted with a situation that was completely out of hand.

Prince Paul's motives

Three main motives had determined Prince Paul's action. In the first place, he was obsessed—and with good reason—by the military unpreparedness into which his régime had allowed the country to drift during the previous seven years, and which had become acute since the fall of Czechoslovakia and the acquisition of the Škoda armament plants by Germany. He knew that the democracies were unable to supply Jugoslavia or Turkey with war material. He and his generals knew, too, that, quite apart from deficiencies of arms and training, the northern frontier was indefensible, that the railway system was entirely inadequate for purposes of war, that the defence of Belgrade could be outflanked both from Temesvar and from the Fruška Gora, and that the sole hope of a successful defence lay in abandoning the four principal cities—Belgrade, Zagreb, Ljubljana and Subotica—to enemy occupation, with unforeseeable consequences.

His second obsession was Bolshevism, which, he was uncomfortably aware, might make its appeal to a people thoroughly tired of

244

THE FINAL CRISIS, 1941

dictatorship and now enraged at the discovery of its military incompetence.

There was a third and probably decisive motive to Prince Paul's action. In 1939 he had genuinely desired a solution of the Serbo-Croat dispute, but had held out stubbornly until Maček consented to base that solution on a direct agreement between himself and the Prince, instead of basing it on a concentration of all parties, and above all, of the three parties which really represented something in Serbia proper. But this would infallibly have meant the end of the dictatorship and the re-establishment of a democratic régime, and to that he was firmly opposed—using the flimsy pretext that there could be no change of régime until the young king came of age in September 1941. In exactly the same way, in March 1941, to have yielded to the popular demand would have involved replacing the Cvetković government (which was entirely unrepresentative of Serbia, and could only exist by the complaisance of the Croat and Slovene parties which really stood for their respective peoples) by a coalition or concentration in the face of which the dictatorship would have shrivelled and collapsed. The signing of the Pact was not only a vital act of foreign policy; it was the Prince's last bid for retention of power at home.

The Coup d'Etat

The journey of the two Ministers to Vienna had been concealed from the general public, but was widely suspected, and on 26 March, when they returned to Belgrade, the news spread like wildfire. That night a bloodless *coup d'état* was effected; MM. Cvetković and Cincar-Marković, the Regents Stanković and Perović, and other high officials, were placed under arrest; King Peter's majority was proclaimed (though he would not be 18 till September 1941); and Prince Paul (who after hearing the report of his two dutiful Ministers had quickly left Belgrade for his castle of Brdo near the Slovene frontier) was stopped at Zagreb by telephonic order of the new government and sent back to Belgrade, where, after a short interval, he and his family followed M. Stojadinović into exile (this time in Kenya, not Mauritius). Finding no support from any direction, he submitted unconditionally, and thus deprived the wilder spirits of any temptation to more drastic action.

The suddenness and complete success of the *coup d'état* were due to the coalescing of a number of different elements; first and foremost, the younger officers, regular and reservist, in marked contrast to 'the Generals', as the phrase ran; then all the old Serbian parties; then the students, and a considerable number of the staff, of Belgrade University; and, not least of all, the Orthodox clergy and hierarchy, led by the Patriarch Gavrilo.

A new cabinet was now formed under General Simović, with Dr Maček and Professor Slobodan Jovanović as vice-premiers, and it can be said without exaggeration that, since the creation of Jugoslavia, no government so representative of all sections of opinion from Left to Right had ever held office.

The tremendous ovations and demonstrations throughout the country which greeted the change of government, left Hitler in no manner of doubt as to popular sentiment. The rebuff came at a specially awkward moment, when the Japanese Foreign Minister was visiting Berlin. It was rubbed in further by public statements from Mr Churchill and Mr Sumner Welles; and the official Moscow journal, *Pravda*, while denying the story that the Soviet government had congratulated Belgrade, took care to add that the Jugoslav people was worthy of its glorious past and deserved congratulations. On the other hand the Nazi propagandist machine launched a violent campaign against Jugoslavia, publishing a mass of entirely imaginary atrocities. The procedure was the same as that against Czechoslovakia in 1938, when elaborate details were woven round places where no incident of any kind had occurred. Chaos, it was claimed, now reigned in Jugoslavia, promoted by 'agents of Britain'.

General Simović issued an Order of the Day, urging calm and bidding people remain at their posts and avoid demonstrations or spreading of rumours. The proclamation of Belgrade, Zagreb and Ljubljana as open cities showed that the government was under no illusions. In Zagreb, Dr Maček issued a remarkable manifesto to the Croats, speaking as 'A Christian who recalls Christ's word, "Blessed are the Peacemakers."' He had done all he could for peace; he would now co-operate with men who had been his allies in most critical times, and who would both respect and extend Croat interests.

The Invasion

At 5 a.m. on Sunday, 6 April, Goebbels broadcast Hitler's message, informing the German people that their troops had already invaded Jugoslavia and Greece during the night, and laying the entire blame upon Britain—'the worst friend which the Continent had possessed for three centuries'. The Vienna Pact, he declared,

THE FINAL CRISIS, 1941

had been welcomed as preventing an extension of the war; but those who signed it were overthrown by a military clique in British pay, 'with the explicit announcement that this was necessary in view of the government's attitude towards Germany'. Even Hitler's habitual recklessness of statement was far surpassed by his assertion that the alleged anti-German incidents of the past week were the work of the same people who drove the world into war by the Sarajevo murders: 'now, as then, this military clique of criminals was financed and incited by the British Secret Service'. Within 48 hours of this manifesto, Hitler was engaged in entrusting the administration of large parts of Jugoslavia to his agents, and it became clear that he had a plan, long since worked out in every detail, for the disruption of Jugoslavia. Specially addressing his troops, Hitler bade them show themselves 'humane wherever your enemy opposes you humanely. Where he shows his innate brutality, you will crush him ruthlessly and relentlessly'. Within two hours of this proclamation, without any declaration of war, the German Air Force was systematically bombarding the open city of Belgrade. Many public buildings were destroyed, including the king's palace at Dedinje, but not the Prince Regent's palace a few hundred yards away, and the loss of life was estimated at 20,000, though exact figures may never be known.

Meanwhile, at 3 a.m.—just two hours before Hitler's manifesto—a Pact of Friendship had been signed between Soviet Russia and Jugoslavia; but, though giving a mutual guarantee of territorial integrity and non-aggression, it did not commit either party to intervene in the event of aggression by a third Power. It was, however, an unmistakable sign that Moscow saw through the game of Berlin. Next day Mr Churchill, speaking in the House of Commons, paid homage to the Jugoslav people and compared their 'universal spasm of revolt and national resurgence' with that which 'in 1808 convulsed and glorified the people of Spain'. Unhappily, in his next statement on 3 May he had to tell the House that the Jugoslavs had 'saved the soul and future of their country, but it was already too late to save its territory.' For the *Blitzkrieg* had swept all before it. The Jugoslav government hurriedly withdrew from Belgrade into the interior of the Šumadija, then by successive stages to Sarajevo and to Nikšić. Almost from the first, both the government and the High Command lost full control of communications between themselves and the operating armies, which had been only partially mobilized at the eleventh hour.

The High Command had expected the Germans to enter Jugoslavia from the north and, in consequence, had concentrated their main resistance there, depriving General Nedić's southern army of equipment, and omitting to form a joint system of defence with the Greeks. But the main German attack came not from the north but from the eastern frontier with Bulgaria, across to Skoplje and over the difficult mountain ranges into the lower Vardar valley. On 4 April the German army had been massed in Western Bulgaria along the frontier and, on the 6th and 7th, mechanized divisions under Field Marshal List crossed the Jugoslav frontier from the direction of Kustendil and, after defeating the Jugoslav 3rd army, occupied Skoplje on the 9th, and cut the Vardar valley route. At the same time other divisions crossed the frontier from Petrić, and drove through the Strumica gap, turning the uncovered left flank of the Greeks and reaching Salonica by 9 April. Another German column, under General von Kleist, crossed the frontier with Bulgaria farther to the north and, by the fourth day of war, 9 April, Niš had been occupied. Two days later Kragujevac, attacked by von Kleist from the south, had fallen, while the Panzer vanguard of the other German forces under List had already reached Bitolj and the north-west shore of Lake Ohrid at Struga, where they joined Italian troops which had advanced from Albania. Bulgarian forces, following in their rear, occupied Ohrid on 13 April.

Meanwhile, in the north-west, the country had not been seriously defended, owing to sabotage, lack of munitions and the breakdown of communications. On 6 April, German troops had invaded Slovenia, occupying Maribor on the 9th, while Italian forces entered from the south-west and took Ljubljana on the 11th. Other German troops crossed the Drava into northern Croatia on the 10th, capturing Zagreb by a rapid thrust of Panzers on the same day. At noon the Ban of Croatia was informed of the withdrawal of the Jugoslav High Command, and was given exactly half an hour in which to evacuate the city.

In the north-east, other armies, Hungarian and German, had invaded the Vojvodina and Slavonia from three directions, the Hungarians concentrating on Bačka and Baranja, while the Germans entered Slavonia from Hungary and the Banat from Temesvar in Roumania. Belgrade was occupied on the afternoon of 12 April by a small detachment of German troops which had crossed the Sava, while the Hungarians penetrated to Novi Sad and Osijek. The capital was formally captured at dawn on 13 April by von

THE FINAL CRISIS, 1941

Kleist's army which had marched up from Niš. On 15 April the government, with King Peter, escaped by plane to Greece and thence to Palestine, eventually reaching London on 21 June. Sarajevo was captured on 16 April by German troops moving west from Kragujevac and south from Zagreb, while the Italians had overrun the whole of the Adriatic coast and were advancing in Hercegovina towards Mostar. On the evening of the next day, following the surrender of their 2nd army, the Jugoslav High Command capitulated, after negotiating for two days at Belgrade and Sarajevo.

SKETCH MAP OF THE BALKANS, 1941

APPENDIX THREE: Conditions in Yugoslavia
April 1941 to June 1944

Montenegro

After 17 April 1941, Italian control was extended to Montenegro and the creation of the 'kingdom' of Montenegro was proclaimed on 12 July. Its boundaries are in general the same as those of the kingdom of Montenegro in 1914 with the exception of the advance of the Albanian frontier to the south-east. Its seaboard is about 20 miles long, extending from Budva Bay to a point between Bar and Komina.

An Italian Civil Commissioner was appointed to Montenegro in May 1941 and delegates were nominated to represent him at the ten most important centres in the country. The Civil Commissioner was to be assisted by a consultative council of five Montenegrins, three of them being former Montenegrin ministers.

The 'National Assembly' which met at Cetinje on 12 July 1941 and proclaimed Montenegro to be an independent constitutional monarchy, also declared that 'the Montenegrins, grateful for the liberation of their country by the Italian Armed Forces . . . decide to associate the life and destinies of Montenegro with those of Italy'. The King of Italy was therefore requested to designate a regent who should issue a constitution for the country. The throne, however, has remained vacant.

In August 1941, it was announced that the Italian military authorities would retain control of administration in Montenegro and that, as was not done in other former Jugoslav territories occupied by the Italian army, the appointment of civil commissioners would be terminated. At the end of November 1941, a 'Governor's Council' was created for Montenegro. The governor was to be appointed from the Italian army and to have his headquarters at Cetinje; he was to command the Italian troops in the country and to control all civil administration through a subordinate civil commissioner. The lira replaced the dinar as currency. It appears that the local authorities in the towns and villages are Montenegrins. In May 1943, a delegation of the Fascist party was attached to the government of Montenegro. It was stated that the country was to be divided administratively into fifteen districts, but in fact the Italians had hardly any control outside the towns of Cetinje, Nikšić and Podgorica and the administrative units and general machinery remained the same as when Montenegro formed part of Jugoslavia. After the Italian collapse, the Germans set up a puppet 'National Administration' of Montenegrins.

Serbia

Since the German occupation in April 1941, Serbia has been reduced to even narrower frontiers than those existing before the First Balkan War.

The northern and western frontiers are those of 1912—to the north, they are marked by the Danube and the Sava, to the west by the Drina. The eastern, south and south-western frontiers have been modified by the Bulgarian and Albanian annexations.

On 30 April 1941 the German commander-in-chief in Serbia established an administrative council and commissioned a number of Serbs as heads of administrative departments to co-operate with the German command. The members of this council were drawn mainly from the Stojadinović and Ljotić political groups   · · ·   The effective ruler of Serbia, under the commander-in-chief, however, was Neuhausen, the former German Consul-General at Belgrade, who, as 'Economic Dictator', was

CONDITIONS BETWEEN APRIL 1941 AND JUNE 1944

entrusted with the reconstruction of Serbian economy. In August 1941, a Serbian government was formed under General Nedić, the former Minister of War • • • to enable 'the German troops to relinquish the tasks which are the concern of the Serbs themselves, if they are willing to co-operate in reconstruction'.

But the central government of Serbia is not that of an independent state. The country is officially the *Gebiet des Militärbefehlshabers Serbiens* and the supreme authority is that of the G.O.C. for the whole area of Serbia. Responsible to him are the head of the Military Administration (*Chef des Verwaltungsstabes beim Befehlshaber in Serbien*) and the economic controller (*General-bevollmächtigter für die Wirtschaft in Serbien*). The Serbian government is under the general control of these supreme German authorities and it has no Ministers for Foreign Affairs or Defence.

The head of the military administration works in close collaboration with the military general headquarters and with the Serbian ministers. In the provinces, Feldkommandants, Kreiskommandants and Ortskommandants held key positions in civil administration and they serve both the military and the civil authorities. Through the Serbian government, the *Chef des Verwaltungsstabes* has control over the whole system of local government. The former *banovine*, of which none has been wholly contained within the reduced Serbia, were abolished and the country was divided into fifteen *okrugi* (counties). Each of these is further divided into about six *srezovi* • • • The head of each county is the *načelnik* who is assisted by officials representing the different departments of government.

The economic controller is in charge of the organization of the main branches of economy within the country. There are German commissioners for industry and raw materials, for bank-note circulation and for clearing; in addition, German officials are attached to the most important economic concerns, such as banks, companies and insurance societies.

The Gestapo has established headquarters at Belgrade, and is divided into six sections. In December 1941, the Serbian State Guard (*Srpska Državna Straža*) was instituted; the various forces of police were thus consolidated into a single service with urban, rural and frontier divisions. This State Guard is under the control of both the Ministry of the Interior (through the chief of State Security) and the chief of the Gestapo in Serbia.

Under the legal system established by the occupying power, the courts of the German armed forces apply German law and have the right to punish any violation of German laws. No specification of offences has been promulgated and the German courts may punish any act they consider harmful to German interests. They have also jurisdiction to try offences committed before the occupation.

The Banat

Since April 1941, the Banat • • • though nominally part of Serbia, has been economically and administratively separated from it. This territory extends between the Tisa, the Danube and the Roumanian frontier.

Immediately after April 1941, the Banat came provisionally under German military control and at first it had no economic or even postal connexion with the rest of Jugoslavia. Entry into the region from Serbia was allowed only with the permission of the German police president at Veliki Bečkerek. The large and prosperous German *Volksgruppe* in the Banat . . . was well organized, and, in March 1942, General Nedić

CONDITIONS BETWEEN APRIL 1941 AND JUNE 1944

formally annexed by Albania. Since that date, the Albanian frontiers have been further extended both to the north-east and to the north-west. To the north-east, Albania has taken the districts of Gusinje and Plav, the plain of Metohija (including Peć), a considerable part of the plain of Kosovo, the upper Vardar valley (including Tetovo) as far as a point north-west of Skoplje, the basin of the Crni Drim from Debar to Lake Ohrid (including Struga) and the northern and eastern shores of Lake Prespa. This north-eastern frontier now starts from a point slightly south-west of Vranje and runs west almost to Mitrovica, leaving Priština to Albania but Vučitrn and the Trepča mines to Serbia; thence it continues westwards, north of Peć, Gusinje and Plav.

To the north-west, Albania was given a small part of the plain of Pod-gorica (extending as far west as Plavnica), together with the district of Ulcinj (Dulcigno), south of Bar (Antivari).

The territory annexed from Jugoslavia has been administered in four prefectures, namely those of Peć (Peja), Priština, Prizren and Debar (Dibra), with sub-prefectures at Djakovica, Orahovac, Suhareka, Tetovo and Rostuše. Albanian officials appointed by the government at Tirana were made responsible for administration in these districts; they were assisted by Italian advisers from the Fascist party. The Italians introduced Fascist institutions in addition to the state machinery, but a marked scarcity of qualified administrators has made efficient administration an acute problem.

Bulgaria

The western boundary of the territory annexed by Bulgaria runs from Mt. Midžor on the Stara Planina, passes between Pirot and Bela Palanka, thence continues east of Grdelica and meets the new Serbo-Albanian frontier west of Vranje. The eastern shore of Lake Ohrid, including the town of Ohrid, as far east as the village of Peštani was ceded to Bulgaria by an agreement with Italy in April 1943. East of a point between Bitolj and Florina, the southern frontier remains as it was before April 1941.

Since January 1942, Bulgarian military forces have occupied the area between Niš and Kragujevac, and a free zone has been granted to Bulgaria in the port of Bar.

In April 1941, a Bulgarian prefect was established at Skoplje. Bulgarian administration was gradually extended throughout the occupied area and three *oblasti* • • • were formed. In the north, the districts of Nišava, Lužnica and Caribrod, in the former Moravska *banovina* and the district of Bosiljgrad, in the Vardarska *banovina*, have been incorporated, under the name of Morava, within the administrative region of Sofia. To the south, the greater part of the Vardarska *banovina* has been formed into the new regions of Skoplje and Bitolj, and these are collectively called Macedonia.

The Independent State of Croatia

On 16 April 1941, Pavelić formally inaugurated the independent state of Croatia and the boundaries of the new state were gradually defined. • • • On the north the frontier follows the Drava and the Danube, as far as the confluence of the Sava with the Danube opposite Belgrade. To the west, the boundary with German and Italian-annexed Slovenia was defined in May 1941; it follows the boundary of the former Dravska *banovina* • • • from its junction with the Drava, south-west to a point on the Kupa, north of Delnice, thence to the sea between Bakar (Buccari) and Kraljevica (Porto Ré). Along the Adriatic coast, Croatia has retained the seaboard from south of Bakar (east of Sušak) as far as Novigrad inlet, as well as the island of Pag and the Velebit (Podgorski) Channel. Farther south, the coast from slightly south-east of Split to a point slightly beyond Cavtat (including the ports of Metković and Gruž), as well as the islands of Brač and Hvar, belong to Croatia. The frontier-line re-enters the mainland between Cavtat and Gruda and runs north-west until it joins the Montenegrin frontier at Mt. Orjen; from this point northwards, it follows the pre-1918 frontier between Montenegro and Austria-Hungary · · · , then, after crossing the Lim at Uvac, it goes east of Višegrad and follows the 1912 boundary of Bosnia and Serbia (Fig. 26) to the Drina, thence along the right bank of the river to its confluence with the Sava, and thereafter along the Sava to its confluence with the Danube (thus enclosing the region of Srem within Croatia).

Until September 1943 the 'Independent State of Croatia' (*Nezavisna Država Hrvatska*) was a monarchy under King Tomislav II (the Duke of Spoleto, who later became Duke of Aosta) who preferred, however, to remain in Italy. In practice, Ante Pavelić, the *Poglavnik* (or 'Leader'), assumed all power on the Führer-principle and governed through a cabinet and a 'council of state' whose functions were to 'draw up all decrees, regulations, orders of proceedings, instructions and authoritative decisions of general significance'. At the beginning of 1942, Pavelić revived the *Sabor* · · · ; surviving members of the former Croatian 'Diet' and several members ot the Peasant Party were invited to attend, but most of the latter either refused or merely ignored the summons; indeed the Peasant Party, on the whole, has consistently refused to collaborate with Pavelić, who is now 'Head' of the state.

Administrative inefficiency has been the main feature of the Poglavnik's rule. The state is divided into 23 prefectures (*velike župe*), which are further divided into 142 districts (*kotari*) and cities. The districts are divided into administrative communes (*općine*). Members of the *Ustaša* party have been appointed heads of most of these administrative units; and the police are under the control of the prefect (*Veliki Župan*). The Ustaš Security Service has taken over the duties of the Jugoslav gendarmerie.

In 1942, the civil administration of the coastal regions was transferred from the Italians to the Croat government, but the Italians retained control over three regions: the Dubrovnik area, part of south-west Bosnia and part of the Lika district crossed by the Ogulin-Split railway.

Alongside of the local administrative officials, the *Ustaša* party has its own organization: there is a *stožernik* in the chief town of each prefecture, a *logornik* in each district and a *tabornik* in each commune; each of these has four to six assistants. The *Ustaša* representatives are not state officials but they are entrusted with the task of developing opinions agreeable to the régime among the population, and they have not been without influence over the state officials.

Although the central government of Croatia is nominally that of an independent state, with the usual departments of government, final decision on all important civil matters rest with the German minister to Croatia. In Zagreb the Gestapo, too, is said to operate freely, and German control has extended to several spheres of civil and economic administration. The German *Volksgruppe*, with its headquarters at Osijek, is organized on the 'leadership principle' and forms a widely autonomous state within a state

CONDITIONS BETWEEN APRIL 1941 AND JUNE 1944

appointed the leader of the *Volksgruppe* as head of the civil administration. Thus the Germans have been able to treat the province virtually as a German colony administered by the *Volksgruppe*. Its relationship to the Serbian government is not clear.

SOCIAL CONDITIONS

General Features

In Slovenia, the Germans have taken extensive measures to Germanize the area by the deportation of Slovenes and by the settlement of German peasants and also to accomplish its economic assimilation to Greater Germany. Food conditions both in this area and in Italian Slovenia appear to be better than in the rest of partitioned Jugoslavia. On the other hand, in Dalmatia, in the Croatian coastal zone, in Bosnia-Hercegovina and in Montenegro the food situation has deteriorated catastrophically and little has been supplied by the occupying power. Little is known of the Albanian-annexed regions, but here, too, the standard of living is likely to have declined considerably. In the 'Hungarian' districts, Jugoslavs who had immigrated since 1918 were ejected and Magyars settled on the land. Food production has not shown any serious decline; indeed the Axis powers have secured useful quantities of grain from Bačka and Baranja. The Bulgarians have pursued a severe policy of Bulgarization in Macedonia, and as a whole the standard of living is very low.

The supply of food to the towns of Croatia, which has a relatively high proportion of urban population, has been a serious problem since the Pavelić régime created the 'independent state'. Apart from the northern belt of the country, all the main foodstuffs are in short supply throughout the state and there are considerable variations in quantities available from town to town. In the more backward areas of the country, especially in the coastal districts, conditions are worse and even the rural districts suffer privation. These shortages have only partly been due to reduced production, since inadequate control over agricultural production has also been a serious factor. In January 1943, Pavelić issued a civil mobilization decree which demanded service from all inhabitants of the state, either for the Ministry of War or for the Ministry of the Interior. The mobilization has been limited, however, to the labour necessary for the functioning of the transport services.

The more complete German control over Serbia has made exploitation more open and more extensive than in Croatia. The new state has been virtually isolated not only from the rest of Jugoslavia but also from other parts of Europe. Since the important agricultural region of the Banat is separately administered, any available surplus has been exported by the Germans to Germany with the result that the southern 'deficient' areas ... have been short of foodstuffs, especially in the towns. The standard of living in Serbia has therefore substantially deteriorated. Further privation has been caused by the burden of occupation costs and of increased taxation. The population has also suffered from shortages of clothing and fuel, from inflation and from the enforcement of compulsory labour. Late in 1942, the German Economic Controller issued an order compelling the peasants to deliver their grain in order to assure supplies for the population, for the occupying forces, for the state guard and for heavy workers; the balance was to be placed at the disposal of the Economic Controller.

Religion

The Orthodox Church. The Serbian Orthodox clergy have played an important part in resisting foreign occupation under the Patriarch Gavrilo's gallant leadership; though he himself was soon imprisoned by the Germans, as were other Serbian bishops. In former Jugoslav Macedonia, the Bulgarians have expelled Serb bishops and priests and have replaced them with their own. In Croatia, too, the Orthodox hierarchy have suffered considerably at the hands of the *Ustaše*. After the independent Croat state had been set up, an Autocephalous Croat Orthodox Church was established to include the 1½ million Orthodox of Croatia, and a Russian bishop of the Karlovci Synod (see p. 221) was put at its head. It is technically in accordance with Orthodox theory that a separate state should have a separate ecclesiastical organization, but the new patriarch and his followers have been indignantly repudiated by the Serb Church, and the newly created Church has been unable to find an adequate supply of priests.

The Roman Catholic Church. The Roman Catholic Church in Slovenia, where most of the priests themselves came of peasant families, has long been the champion of Slovene nationalism • • • and it is not surprising that the clergy in the German-occupied part of the country were savagely persecuted by the new rulers. They were subjected to the grossest indignities, and the churches did not escape from sacrilege. Within a short time, the number of priests in the diocese of Maribor was reduced from 474 to 7, and there was a similar reduction in the German-annexed parts of the diocese of Ljubljana. The exiled Slovenes, 60,000 of whom have been transported to Serbia, and those priests who succeeded in escaping, have been received with great kindness, not only by the Croats but also by the Serbs, headed by the Orthodox clergy. In Italian-occupied Slovenia, the Church enjoys a more favoured position and the clergy are unrestricted. In Croatia, the Pavelić régime has done its utmost to gain the full support of the Church, but the Roman Catholic clergy, following the lead of Mgr Stepinac, Archbishop of Zagreb, have protested strongly both against the *Ustaš* persecution of Serbs and Jews and against the government's attempts to force conversion to Roman Catholicism.

The Moslems. Soon after the establishment of the independent state of Croatia, the Moslems were assured complete religious and cultural autonomy. They have been given considerable financial assistance; state subsidies to Moslem schools have been substantially increased and several new ones have been founded. In the summer of 1942, Pavelić ordered the construction of a mosque in Zagreb for the 3,500 Moslems in Croatia-Slavonia. There is a large Moslem element both among the officials of the Croat government and among the *Ustaše*.

The Jews. Towards the end of April 1941, the Germans enforced severe anti-Jewish measures in Serbia, and several concentration camps were set up. The Jews of Bulgarian-annexed Macedonia were deported early in 1943. The German example has been followed in Croatia since April 1941, and Jewish laws have been vigorously applied. For example, in July 1941, Pavelić decreed that all the Jewish inhabitants of Zagreb should be deported to an island in the Adriatic; later, all Jewish synagogues in Zagreb were ordered to be demolished. Intensified anti-Semitic measures have also been introduced in Sarajevo. Confiscation of property, persecution and extermination have been the results of the carefully planned anti-Jewish laws.

King Petar II

FORCES OF RESISTANCE

The resistance of the Jugoslav peoples to enemy oppression has been on a large and heroic scale. Civil disobedience has been almost general. Sabotage has been widespread and effective. Open warfare has broken out at one time or another in almost every district under German, Italian or *Ustaš* control. Jugoslav resistance has successfully diverted many enemy divisions besides large Croatian forces which might otherwise have been employed to swell the German armies.

Several factors have helped to strengthen popular resistance. First, large numbers of Jugoslav soldiers were able to escape after the first thrust of the German invasion. Some of these dispersed to their homes, retaining their arms or hiding them in secret dumps. Small bands of others remained in difficult country which was not cleared by the Germans. Again, Jugoslav mobilization had been far from complete; units were still assembling in the western regions while the invasion proceeded and they dispersed either unattacked or without serious fighting. Since the capitulation, constant German demands for labour or produce (Pavelić has sent over 100,000 Croat workers to Germany) and conscription for the Croat army have also strengthened resistance. Finally, there is a strong tradition of the glories of irregular warfare, and memories of the never-despairing struggle for freedom in former centuries have been a powerful incentive to hope and action. The physical features of the country, too, have made successful

256

CONDITIONS BETWEEN APRIL 1941 AND JUNE 1944

guerilla activity possible, and soon after the capitulation in 1941, several groups of Jugoslavs were taking part in some sort of organized active resistance.

In Serbia, the largest group was that formed under the leadership of Colonel Mihajlović. It consisted of Serbian remnants of the Jugoslav army, of members of the semi-military and Serb nationalist Četnik organization and of ordinary citizens. There were also Partisan formations organized and directed by Communists. In 1941, Četnik and Partisan collaboration in Serbia resulted for a time in their holding four-fifths of the whole country, but a powerful German punitive expedition soon followed and by the end of the year organized fighting had ceased. Extensive areas had been laid waste and thousands of people, many of whom had taken no part in the revolt, were shot. The Partisans either dispersed or withdrew to Montenegro and Bosnia, where they joined other Partisan guerilla bands. Some of the Četniks, too, withdrew to the west to carry on the battle, while others scattered apparently to await a more opportune moment.

The areas under Croat rule have suffered less systematic repression than the rest of Jugoslavia, despite the terrorist practices of the *Ustaše* and their well-planned onslaughts on the Serb population, especially in northern and western Bosnia. Pavelić and his ministers have openly proclaimed their intention of removing the Serb element from the population and the *Ustaše* were given a free hand to use 'the steel broom' for this purpose. Nevertheless, Partisan forces hostile to the régime, including many thousands of Bosnian Serbs, gave battle to the *Ustaše* and joined up with other Partisans from Serbia. Throughout 1942 the Partisan forces continued the guerilla war in central and western Bosnia and in southern Croatia, but there was no news of guerilla activities in Serbia or Slovenia, although highly organized civil disobedience was effectively employed throughout the country.

Not only was actual fighting becoming confused, but the political issues presented an even more complex pattern. Of the many different groups taking part in some form of organized active resistance, the two main forces were the troops of Mihajlović operating on the borders of Serbia and Montenegro, and the National Army of Liberation (N.L.A.), commanded by Marshal Tito. By the beginning of 1943 a rift appeared between General Mihajlović and the Partisans; the latter alleged that some of the Četniks were collaborating with the Axis against the Partisans. Meanwhile, fighting was concentrated in three areas—around Karlovac in western Croatia, in the Bihać district of west Bosnia, and in south Bosnia around Travnik. A German and Italian drive against the Partisans in western Bosnia and southern Croatia was launched in the early months of 1943. There were also Partisan activities in Slavonia and in Slovenia, around Ljubljana, where the groups were in contact with Partisans from Croatia. After an offensive of two months' duration, the Axis forces had succeeded in occupying several major places, but they had entirely failed in their main purpose, namely, the encirclement and the annihilation of the N.L.A. On the contrary, Partisan troops had now regained the initiative in various sectors and they dominated the heights along the Sarajevo-Mostar railway. War reports published by the N.L.A. through Radio Free Jugoslavia often cover considerable periods of time, but it is clear that between March 1943 and January 1944, the Partisans, aided by supplies from the Allies, gained control of large areas in the interior of Jugoslavia, especially the mountainous regions of Bosnia, Dalmatia, Montenegro and the Sanjak, the hills of Slavonia, the Croat-Slovene border and many districts in Slovenia. On the other hand, the German forces, together with the 'government' forces of Croatia

CONDITIONS BETWEEN APRIL 1941 AND JUNE 1944

and Serbia, were in control of the main lines of communication, the river valleys, most of the Adriatic coast and islands, and the more accessible parts of Croatia, Slavonia, Bosnia and central Serbia. But the border-line between liberated and enemy-controlled territory cannot be clearly demarcated for it varies according to the fortunes of war. In his survey before Parliament on 22 February 1944, Mr Churchill described the state of resistance in Jugoslavia and in referring to the Partisans he stated that 'the whole movement has taken shape and form, without losing, as I say, the guerilla quality without which it could not possibly succeed. These forces are, at this moment, holding in check no fewer than 14 German divisions, out of 20 in the Balkan peninsula. Around and within these heroic forces, a national and unifying movement has developed. The Communist element had the honour of being the beginners, but, as the movement increased in strength and numbers, a modifying and unifying process has taken place, and national conceptions have supervened. In Marshal Tito, the Partisans have found an outstanding leader, glorious in the fight for freedom'.*

Under Marshal Tito, the anti-Fascist council for the liberation of Jugoslavia (AVNOJ) claims to represent all the sections of the Jugoslav people according to their relative strengths; its aims are stated to be, first and foremost, the liberation of Jugoslavia from German domination, and, secondly, the formation of a new Jugoslav state on a democratic and federal basis. The name of Dr Maček, whom Pavelić has kept in strict confinement, remains venerated in Croatia, and the Peasant Party, though weakened, is still supported by the majority of the people though some of its leaders have joined the Partisans. In Slovenia, the Freedom Front (O.F.) continues the struggle for national liberation. In Serbia, however, active resistance is almost at a standstill.

On 24 May 1944, Mr Churchill again spoke of the resistance movement in Jugoslavia and summed up the position thus: 'The reason why we have ceased to supply Mihajlovitch with arms and support is a simple one. He has not been fighting the enemy and, moreover, some of his subordinates have made accommodations with the enemy from which have arisen armed conflicts with the forces of Marshal Tito, accompanied by many charges and counter-charges, and the loss of patriot lives to the German advantage. We have proclaimed ourselves the strong supporters of Marshal Tito because of his heroic and massive struggle against the German armies. We are sending, and planning to send, the largest possible supplies of weapons to him and to make the closest contact with him. . . . It must be remembered, however, that this question does not turn on Mihajlovitch alone; there is also a very large body, amounting to perhaps 200,000, of Serbian peasant proprietors who are anti-German but strongly Serbian and who naturally hold the views of a peasant ownership community in regard to property, less enthusiastic in regard to communism than some of those in Croatia and Slovenia. Marshal Tito has largely sunk his communist aspect in his character as a Yugoslav patriot leader. He repeatedly proclaims he has no intention of reversing the property and social systems which prevail in Serbia, but these facts are not accepted yet by the other side.'†

* *Parliamentary Debates (Hansard)*, vol. 397, pp. 692–94 (22 February 1944).
† *Parliamentary Debates (Hansard)*, vol. 400, pp. 776–7 (24 May 1944).

[Editor's Note: The Author of this book, Mr. Milija Lasic-Vasojevic, specifically refutes Mr. Churchill's naive comments above through the events recounted in the text of this book.]

Miljan Vukov-Vesovic, Duke of the Vasojevic "tribe" and senator in the parliament of the then-independent nation of Montenegro late in the 19th century. He was head of the clan from which many of the persons mentioned in this book were members.

APPENDIX FOUR: A Brief History of Montenegro

'When God finished making the world,' runs an old Montenegrin ballad, 'He found that he had a great many rocks left in His bag; so He tumbled the whole lot on to a wild and desolate bit of country —and that is how Montenegro was formed.' This legend embodies the most important fact about the geography and history of Montenegro. The barren limestone country around Cetinje was a very inaccessible fortress, and its caves and rocks gave ample opportunity for guerilla warfare. It was the only corner of the Balkan lands to escape the domination of the Turk from the fourteenth century onwards; here, a few Christian shepherds and goatherds always maintained their liberty. It is true that the Turks sometimes managed to penetrate into the wild country, but they could never maintain their forces for long. Montenegro remained a small island of freedom in the great Turkish sea. That is her essential role in the history of the Balkans.

The early state, 1356–1516

The early history of the area that became Montenegro forms part of the story of the rise of medieval Serbia ; and it was not until the break-up of Stephen Dušan's realm, after his death in 1355, that the distinctive unit to be known as Montenegro emerged as an independent principality. This area north of Lake Scutari had been known as the 'Zeta'. It had formed one of the divisions of Dušan's realm, and, in the confusion after his death, a noble named Balša succeeded in establishing himself as master of the Zeta, and in founding a dynasty that lasted until 1421. The territory of the Balšas seems to have reached the Adriatic at Antivari (Bar) and Budva, and its capital, for a time at any rate, was Scutari itself.

The name 'Montenegro', which came into general use early in the fifteenth century, is the Venetian form of the Italian 'Monte Nero', called 'Crna Gora' in Serbian. This term 'Black Mountain' was derived, according to one view, from the dark appearance, at some seasons of the year, of Mount Lovćen in the country immediately to the north of Lake Scutari. The name itself, then, is an indication of the close relations that existed with the Venetians; the Balšas and Venice were sometimes in dispute about Scutari and other places, and at other times in alliance against the Turk.

When the male line of the Balšas became extinct in 1422, a new dynasty was founded by Stephen Crnojević, who established his capital at Zabljak on the north-eastern edge of Lake Scutari. By this time the Ottoman Turks had advanced well into the Balkan peninsula; and, after the great Christian defeat at Kosovo in 1389, the Zeta in the west had provided a refuge for many who fled before the Turkish conquerors. In the next century, it was entirely surrounded by Turkish territory; Bosnia fell in 1463; Albania in 1478; Hercegovina in 1482. Thus it was that Stephen's successor, Ivan the Black, was forced, after a vigorous resistance, to abandon Zabljak, and to withdraw to the more inaccessible country to the north. Here, not far from Mount Lovćen itself, he established his new capital at Cetinje, and this was to remain the capital throughout all the later history of the principality. 'The history of the Zeta becomes narrowed down into the history of the Crnagora.'* Deprived of the fertile plains of Lake Scutari, and cut off from the sea-coast, the destiny of the Montenegrins was to wage incessant warfare against the Turk for almost four centuries.

A whole cycle of legends has gathered around the name of 'Ivan the Black', telling of his valorous deeds against the Turks, and of how one day he would arise to drive the Turks from Europe. Amongst his other preoccupations, Ivan found time to import a printing press from Venice. It was set up at Obod, to the south of Cetinje, and from here, after 1493, were issued some of the earliest books printed in Cyrillic characters. Ivan built a monastery at Cetinje, and also made it the see of a bishopric. It was into the hands of these bishops, or 'vladikas', that the destiny of the country passed when the descendants of Ivan ceased to rule in 1516.

The elective Vladikas, 1516–1696

The Crnojević dynasty came to an end in 1516, when Montenegro was transformed from a temporal into a theocratic state. The details of the change-over are obscure and not easy to explain, but the monks of Cetinje, from among whom the bishop was elected, had always been a powerful influence in Crna Gora. Their fanaticism had supported the struggle against the Turks; and, during the absences of the later Crnojević rulers, who seemed frequently to have gone to Venice, the bishops may have taken control. At any rate, tradition records that the last Crnojević transferred his power to the bishop before leaving finally for Venice.

* F. S. Stevenson, *A History of Montenegro*, p. 100 (London, 1914).

From this time onward until 1851, the Montenegrins were ruled by the bishops of Cetinje. The bishops, or vladikas, were elected by local assemblies, and after 1557 were consecrated by the patriarch of Peć. 'The word Vladika meant originally a powerful person, or ruler. . . . and in several Slavonic languages, as for example in Czech, it has preserved unimpaired its original signification. Among the Serbs, however, it was gradually specialized, and came to denote a bishop. The title of Vladika which belonged to the rulers of Montenegro . . . though used in the Serbian sense of the word, may be said to unite in itself the notion of secular power with that of episcopal rank in the ecclesiastical hierarchy.'* This union of temporal and spiritual power may well have saved Montenegro. The vladika, as an ecclesiastic, was unlikely to desert to Islam, while his office was by its nature beyond the ambitions of civil chieftains. A civil governor still continued to exist, but his office was entirely subsidiary to that of the vladika.

The seventeenth century was marked by repeated attacks from the Turks; Cetinje itself was captured in 1623 and again in 1687; and it has even been asserted that the Montenegrins were forced to pay tribute for a short time. But the Turks soon withdrew, for, in the mountains of Montenegro, 'a small army is beaten, a large one dies of starvation'. At this time, two Montenegros may be said to have existed—a free Montenegro centred on Cetinje, and an 'unredeemed' Montenegro peopled by Islamized Slavs and Albanians to the south.

The hereditary Vladikas, 1696–1851

The reign of Danilo I, 1696–1737. Before the end of the century a great change took place in 1696 when Danilo Petrović of Njeguši was elected vladika. His successors continued to rule the state until it came to an end in the war of 1914–18. The new feature introduced in 1696 was the power of the vladika to nominate a successor from among his relations. As an Orthodox bishop, he was perforce celibate, and the succession was usually continued from uncle to nephew. It was in this strange form that the theocratic state adopted the hereditary principle. The central power was thus established upon a more stable basis, and with this new cohesion the state was better able to withstand changes from without.

During the reign of Danilo I, every effort was made to revive the fortunes of Montenegro, and there were important developments

* F. S. Stevenson, *History of Montenegro*, pp. 128–9 (London, 1914).

both at home and abroad. Some Montenegrins had adopted Islam, and these renegades had given aid to the Turks. In order to strengthen the state, therefore, desperate action was taken, and on Christmas Eve 1702, a wholesale massacre (the 'Montenegrin Vespers') rid the country of all Mohammedan men—whether Turks, Slavs or Albanians. After this, the struggle was continued with fury on both sides. In 1712, the Turks were defeated, but two years later they were able, after many reverses, to occupy Cetinje for a third time. The Turkish army, however, harassed by guerilla warfare, and suffering from lack of provisions, was forced to leave the desolation of Crna Gora to its hardy inhabitants.

In the meantime, a new factor had entered into Montenegrin history. Russia, under Peter the Great, was in conflict with the Turks, and had become increasingly interested in the Balkan lands. · · · In 1711, Russian envoys came to the Montenegrins, as to other Balkan peoples, and the Czar was hailed as the champion of Montenegrin liberty. In 1715, the vladika visited Peter the Great, who recognized Montenegrin independence, and granted a subsidy to enable the Montenegrins to rebuild their devastated villages. It was the first of many subsidies, and each of Danilo's successors repeated his visit to the Czar. From now on, sometimes in conjunction with the Venetians, Danilo was able to win many victories over the Turks, and, by his death in 1737, Montenegrin independence had survived some of its most fierce trials.

The reign of Sava, 1737–82. Danilo was succeeded in 1737 by his nephew Sava, a man of very different temperament, and little suited to be the ruler of a hardy people in stirring times. He was unable to check the feuds and independence of the local chieftains, and it was a confused period. For the greater part of his reign, Sava remained in the background, and the effective power was wielded for a time by his cousin Vasilije (1750–66), and then by an adventurer, Stephen Mali (1768–74), who claimed to be none other than the Russian Emperor Peter III, the murdered husband of Catherine II. Despite these complicated internal politics, the Turks were on several occasions defeated, and were never able to subdue Crna Gora.

The reign of Peter I, 1782–1830. A new era dawned in 1782 with the death of Sava and the accession of his nephew Peter I, called by later generations 'the great and holy vladika'. He did much to reconcile the dissensions among the various factions of the state; the administration was reorganized, and in 1798 the first Montenegrin code of laws was established. 'He found a loose coalition of clans and tribes, he left a relatively united state'.* Peter, too, took part in the war of Austria and Russia against Turkey, though the Montenegrins gained nothing out of the peace treaties made by their allies in 1791 (Sistova) and 1792 (Jassy) respectively. He was able, however, to inflict a defeat on the Turks, and, in the year 1799, Turkey not only formally recognized the independence of Montenegro, but declared that 'the Montenegrins have never been subjects of our Sublime Porte'—an admission that was to constitute an important precedent. About this time, also, the region of the Brda (to the north-east), whose inhabitants had often acted in concert with those of Crna Gora, was finally incorporated into Montenegro. It was a considerable accession of territory at the expense of Turkey.

During these years, too, the little principality became involved in the complicated affairs of Napoleonic Europe. In 1806, the Montenegrins, in conjunction with the Russians, opposed the French in Dalmatia by contesting Ragusa and occupying the shores of the Gulf of Kotor (the Bocche di Cattaro). . . . The Treaty of Tilsit in 1807, however, left the gulf to the French until 1813, when the Montenegrins, in combination this time with the British fleet under Admiral Fremantle, drove them out. For five months, the shores of the gulf became Montenegrin territory, and the capital of Montenegro was even moved to Kotor (Cattaro). But at the Congress of Vienna, 1814–15, the area was handed back to the Austrians, and, on the advice of Russia, Montenegro yielded up the port together with the opportunity of an outlet on the Adriatic; the state remained landlocked until 1878–80.

For the last fifteen years of his life, Peter was at work uniting the various elements of the state in the face of constant threat from the Turks. He attempted to put an end to the blood feuds which, handed down from one generation to another, had divided families and weakened the country. Under his guidance, the government was assuming a more stable and consolidated character, and the way was prepared for the reforms of his successors. Turkish invasions were repelled in 1819–21 and again in 1828–9. When he died in 1830, at the age of eighty-one, he was venerated as a saint. He had nearly doubled the area of his country; he had cemented relations with Russia; and he had maintained the integrity of the state in the face both of internal friction and of Turkish peril.

* H. W. V. Temperley, *History of Serbia*, p. 154 (London, 1919).

MONTENEGRO

The reign of Peter II, 1830–51. Peter I was succeeded in 1830 by his nephew Peter II, who became famous as a reformer, warrior and poet. His famous epic 'The Mountain Garland' tells of the struggle against the Turk. He set up a printing press at Cetinje, and did much to further the humanizing work of his predecessor. Important changes were made, too, in the administration of the country, in order to increase the central authority at the expense of the unruly chiefs. A permanent senate of twelve members was established at Cetinje in 1831; and a year later the office of civil governor, which had existed since 1516, was abolished; the ecclesiastical power thus completely swallowed the temporal authority.

Abroad, the first half of Peter II's reign was marked by continued struggle against the Turks. The Montenegrins were offered the town of Scutari, and a frontage on the Adriatic together with a part of Hercegovina, if they would but acknowledge Turkish suzerainty. But Peter II refused to accept the bargain, and war broke out in 1832. Although the Montenegrins invaded both Albania and Hercegovina, they were unable to acquire any permanent territory. On one occasion a body of Montenegrins seized Zabljak and held it against the Turks until Peter II ordered its restoration on ground of expediency (1835). There were also disputes with Austria. The Pastrović clan, along the Adriatic shore between Budva and Spizza (Spič), sold its territory to Montenegro, always eager for a chance of an outlet to the sea. But Austria objected to this infringement of its sovereignty, and Montenegro had to yield up the territory in return for monetary compensation, and the Austro-Montenegrin frontier was delimited in 1838–40.

The total population of the state at this time was estimated at about 120,000 people. It was not a large number, but there were difficulties towards the end of Peter II's reign when the crops— chiefly potatoes and maize—failed. The famine was so severe that the Crnička district and part of the Brda, already discontented with the centralizing tendencies of the period, attempted to secede, and were reunited only after a short period of civil war (1847). In the following year, the Montenegrins, like the Serbians, were stirred by the action of the Austrian Serbs in the revolution of 1848 . . . Peter II offered aid to Jelačić, Ban of Croatia, who, however, did not wish to accept outside help in a civil war with the Hungarians. Peter II died in 1851—the last of the vladikas.

The reign of Danilo II, 1851–60. The reign of Danilo II was marked by a radical change in the ancient constitution of the country a change which perhaps was inevitable sooner or later. He wished to marry, but the custom which compelled the ruler to be consecrated as bishop would not allow this. He therefore proposed to separate the civil and ecclesiastical offices of his predecessor. In 1852 he assumed the title of 'gospodar' or prince of Crna Gora and of the Brda; the succession was declared to be hereditary in the male line; while the office of bishop was to be held by a member of the Montenegrin aristocracy. Despite these startling changes, and indeed partly because of them, Danilo II was able to continue the work of his predecessor in consolidating the state. In 1855, a new legal code was introduced, providing for civil and religious liberty, and aiming at putting down brigandage. Both in its administration and in its civilization, Montenegro was assuming a more 'western' character.

Parallel with these changes at home, there were various foreign complications. The new constitution of 1852 had been introduced with the approval of both Austria and Russia, but Turkey objected and revived its claim to the suzerainty of the province. In the war that followed, the Turks, after many reverses, were compelled by diplomatic pressure from Austria and Russia to cease fighting. The Austrian delegate, at the peace negotiations of March 1853, made special reference to the Turkish acknowledgement of 1799 that Montenegro was in no sense a vassal state. Thus Austria championed the little state that, within a generation, was to regard her as a deadly foe.

When the Crimean War broke out between Turkey and Russia in October 1853, the latter expected support from Montenegro, but Danilo II refrained from war on the advice of Austria. This peaceful policy produced great discontent which culminated in revolt; the people of the Brda region declared themselves an independent state, and were induced to submit only after civil war. At the Treaty of Paris which ended the Crimean War in 1856, the Russian delegates, under pressure from Austria, disclaimed any special interest in Montenegro beyond that of 'friendly disposition'. Turkey seized the opportunity, however, to state that it regarded Montenegro as 'an integral part of the Ottoman Empire', but it was careful to add that it 'had no intention of altering the existing state of affairs'. The Turkish claim was at once denied by Danilo II in a memorandum addressed to the Powers. He pointed out that 'for 466 years the Montenegrin people had never been subjected to any Power' (i.e. since the battle of Kosovo), and that 'for four and a half centuries it had waged continual warfare with Turkey'. The memorandum,

Vasojevic Tribal Commander Miras Djolev Zonjic-Dabetic

Foreground: Tribal (Clan) Commander Bozina Djolev Dabetic-Lekic;
Background: Tribal Commander Vuko Dabetic.

moreover, claimed: (1) the official recognition of Montenegrin independence; (2) an extension of frontiers towards Albania and Hercegovina; (3) proper delimitation of the Turco-Montenegrin frontier; (4) the annexation of Antivari (Bar), in order to provide an outlet to the sea. But nothing came of these demands, despite a Turkish offer of increased territory in return for a recognition of Turkish sovereignty.

In the years that followed, Danilo was anxious to maintain peaceful relations with Turkey, but it was a desire that his subjects did not share. Frontier incidents in 1858 led to war, which was marked by a brilliant Montenegrin victory at Grahovo. It was hailed as the 'Marathon of Montenegro', and was followed by the appointment of an international commission to delimit the Turco-Montenegrin frontier. As a result, the district around Grahovo was added to the principality.

Danilo II died in 1860 after being shot by a Montenegrin rebel whom he had exiled. He left only a daughter, and the throne passed to his nephew Nicholas.

The reign of Nicholas I up to 1914

Territorial Expansion, 1860–80. Nicholas was only nineteen years old when he began his long reign (1860–1918). In 1861, the neighbouring Hercegovinians rose against the Turks · · · and, though the Montenegrin government carefully kept out of the war on the advice of the Powers, individual Montenegrins crossed the frontier to take part in the struggle of their fellow-Slavs. Seizing this pretext, Turkey declared war on Montenegro early in 1862, and advanced from Nikšić and Spuž into the short neck of territory (barely twelve miles wide) that connected Crna Gora and the Brda. Despite fierce resistance, the Montenegrins were defeated, though the subsequent Convention of Scutari acknowledged the frontier of 1859, and allowed the Montenegrins free trade through the port of Antivari (31 August 1862). During the fourteen years that followed, Montenegro was at peace, and at one time almost succeeded by negotiation in gaining a direct outlet on to the Adriatic at Novasella near Spizza (1866), but this was vetoed by England and France because it would have meant an increase of Russian influence in the Mediterranean.

In October 1874, the murder of twenty-two Montenegrins by the Turks at Podgorica nearly started war again, but the crisis was smoothed over by the Great Powers. In the following year, however, the revolt of Bosnia and Hercegovina soon started a train of events that could not be smoothed out. ⋯   The revolt aroused very great sympathy among the Montenegrins, and, in July 1876, Nicholas, in concert with Prince Milan of Serbia, declared war on Turkey. Within a few months, Montenegrin victories at Danilov Grad, Medun and elsewhere brought an armistice (November); but, in April 1877, Russia declared war on Turkey, and the Montenegrins reopened hostilities. It was a year of great victories, and the Turkish attempt again to separate Crna Gora and the Brda was defeated. Nikšić and Bileća (Bilek) in Hercegovina were taken, and, on the Albanian side, Dulcigno (Ulcinj), Antivari and the territory south of Lake Scutari were occupied; the seaboard was at last in Montenegrin hands.

The Treaty of San Stefano (3 March 1878) allowed Montenegro to retain her recent conquests, and the state was roughly trebled in area ⋯   the independent status of the county was, moreover, once more formally recognized by the Turks. But the fate of Montenegro was bound up with the wider policies of the Great Powers in Europe, and the Treaty of Berlin a few months later (13 July 1878), while affirming her independence, reduced her area from 5,272 to 3,680 square miles. In particular, Dulcigno (Ulcinj) was restored to Turkey and Spizza ceded to Austrian Dalmatia. Antivari (Bar) was still left to provide an outlet to the Adriatic, but, in order to prevent this port from becoming a possible Russian base, the treaty provided that Montenegrin waters should 'remain closed to the ships of war of all nations'; that Montenegro should have no fleet; and that the maritime policing of the coast should be undertaken by Austria-Hungary. The Montenegrin frontier on the Albanian side remained in dispute for some time owing to the lawless independence of the local tribes; and, after much negotiation, Montenegro, in 1880, gave up the districts of Gusinje and Plav in return for Ulcinj, together with the strip of coast as far as the river Bojana—thus making altogether a seaboard of some thirty miles. ⋯   But even after this, the frontiers still remained in dispute at some points, partly owing to the restless border tribes; there were further rectifications, and, as late as 1911, there were still some undefined areas along the frontier.

Peaceful Development, 1880–1912. As a result of the struggle with the Turk, the tradition of fighting in Montenegro went back for five centuries or so, and it was no easy task to change this Homeric society of mountain chieftains into an organized nineteenth-century state.

MONTENEGRO

Despite occasional border unrest, however, the thirty years following 1880 were marked by considerable economic, social and political developments. Motor roads were built, and, in 1908, a railway between Antivari and Lake Scutari was opened; a bank was founded;

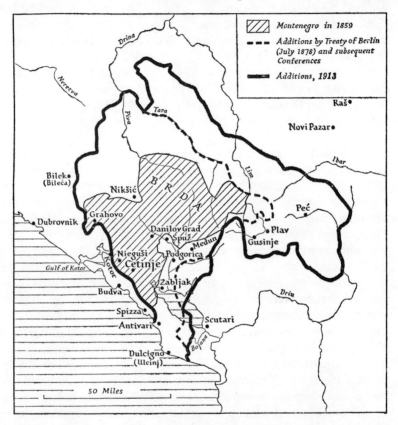

The growth of Montenegro

Based on (i) E. Hertslet, *The Map of Europe by Treaty*, vol. IV, p. 2782 (H.M.S.O., London, 1891); (ii) *Enciclopedia Italiana*, vol. XXIII, p. 744 (Milano, 1934). For the complicated frontier changes between 1878–87, see E. Hertslet, *op. cit.*, vol. IV, maps opposite pp. 2674, 2782, 2956, 3018 and 3140.

agriculture (particularly the cultivation of vines and tobacco) was improved, and an agricultural college was opened at Podgorica. By 1910, there were twenty-one post offices, and before the outbreak of war in 1914 the number had been trebled; and this may be taken as symptomatic of the accelerated progress of the country in general. As might be expected in a country where capital was scarce, much of this development was in the hands of foreigners, particularly Italians, and there was a cry of 'Montenegro for the Montenegrins'. It must be added, however, that all this improvement did not prevent the occasional recurrence of famine and the continual emigration of younger men to Serbia, to the U.S.A. and elsewhere.

Parallel with economic development, there was considerable social and intellectual progress, and a public library, a theatre and a museum were opened in Cetinje. In 1893, the four-hundredth anniversary of the foundation of the printing press at Obod was celebrated amidst many representatives from foreign universities. Theoretically, at any rate, primary education was compulsory and by 1906 there were 112 primary schools with 150 teachers and 9,756 pupils; there were also secondary schools at Cetinje and Podgorica. Higher education, however, had to be sought abroad, usually at the University of Belgrade, and this Serbian link was not without important political effects, for the younger generation came back with new ideas of democracy that soon clashed with the autocracy of their ruler.

In the third place, there were important political developments. The old legal code of 1855 was revised in 1888; and, to the surprise of Europe, parliamentary institutions were introduced in 1905, and the first Montenegrin parliament met on 19 December. It consisted of 14 *ex officio* members, and 62 elected by manhood suffrage. The experiment, however, was not an unqualified success. Party feeling ran high, and cabinet crises were frequent. There were complaints, too, that the dominant personality of Nicholas was autocratic. The international status of the country had been improved by the marriage of one of the daughters of Nicholas to the heir to the Italian throne; another of his children married the exiled Peter Karageorgević, who was later to become king of Serbia, while four married into German and Russian royal families; indeed, Nicholas was described as 'the father-in-law of Europe'. In 1898 he visited Queen Victoria at Windsor; in 1900 he assumed the style of 'Royal Highness', and, finally in 1910, he took the title of king.

In the meantime, the annexation of Bosnia and Hercegovina by Austria in 1908 had aroused antagonism in Montenegro, but Montenegrin acquiescence was purchased in the following year by the removal of the Austrian restrictions upon Antivari and the rest of the Montenegrin coastline.

The Balkan Wars, 1912–13. The generation of peace since 1878 was soon to be shattered by the wider complications of the Eastern Question. In 1912, Serbia, Montenegro, Greece and Bulgaria

Avro Cemovic, Brigadier of the Vasojevic Tribe.

Duke of the Vasojevic Tribe and Minister for Montenegro (Crna Gora)
Gavro Vukovic-Vesovic

challenged Turkey, just weakened by the Italian war and the loss of Tripoli. . . . On 8 October, Montenegro, claiming a rectification of her frontier, declared war on the Turks, and was joined by her allies. Plav and Gusinje, which had been yielded up in 1880, were occupied; so was Peć, and, after a long siege, Scutari itself (the old residence of the Balšas) surrendered. The Great Powers, particularly Austria and Italy, were averse from seeing too great a Slav frontage on the Adriatic, and they intended that Scutari should form part of a new Albanian state; it had therefore to be evacuated by the Montenegrins. The Treaty of London (30 May 1913) ceded all Turkish territory west of the Enos-Midia line to the Balkan allies, with the exception of Albania; the division of the spoil and the details of the frontiers were left to be adjusted. In the Second Balkan War, caused by the failure of the allies to agree about the division, Serbia, Greece and Montenegro together with Roumania defeated the Bulgarians. The subsequent adjustment of frontiers gave Montenegro a considerable increase of territory, for the sanjak of Novi Pazar was partitioned between Serbia and Montenegro.

The area of the enlarged state amounted to about 6,250 sq. miles; its population was variously estimated, and probably numbered something under half a million. The greater part of this population was Serb in speech and Orthodox in religion, but it included about 25,000 Roman Catholics and about 105,000 Moslems; the latter were mostly Albanians, and some 80,000 of them lived in the new territory added in 1913.

The partition of the sanjak of Novi Pazar had at last brought the two Serb peoples of Montenegro and Serbia into territorial contact; and, early in 1914, proposals for uniting the two countries were discussed. This would have involved a customs union, a fusion of the two armies and a joint foreign policy, but the two states would have retained their separate dynasties. Austria objected to the proposal, but despite this, and despite personal differences between Nicholas and the king of Serbia, the movement for union between the two peoples was rapidly growing when the war of 1914 broke out.

APPENDIX FIVE: Some Aspects of Yugoslavian Culture

MEDIEVAL DEVELOPMENT

INTRODUCTION

When the Southern Slavs filtered into the Balkan peninsula in the seventh century, they brought with them a complex collection of pagan beliefs and practices to a country rich in mythology and monuments of the ancient classical world of which it had been an integral part. The tradition of the pre-Christian Slavs persists to this day in altered form in the oral tradition, in peasant customs and beliefs; monuments of classical antiquity are either uncovered by archaeological excavation as, for example, in the Necropolis at Trebenište in South Serbia, in Salona near Split (Spalato), and at Vinča near Belgrade, or have solidly withstood the ravages of time, as the famous gigantic palace of Diocletian at Split. The pagan Slavs soon experienced the impact of medieval Christian culture both from the Western and Eastern Roman Empires, later differentiated into the Western Catholic world, which moulded the Slovenes and the Croats, and the Byzantine Orthodox world to which belonged the Serbs. Neo-Manichaean influence penetrated into the Balkans from the Near East in the ninth and tenth centuries and formed the basis of the Bogomil sect, which arose in Macedonia in the tenth century, infiltrated into Serbia in the twelfth century and into Bosnia, where they were known as Patarenes. Moslem culture, which came in with the Turkish domination from the fourteenth century, has left deep traces and particularly in Bosnia and Macedonia.   · · ·
Finally, the peoples of Jugoslavia have also been influenced by the rationalistic, scientific outlook, gaining ground in Europe since the sixteenth century and this has been progressively regarded as the source of enlightenment and emulation. Each of these cultures has produced its monuments and continues to play its part in Jugoslavia.

MEDIEVAL DEVELOPMENT

Most of the medieval literature was produced in the monasteries, written on parchment with a goose quill. Some have elaborate capital letters in red, some are illuminated, some were specially ordered for kings or high dignitaries, the patrons of letters. The rulers of the Serb medieval state are known to have had libraries of manuscripts. Of these manuscripts, the finest and earliest is the Miroslav Gospel, attributed to the twelfth century.

Serbia in the Middle Ages was fully part of Europe and a bridge between Byzantium and the Orient on the one hand, and Rome and Western Europe on the other. This period of Serbian culture ends with the Turkish conquest when Serbia was cut from cultural contacts with the rest of the world. But this monastic culture was not in vain: for 500 years in the seclusion of the monasteries the memory and practice of Serbia's medieval achievement were cherished and grew into a tradition which passed orally to the people in the cult of a national epic poetry.

THE JUGOSLAV ORAL TRADITION

GENERAL FEATURES

A rich oral tradition has been for centuries a special feature of the culture of the Jugoslavs. For the last hundred years it has been rapidly yielding to the pressure of modern influences owing to the inevitable impact with Western European ideas. Already it has disappeared in the towns, together with the national costume. With the spread of education, the final liquidation of illiteracy, the growing influence of the newspaper, radio, cinema, urbanization and industrialism, it is doomed eventually to disappear. Meanwhile, since the majority of the population are peasants, the oral tradition is perceptible as soon as one leaves the towns, whereas in remote regions along the periphery and away from the main centres of civilization, and therefore more inaccessible and refractory to the encroaching process of modernization, traditional life strongly persists and the oral tradition is still active.

Folk-magic expressed in formulae is used particularly in healing ritual and as a potent force for good or evil in every aspect of human activity, such as fishing, hunting, bee-keeping, cattle breeding, warfare, birth, marriage and death. . . . In these beliefs and formulae Christian, Moslem and pagan elements are inextricably interwoven, and parallel formulae can be found among the other Slav peoples, thus making the question of origins obscure.

This oral tradition is further expressed anonymously in folk tale and poetry, which, though now mostly collected and printed, have not yet become literature, something invented or recorded and considered as apart from everyday life. Folk-poetry can be conveniently divided into lyrics and epic poetry.

Lyrics

The lyrics are known as women's songs—*ženske pesme*—though they need not necessarily be sung by women. They vary in metre and length, though they are mostly short, and their themes poetically reflect many subjects. They are sung to a variety of beautiful folk-tunes, but they are unaccompanied by any instrument; they are sung at work and at play—for the Jugoslav lives his poetry—whenever men are gathered together, at a *slava* . . . round a camp fire, at harvesting, at food or drink, or when dancing the *kolo* . . . when women are spinning or rocking a cradle, when they are thinking of a beloved, or visiting a grave, or lamenting the dead. Special mention should be made of the Bosnian love songs called *sevdalinke* and the *dert* love songs of Vranje and the propitiatory songs—the *dodolske* and the *kraljičke*. All these are delightful, naïve and sincere in sentiment, unexpectedly fresh in imagery and touchingly simple, but most of them lose their beauty in translation and in the original they do not surpass the lyrical folk-songs of other peoples in Europe.

Epic Poetry

General Features

The Jugoslav epic poems (*narodne pesme*)—and the Serbian in particular—are the great glory of the Jugoslav oral tradition. It is the most characteristic expression of the creative genius of the people, it is their pride, the dynamic source of their hope, and their instigation to collective action in historical moments, such as in their fight for liberation, be it from the Turk or from the German. There is not a Jugoslav, literate or illiterate, who does not know the historical or legendary heroes of the *narodne pesme*; these are the history book of the people, an example to follow and one of the greatest moulding influences. A study of the national epic poetry which the Jugoslavs have created is the surest way to understand their mentality and spiritual outlook.

This narrative poetry based on historic events is mainly the

A guslar player

Guslarske

The *guslarske* ballads and their variants have been collected in
their thousands, and the metre—a line of ten syllables with a pause
after the fourth—has not varied for more than two centuries. The
number of variants show that improvisation rather than static
memorization is a faculty cultivated by Jugoslav *guslars*, or bards.

These remarkable ballads, generally considered by experts to be
the finest ballad poetry in Europe and not more widely known only
because Serbo-Croat is so little studied, are recited to the accompaniment of a *gusle*, a primitive single stringed fiddle with a deeply
rounded body made of maple. The Jugoslav Moslems use a tambura,
a kind of mandoline with two metal strings. The bridge of the gusle
rests on a piece of taut vellum. The neck of the instrument is
elaborately carved with the figures of the ballad heroes or with the

heads of animals. The bow is shaped like a curved snake and is strung with horsehair. The guslar sits, holding the gusle body downwards like a violoncello. He closes his eyes, he fingers quickly and deftly, then for an introduction he draws his bow to and fro across the string, producing a harsh grating sound which arrests the attention. A series of eerie sounds, like a plaintive wail, has a hypnotic effect on the listeners. Then a pause, after which the guslar plunges into his rapid recitative, his voice pausing every four or five lines, although the *narodne pesme* are not broken up into stanzas. But it is not the chanting that is the main interest, but the glorifying of men's deeds.

The *guslarske narodne pesme* can be divided into non-historical and historical poems.

Non-historical poems

Among the non-historical 'The Wife of Hassan Aga', the first to become known in translation in Western Europe (in Italian in 1774, in German in 1789) is one of the most moving. It is a tragic story based on the life of the Moslem Serbs. Hassan Aga's faithful wife is too shy to visit him when he is wounded after battle for fear of meeting another man on the way. He avenges himself by divorcing her, sends her back to her mother and separates her from her five children. Her brother promptly arranges to wed her to the great Cadi of Imoske. Broken-hearted and on her way to her new home, she is allowed the favour to stop and give gifts to her orphan children. The infuriated Hassan again misjudges the poor woman: 'Hither, my children, motherless! And from her stand apart! Pity and mercy has she none within her stony heart'. Unable to bear this cruelty she fell on the ground 'and her soul departed as she saw her children motherless'.

Another popular *pesma*, 'Predrag and Nenad' ('The most dear and the unexpected one'), is the same story as Malory's 'Balin and Balan' repeated by Tennyson. It is the tragedy of one warrior brother going out to seek another. Three times he meets his brother's men—a symbolic testing of the spirit. To the first two groups he appeals with reason and passes unhurt, but the third attacks him and in self-defence he fights. His brother sends an arrow through his heart. Dying he reveals his identity: in remorse his brother stabs himself, 'Down brother fell by brother, the dead lay with the dead'.

Historical Cycles

The historical *pesme* are divided into cycles which give a vivid history of the Serbs from the twelfth century to the present day. Three of the main and best known cycles are described below.

The Nemanjid Cycle contains *pesme* about Stephen Nemanja, the founder of the Serbian medieval state, about his son St Sava (these are considered to be of literary or written origin) and about the strong Stephen Dušan, about Uroš and the Mrnjavčevići—Vukašin, Uglješa and the unhistorical Gojko—who all illegally claimed the throne. In one of the *pesme*, Vukašin's son Marko judges that Uroš is the lawful heir. Marko escapes his father by seeking sanctuary in a church. Vukašin stabs at the wooden door. Blood rushes from it. He thinks he has killed his son, but a voice from the church says that an angel of the Lord has been slain. Vukašin then curses Marko, but Uroš blesses him: 'Be thy name renowned everywhere while sun and moon endure'. And so it was, for Marko, the most popular hero in the *pesme*, has a cycle to himself.

The Marriage of King Vukašin gives a lurid picture of the social conditions of the period, of its cruelty and courage. Vukašin, a contemporary of Stephen Dušan, woos Vidosava in a letter and begs her to poison or betray her husband, Momčilo. She falls to the temptation: at her suggestion Vukašin comes to slay Momčilo when he is out hunting. She helps Vukašin by singeing her husband's winged horse, by sealing fast his sword with salt blood, so that, helpless against his foe, Momčilo flees to his castle which is bolted and barred. His sister Jevrosima, tied by her hair to a beam, swung her head with all her strength so that all her hair was torn off and remained on the beam. She then threw Momčilo a length of linen cloth up which he scaled, but his wife with a sharp sword severed the linen sheet above his hand. He fell on swords and war spears, and King Vukašin pierced him through the living heart. The dying Momčilo warns the king to marry his sister Jevrosima rather than his own faithless wife. Vidosava welcomes the murderer in the castle and brings him Momčilo's armour and apparel. Its size and weight makes Vukašin realize that 'If to-day she betrays such a knight of prowess, whose match there is not in all the world, how should she not betray me to-morrow?' So he had Vidosava bound to the tails of horses. 'And the horses rent her living body asunder'. The king then married the fair Jevrosima who bore him a hero; his name was Marko Kraljević.

ASPECTS OF MEDIEVAL AND MODERN CULTURE

The Walling of Skutari is a cruel *pesma* in which a *vila*—a spirit who lives in wooded mountains and in rocky places round lakes and rivers—wrecks by night what the three brothers Vukašin, Uglješa and Gojko build by day. She demands a propitiatory sacrifice: whichever of the three wives next brings the masons' dinner must be walled into the tower's foundations that it may stand. The brothers pledge secrecy before God and swear to leave the victim to chance. Vukašin and Uglješa break their pledge to save their wives, but Gojko keeps his word. His unsuspecting wife leaves her babe and carries the dinner out of her turn to oblige her sisters. Gojko weeps at the sight of his wife, but cannot save her. She is walled in: 'and the slender girl laughs lightly, thinking haply they jest'. In a sudden agony of realization she begs that they leave a window for her eyes and one for her breast that she might see and feed her babe. They grant her prayer. After seven days, her voice was gone, but she suckled her babe for a year. The fortress held—the *vila* had been appeased, and 'yea, even to-day, the white milk flows, for a miracle most high and a healing draught for women, whereof the breasts are dry'.

The Kosovo Cycle, the most significant of all, unlike most of the other cycles, forms an organic whole consisting of many *pesme*. The legend of Kosovo has grown gradually. It was inspired by the belief that the Battle of Kosovo (1389) was the greatest tragedy the Serbs had had to face. It was the end of their medieval greatness, the end of their freedom for over five hundred years. ... The Kosovo *pesme* are Homeric in simplicity and in grandeur. Against overwhelming odds Stephen Lazar makes the choice not to accept Turkish vassaldom without fighting and this has become a prototype for the Serbian people whenever they are faced with a spiritual choice in historical moments:

> 'God of my fathers, what shall I do?
> If a heavenly empire, then must I lose
> All that is dearest to me upon earth;
> But if that the heavenly here I refuse,
> What then is the earthly worth?
> It is but a day, it passeth away,
> And the glory of earth full soon is o'er.
> But the glory of God is more and more.
> What is this world's renown?
> (His heart was heavy, his soul was stirred)
> Shall an earthly empire be preferred
> To an everlasting crown?

His choice was made, the battle was a defeat, but it stands as a moral victory. And so Kosovo and all it symbolizes for the Jugoslavs has grown into a cult. Death and honour must be chosen rather than capitulation and a life of shame. In these *pesme* which are dramatic in intensity and charged with an inexorable doom, equalled only in Greek tragedy, all Lazar's people play a fittingly dignified and heroic part: the Tsarica Milica bravely parts with her lord and her nine brothers, none of whom put personal love before public duty; Miloš Obilić, slandered as a traitor, redeems his honour at the price of death by stabbing Lazar's enemy, the Sultan Murad; Goluban the servant, joins Lazar because it is more important to fight the enemy than to attend to the tragic Tsarica, and that same Goluban, wounded, later brings back to her news of defeat and gory details of the death of Lazar and all the heroes of Kosovo; the mother of the nine dead brothers Jugovići mourns in noble silence while the nine widows weep. She does not shed a single tear at the sight of their tears nor at the plaintive neighing of her sons' horses, but when she recognizes the severed hand that two coal-black ravens drop into her lap as being the hand of her beloved son Damian, she breaks her silence:

> '"O my hand, my fresh green apple,
> Where didst thou grow, where werst thou plucked?
> T'was on my breast that thou didst grow,
> The plucking was on Kosovo."
> Speaking, she breathed her life away.'

The Maid of Kosovo has lost her betrothed in battle but with dignified, selfless tenderness she wanders among the dead on the battlefield, tends the wounded and relieves their suffering, while her own sorrow is such that if she were to touch a pine tree 'young and green, it would dry up and shrivel'.

The Cycle of Kraljević Marko (Prince Marko) contains the largest number of *pesme* and is popular not only among the Serbs and Croats, but also with the Slovenes, Bulgarians, Turks and Albanians. Marko is the son of Vukašin, the king of Prilep, who was drowned with thousands of his Serbs when routed by the Turks. Marko became ruler of Prilep, but under Ottoman pressure in 1385 went over to the service of the Turks. Tradition says that he was killed at the Battle of Rovina in 1394. This hazy historical figure has become Serbia's grandest national hero in traditional poetry. He is the Serbian Hercules, dark-eyed, with a black moustache as large as

ASPECTS OF MEDIEVAL AND MODERN CULTURE

a lamb, his cloak is a wolfskin, his cap is pulled down to his eyebrows, he drinks, he brawls, he wins in fights. The Serbian people
have attributed to Marko all their own good and bad qualities. He
is essentially human. He is tender to his mother, yet he is cruel to
his wife whom he forgets for nine years, but when he learns that
another man has carried her off, he returns from the other end of
the land, rescues her, only to abandon her again. He is crude, but
he is noble; he is cruel, but he is just; his evil deeds he atones by good
ones; he helps the weak and the poor against the strong and the
tyrant. He abolished the oppressive marriage tax for all by killing
the lord who extorted it; he even intimidates the all-powerful sultan.
He observes the religious tradition of his people; he will not shed
blood on his *slava*. He flees from his father so that the latter may not
shed the blood of a son; he wants nothing for himself but would do
anything for the people. He lives on the roads and in inns, he is of
a piece with the Balkan landscape, his life, full and varied in the
expenditure of boundless energy, is one long adventure against the
Turk. But though so human, he is a man apart: he is in league with
the *vile* and the dragons; he lives some three hundred years. His
faithful companion is Šarac, the piebald horse who drinks half his
wine. But death must come even to Marko. The *vila* warns him, he
looks into a mountain well and sees in the water when he is to die.
With his sabre he cut off Šarac's head so that it should not fall into
the hands of the Turk. He buried his horse better than he had buried
his own brother. He broke his sharp sword into four pieces, he
broke his war spear into seven. His mace he cast from the mountain
into the sea:

> '"When my mace shall come up out of the sea,
> Another Marko shall appear upon earth."'

Then he wrote a letter which he fixed to a pine tree together with
three purses of gold:

> '"One purse I give to him that findeth me
> That he may bury my body.
> Another purse I give for to adorn the churches,
> The third I give to the maimed and the blind,
> That the blind may go into all the world
> To sing and to celebrate Marko."'

Then he lay down by the well and died. Whoever passed by made
wide his path round about him for fear lest he should wake Marko,
until the Abbot of the White Church Vilindar (Hilendar) on the

Holy Mountain (Athos) found him. And he set the dead Marko on his horse and brought him to the seashore and took him by ship to the Holy Mountain and buried him in the middle of the church of the White Vilindar:

> 'But he left no sign thereon,
> That none should know the grave of Marko
> And that the enemies should not revenge them on the dead.'

Later Cycles

The other cycles belong to the period when Serbia was subjugated to the Turks. They celebrate the deeds of the Brankovići, the ruling despots of Serbia until 1459, of the Crnojevići, the last rulers of the Zeta dynasty (until 1496), of the bold Hajduks, guerilla warriors who took to the mountains from where they were always ready to harass the Turks who tyrannized over the Serbian people. The Hajduks kept alive the spirit of independence; particularly fine are the *pesme* about Starina Novak, a famous Hajduk of the sixteenth century and his faithful men, about Bajo Pivljanin of the seventeenth century and his men, especially Limun Hajduk and about the Bosnian Hajduks. Another cycle deals with the Uskoks, the men who sought refuge after the fall of Hercegovina in 1482 in Dalmatia and the Croatian coast where, as mercenaries of the emperors or of the *doge* of Venice, they protected the borders from the Turks and often made successful raids against them.

The struggle of the Montenegrins against the Turks in the eighteenth century and the liberation of Serbia in the nineteenth century have given rise to two cycles in which the events are described if less poetically then more accurately historically. Particularly fine are 'Kara George's Farewell to Serbia', 'The Beginning of the Revolt against the Dahijas' and 'The Battle of Mišar', in which two black ravens describe the battle to Kulin's mourning widow.

There are also cycles which deal with Dalmatian and Bosnian subjects. In the Bosnian *pesme* no historical events are described older than the sixteenth century, and, unlike the other *narodne pesme*, women and love themes are prominent. Of particular interest is the modern cycle in which recent events are sung. These deal with the Balkan Wars of 1912, 1913, the war of 1914–18, the assassination of King Alexander and the French Foreign Minister Barthou (who is called 'Bartulović'). No doubt there are new *pesme* being recited to-day about the Jugoslav resistance and the exploits of the guerillas since 1941.

285

ASPECTS OF MEDIEVAL AND MODERN CULTURE

The professional bard, the guslar is disappearing, though he can still be heard mostly in Bosnia, Hercegovina and Montenegro, but the reciting of the *narodne pesme*, even without a musical accompaniment, is not dying out. Here we may observe the effect of the printed word on the oral tradition. Before the nineteenth century, few of the *narodne pesme* were written down. Now thousands are printed in variants. The first to be written down were in Peter Hektorović's *Ribanje* ('Fishing') heard from Hvar fishermen and published in 1568. Some more were found in manuscripts in the seventeenth and eighteenth centuries, but systematic collecting was only begun by Vuk Karadžić (1787–1864) who published two volumes of *pesme* in 1814 and 1815; a further collection was printed in four volumes in 1824–1833; a third, augmented edition, was published in six volumes in 1841–1866; a state edition in nine volumes appeared in 1887–1902 and has been reprinted many times since, the last being dated 1936. Vuk Karadžić set the trail for other collectors such as Sima Milutinović, Njegoš, Jukić, Martić, Petar Nović and others. Many *narodne pesme* have been printed in the *Matica Hrvatska* and the *Bosanska Vila*, and when printed they were a revelation. Translations of them began to appear in French, German and English; Goethe, Herder, Madame de Staël, Walter Scott, Grimm, Lamartine, Mérimée, all appreciated them. Here was the heroic story of men of integrity and courage for whom the principles of faith and honour stood above all else and who sang of them in all simplicity, without boasting or didacticism. These *pesme* became a cult and an inspiration to those Slavs who were still under foreign domination. Literary men have found in them a source for new subjects. Particularly important is the fact that the language of the *narodne pesme* became the basis for a new Serbo-Croat literary language which was nearer to the simple spoken language of the people than the conventional literary medium which was heavily charged with Old Church Slavonic (see p. 210).

To-day, the Jugoslavs are justly proud of their *pesme* and they are aware how great a part of their national heritage they are. Small wonder then that their study in printed editions has been included in the obligatory curriculum of all the schools in Jugoslavia, and there is, therefore, not a single Jugoslav who cannot recite some lines by heart. This will ensure the survival of the *narodne pesme* as an inspiration both for literature and for life, though much of the rest of the folklore and popular customs, which have been handed down in oral form from generation to generation, will inevitably disappear.

APPENDIX SIX: A Note of the Status of Women in Yugoslavia, 1939

The status of women, which is fairly high in the north-west of the country, diminishes towards the south-east. In Slovenia, the Vojvodina, the northern part of Croatia and northern Serbia it is similar to that of the adjacent countries of Austria and Hungary. In South Serbia, Bosnia and Hercegovina, Montenegro and Dalmatia women have a very subordinate position and have to defer to all men and even to youths.

Everywhere women work in the fields at such tasks as planting, hoeing, hay-making and fruit-picking, the work being most arduous in Bosnia and Montenegro, where women take part in every kind of agricultural work, including ploughing and reaping. Many Montenegrin men do not even carry a parcel, a state of affairs which appears to date from the time when every man had to be ready to fight at an instant's notice. In parts of Bosnia the women eat only after the men have finished, they carry heavier loads, and go on foot while the men ride. Moslem women live in a state of seclusion and subordination which has been abandoned in Turkey itself.

The relative status of women in the different parts of the country is reflected very closely in the literacy figures. In the Dravska *banovina*, which corresponds to Slovenia, only 5·8% of females over 10 years old were illiterate at the census of 1931, and only 15% in the Belgrade prefecture. In the Savska, roughly corresponding with Croatia and Slavonia, there were 35%, and 40% in the Dunavska, or the Vojvodina. The Primorska (coastal) *banovina* had 70%, and there were over 80% in the five remaining areas.

More liberal ideas concerning the status of women were gaining ground among the younger generation in recent years, even to some extent in the south, especially in the more accessible valleys and in the developing towns where women could obtain some gainful occupation.

Paid occupations for women are few. Only 188,729 came under the national insurance scheme in 1938. Women are employed as servants in hotels and in private houses in towns, and also as shop assistants. There are few openings for women in industry, as the country has so few of the secondary or lighter factory industries, but some are employed in the textile factories. There are some openings for women in offices as typists, and in the lower grades of the postal service as telephonists. The teaching profession is open to women, and also nursing, the latter work being often undertaken by nuns. There are a few women dentists and doctors. In a poor and undeveloped country, however, where there is not enough work for men there will be few openings for women.

INDEX OF NAMES MENTIONED IN TEXT